PE
Third Edition

OCR GCSE (9–1)

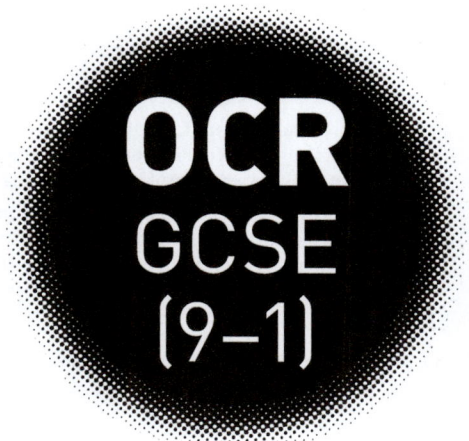

PE

Third Edition

JOHN HONEYBOURNE

An OCR endorsed textbook

Boost
OCR Oxford Cambridge and RSA
HODDER EDUCATION
AN HACHETTE UK COMPANY

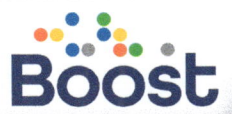

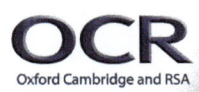

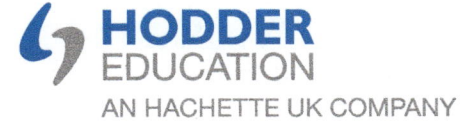

The teaching content of this resource is endorsed by OCR for use with specification OCR GCSE (9–1) Physical Education J587. In order to gain OCR endorsement, this resource has been reviewed against OCR's endorsement criteria.

This resource was designed using the most up to date information from the specification. Specifications are updated over time which means there may be contradictions between the resource and the specification, therefore please use the information on the latest specification and Sample Assessment Materials at all times when ensuring students are fully prepared for their assessments.

Any references to assessment and/or assessment preparation are the publisher's interpretation of the specification requirements and are not endorsed by OCR. OCR recommends that teachers consider using a range of teaching and learning resources in preparing learners for assessment, based on their own professional judgement for their students' needs. OCR has not paid for the production of this resource, nor does OCR receive any royalties from its sale. For more information about the endorsement process, please visit the OCR website, www.ocr.org.uk.

For answers to exam practice questions, please visit:
www.hoddereducation.co.uk/OCR-GCSE-PE-Answers

Please note that these answers are not endorsed by OCR.

The Publishers would like to thank the following for permission to reproduce copyright material.

Photo credits

p.1/p.37 © Kevin Warburton - A Moment in Sport/ProSports/Shutterstock; **p.5** © Adrian Dennis/AFP/Getty Images; **p.6** © Andyross/iStock/Thinkstock; **p.12** © Daniel Swee/Alamy Stock Photo; **p.15** © Photosbyjim/iStock/Thinkstock; **p.25** © Warrengoldswain/iStock/Thinkstock; **p.26** © RIA Novosti/TopFoto; **p.30** © Wavebreak Media/Thinkstock; **p.34** © DigitalVision/Thinkstock; **p.36** © LUNAMARINA/iStock/Thinkstock; **p.38** © Crdjan/iStock/Thinkstock; **p.39** © BSIP/Universal Images Group/Getty Images; **p.43/p.45** © David Noton Photography/Alamy Stock Photo; **p.49** © Leo Mason sports photos/Alamy Stock Photo; **p.50** © Demid/iStock/Thinkstock; **p.52** © Morne de Klerk/Getty Images; **p.53** © ShariffC/iStock/Thinkstock; **p.54** © BanksPhotos/E+/Getty Images; **p.55** © Sergejs Nescereckis/Alamy Stock Photo; **p.57** © Lee Jin-man/AP/Shutterstock; **p.59** © .shock/stock.adobe.com; **p.61** © Mark Dadswell/Getty Images; **p.64** © Songbird839/iStock/Thinkstock; **p.70** © lightpoet/123RF; **p.74** © Arnold Slater/Shutterstock; **p.75** © Martin-dm/E+/Getty Images; **p.76** © Aflo/Shutterstock; **p.78** © Alan Edwards/Alamy Stock Photo; **p.81** © Simon Dael/BPI/Shutterstock; **p.83** © Harry Hubbard/The FA Collection/Getty Images; **p.85** © Ryan Crockett/JMP/Shutterstock; **p.91/p.104 (bottom)** © Mark Baynes/Alamy Stock Photo; **p.98** © Dennis MacDonald/Alamy Stock Photo; **p.99** © Txking/iStock/Thinkstock; **p.101 (top)** © Ross D Franklin/AP/Shutterstock; **p.101 (bottom)** © Paul Kitagaki Jr./ZUMA Wire/Alamy Stock Photo; **p.104 (top)** © Marino/stock.adobe.com; **p.106 (top)** © Erickson Stock/Alamy Stock Photo; **p.106 (bottom)** © PCN Black/PCN Photography/Alamy Stock Photo; **p.107** © Juergen Hasenkopf/Alamy Stock Photo; **p.109** © Moodboard/Thinkstock; **p.110** © Dmac/Alamy Stock Photo; **p.119** © Fred van Wijk/Alamy Stock Photo; **p.123** © Steve Bardens/The RFU Collection/Getty Images; **p.125** © Armando Babani/epa european pressphoto agency b.v./Alamy Stock Photo; **p.130** © Sport Picture Library/Alamy Stock Photo; **p.133/p.140** © Jamie Wiseman/ANL/Shutterstock; **p.135 (top)** © Bagu Blanco/BPI/Shutterstock; **p.135 (centre)** © Sport In Pictures/Alamy Stock Photo; **p.137** © Visage/Stockbyte/Getty Images; **p.141 (top)** © Ron Chapple Studios/Thinkstock; **p.141 (bottom)** © Action Plus Sports Images/Alamy Stock Photo; **p.143** © Mike Booth/Alamy Stock Photo; **p.146** © Daxiao Productions/stock.adobe.com; **p.148** © Gary Mitchell, GMP Media/Alamy Stock Photo; **p.150** © Chad Case/Alamy Stock Photo; **p.151** © Wavebreakmedia/Shutterstock.com; **p.152** © Fuse/Thinkstock; **p.157/p.176** © Thitikorn Suksao/EyeEm/Getty Images; **p.159** sourced from gov.uk 2020; **p.160** © Monkeybusinessimages/iStock/Thinkstock; **p.161** © Ljupco/iStock/Thinkstock; **p.167** © Minadezhda/iStock/Thinkstock; **p.168** © Dave Shopland/BPI/Shutterstock; **p.177** © Action Plus Sports Images/Alamy Stock Photo

Acknowledgements

p.60 Exercise essential to healthy aging by Christine Hinzmann, Glacier Community Media, 2020; **p.70** Courtesy of Hearst Magazines UK; **p.112** © Sabrina Barr/The Independent; **p.177** © bbcgoodfood.com/Immediate Media.

Every effort has been made to trace all copyright holders, but if any have been inadvertently overlooked, the Publishers will be pleased to make the necessary arrangements at the first opportunity.

Although every effort has been made to ensure that website addresses are correct at time of going to press, Hodder Education cannot be held responsible for the content of any website mentioned in this book. It is sometimes possible to find a relocated web page by typing in the address of the home page for a website in the URL window of your browser.

Hachette UK's policy is to use papers that are natural, renewable and recyclable products and made from wood grown in well-managed forests and other controlled sources. The logging and manufacturing processes are expected to conform to the environmental regulations of the country of origin.

Orders: please contact Hachette UK Distribution, Hely Hutchinson Centre, Milton Road, Didcot, Oxfordshire, OX11 7HH. Telephone: +44 (0)1235 827827. Email education@hachette.co.uk Lines are open from 9 a.m. to 5 p.m., Monday to Friday. You can also order through our website: www.hoddereducation.co.uk

ISBN: 978 1 3983 2700 9

© John Honeybourne 2021

First published in 2009
Second edition published in 2016
This third edition published in 2021 by
Hodder Education,
An Hachette UK Company
Carmelite House
50 Victoria Embankment
London EC4Y 0DZ

www.hoddereducation.co.uk

Impression number   10 9 8 7 6 5 4

Year   2025 2024 2023

All rights reserved. Apart from any use permitted under UK copyright law, no part of this publication may be reproduced or transmitted in any form or by any means, electronic or mechanical, including photocopying and recording, or held within any information storage and retrieval system, without permission in writing from the publisher or under licence from the Copyright Licensing Agency Limited. Further details of such licences (for reprographic reproduction) may be obtained from the Copyright Licensing Agency Limited, www.cla.co.uk

Cover photo © Monkey Business – stock.adobe.com

Typeset in India by Aptara, Inc.

Printed and bound by CPI Group (UK) Ltd, Croydon, CR0 4YY

A catalogue record for this title is available from the British Library.

Contents

Introduction — vi

Section 1 Applied Anatomy and Physiology
1.1 The structure and function of the skeletal system — 2
1.2 The structure and function of the muscular system — 11
1.3 Movement analysis — 15
1.4 The cardiovascular and respiratory systems — 20
1.5 The effects of exercise on the body systems — 33

Section 2 Physical Training
2.1 Components of fitness — 44
2.2 Applying the principles of training — 67
2.3 Preventing injury in physical activity and training — 81

Section 3 Socio-cultural Influences
3.1 Engagement patterns of different social groups in physical activities and sports — 92
3.2 Commercialisation of physical activity and sport — 117
3.3 Ethical and socio-cultural issues in physical activity and sport — 123

Section 4 Sports Psychology
4.1 Characteristics of skilful movement and classification of skills — 134
4.2 Goal setting — 139
4.3 Mental preparation — 144
4.4 Types of guidance and feedback — 150

Section 5 Health, Fitness and Well-being
5.1 Health, fitness and well-being — 158
5.2 Diet and nutrition — 167

Glossary — 180
Index — 184

Introduction

This brand new edition of our bestselling OCR endorsed textbook is designed specifically to cover the specification content for the OCR GCSE Physical Education qualification (J587). Each section of the book covers a different main topic area of the OCR specification and each chapter explores in more detail the specification content, along with material that will fully develop each candidate's understanding of each topic area. The book includes extension material to stretch and challenge candidates and to give context to the theoretical principles covered.

What's new in this edition?

- The assessment material, including Check your understanding and Practice questions, has been updated to reflect past exam papers. This includes more analysis (AO2) and evaluation (AO3) longer-form and higher mark questions.
- New sport activities included on the DfE's latest OCR GCSE PE activity list have been included as examples throughout the book.
- More support and some additional content have been added to topics that students often find challenging, in particular in Chapter 1.3 Levers and planes and Section 3 Socio-cultural influences.
- Sporting examples – including reference to specific sportspeople, data and statistics have been updated to reflect current events.

How to use this book

Understanding the Specification
Outline of the main ways the content is related to the specification.

IN THE NEWS
References to contemporary real-life events that are designed to demonstrate the importance of PE to the world around us.

Key terms
A short definition of key vocabulary. Whilst not all of the key terms appear in the OCR GCSE PE Specification, they all provide a short definition of key vocabulary that enables students to fully understand underlying concepts found in the Specification.

Activities
Short tasks and activities to help reinforce learning.

❓ Extend your knowledge
Extension material for each chapter that might go slightly beyond what is stated in the OCR GCSE PE Specification but gives extra information for possible use in extended answers.

✔ Check your understanding
Short, knowledge-based questions to help you check you've understood different topics.

Practice questions
Questions designed to offer study practice.

STUDY HINTS
Handy tips for studying OCR GCSE PE.

SUMMARY
Summary of key points of each chapter.

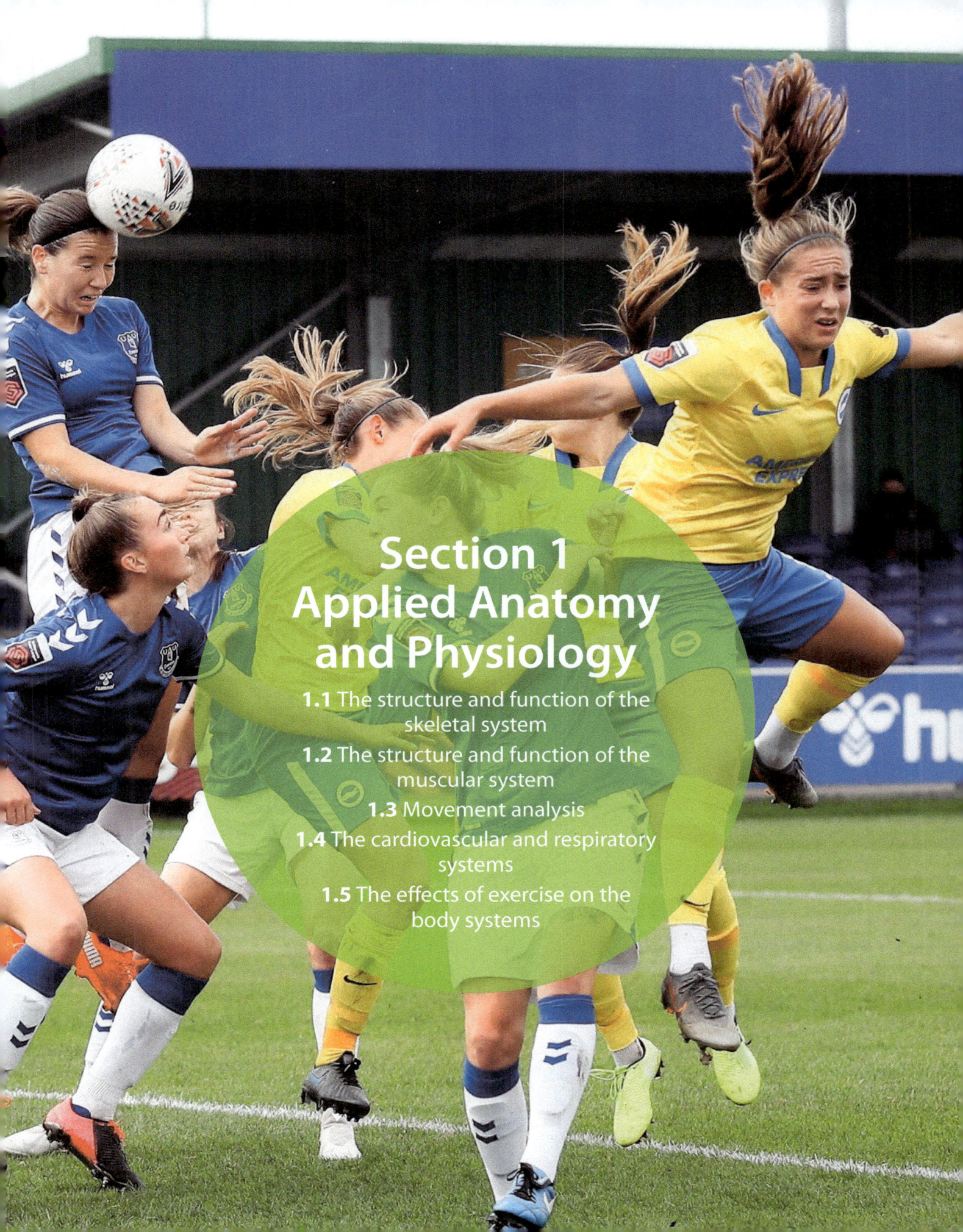

Section 1
Applied Anatomy and Physiology

1.1 The structure and function of the skeletal system
1.2 The structure and function of the muscular system
1.3 Movement analysis
1.4 The cardiovascular and respiratory systems
1.5 The effects of exercise on the body systems

Chapter 1.1
The structure and function of the skeletal system

Understanding the Specification

This topic area will help you know and understand the location of the major bones in the body. By the end of the topic, you will be able to apply examples to the functions of the skeleton. You should know the major joints and the articulating bones (bones that make up the joint) in the knee, elbow, shoulder and hip. You should also know about types of movements at hinge joints and ball and socket joints and be able to use practical examples to show and analyse different movements.

Activity

Write the names of the major bones of the body on separate sticky notes. With a partner, put each sticky note on the appropriate area for the bone, either on a picture or on yourselves.

? Extend your knowledge

The **axial skeleton** is the central part of the skeleton and is the main source of support. It includes the cranium (the skull), the vertebral column (bones that make up the spine) and the rib cage, including 12 pairs of ribs and the sternum.

The **appendicular skeleton** consists of the remaining bones and includes the structures that join these bones on to the axial skeleton.

Location of the major bones

More than 200 bones make up the human skeleton. For us to understand how the body moves effectively in sports activities, it is important to know the location of the main bones.

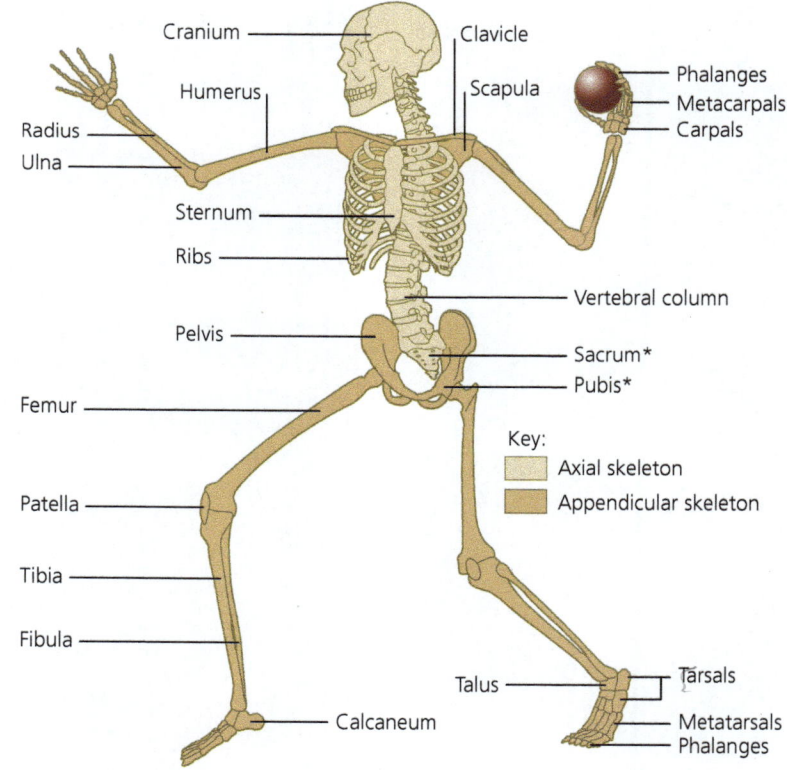

* not required knowledge for OCR GCSE PE Specification

▲ Figure 1.1.1 Location of the major bones in the human body

2

You should know the location of the following bones:
- cranium
- vertebrae
- ribs
- sternum
- clavicle
- scapula
- humerus
- ulna
- radius
- carpals
- metacarpals
- phalanges
- pelvis (ilium)
- femur
- patella
- tibia
- fibula
- tarsals
- metatarsals.

Functions of the skeleton

The skeleton has several major functions:

1. To give shape and support to the body – therefore giving the body posture. This support enables us to stand. The bones of the body are held together by ligaments. The skeleton gives a structural framework to which the muscles are attached via tendons. A practical example of the skeleton providing support is for a gymnast who maintains a controlled shape with straight legs and pointed toes in a handstand.

2. To allow movement of the body – by providing areas or sites for muscle attachment. This also provides a system of levers that helps us to move. A practical example of the skeleton allowing movement is a squash player being able to play a forehand drive.

3. To give protection to the internal organs – such as heart (ribs), lungs (ribs), spinal cord (vertebral column) and the brain (cranium). A practical sports example of the skeleton providing protection is an amateur boxer's ribs protecting the lungs when receiving a blow to the chest.

4. To produce blood – red and white blood cells. Red bone marrow is contained within the ends of long bones and many other types of bones such as the ribs. It produces red blood cells that carry oxygen. A practical example of the importance of blood cell production to the sports performer is a wheelchair basketball player who relies on high levels of oxygen being delivered to the arms via the red blood cells to keep the wheelchair moving. White blood cells form part of the immune system and help fight off infections and other diseases.

5. To store minerals – such as phosphorus, calcium, potassium and iron, etc. Iron helps to transport oxygen to working muscles, and calcium is needed to build and repair bones. A practical sports example of the importance of minerals is a rugby league player who relies on good bone strength to be able to tackle effectively and reduce the chances of injury to bones, e.g. fractures.

Types of synovial joint

A joint is where two or more bones meet. There are many different types of joint in the human body, including some that do not allow movement, or allow very little. Joints are very important in movements related to sport. The type of joint that we are more concerned with is the **synovial joint**.

This is the most common joint and, since it allows for a wide range of movement, is very important to people playing sports. It consists of a joint capsule, lined with a synovial membrane. There is lubrication provided for the joint in the form of synovial fluid. This is secreted into the joint, e.g. the knee joint, by the synovial membrane.

Key term

Synovial joint This is a freely movable joint in which the bones' surfaces are covered by cartilage, called articular cartilage, and connected by a fibrous connective tissue capsule (joint capsule) lined with synovial fluid.

Section 1 Applied Anatomy and Physiology

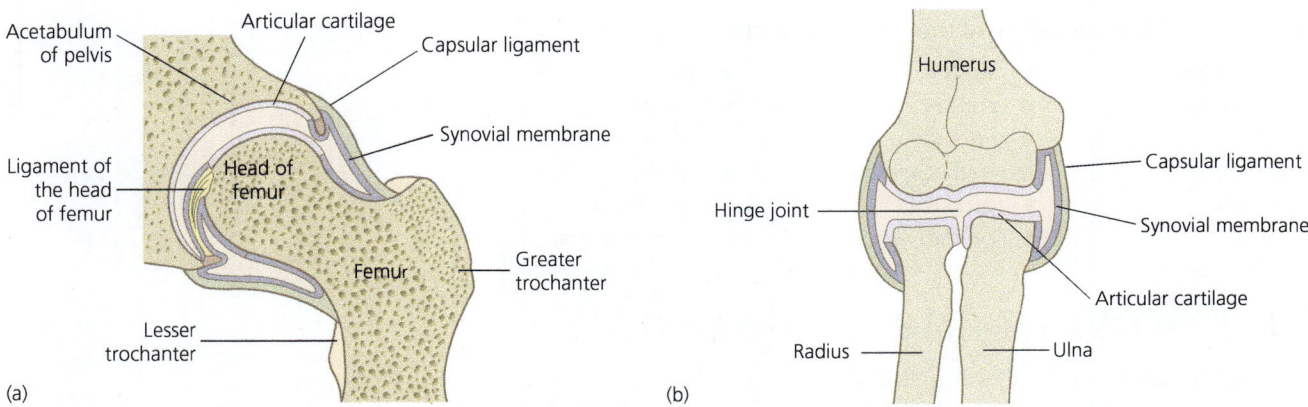

▲ Figure 1.1.2 Diagram of (a) the hip joint and (b) the elbow joint. These are synovial joints

The many different categories for joints relate to the degree of movement that they allow, ranging from fibrous (fixed) to synovial (allowing significant movement). Synovial joints are then further categorised into the type of movement they allow, whether rotational, hinged (hinge) or from side to side (on a plane).

> **? Extend your knowledge**
>
> Other types of joint are:
> - **Fibrous or fixed**: this does not allow any movement. There is tough, fibrous tissue that lays between the ends of the bones, e.g. the sutures or thin joints of the cranium.
> - **Cartilaginous or slightly movable**: this allows some movement. The ends of the bones have tough fibrous cartilage, which allows for shock absorption but also gives stability, e.g. the intervertebral discs between each bone in the vertebral column.

Hinge joint

The hinge joint allows movement in one plane only, just like a door hinge moves (uniaxial), e.g. knee joint and elbow joint. An example of a physical activity that uses the knee joint is sprinting, with the **articulating bones** being the femur and the tibia. For the elbow joint, a physical activity is the biceps curl in weight training, with the articulating bones being the humerus, the radius and the ulna.

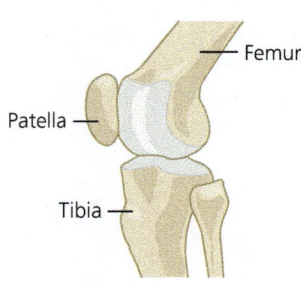

▲ Figure 1.1.3 The knee joint is used extensively in sport and exercise

Key term

Articulating bones These are the bones that move within a joint.

The articulating bones for the knee joint are the:
- femur
- tibia.

The articulating bones for the elbow joint are the:
- humerus
- radius
- ulna.

Ball and socket joint

This allows a wide range of movement and occurs when a round head of bone fits into a cup-shaped depression, e.g. the shoulder joint and the hip joint. An example of a physical activity that uses the shoulder joint is an

Chapter 1.1 The structure and function of the skeletal system

▲ Figure 1.1.4 The javelin thrower needs a healthy and strong shoulder joint

STUDY HINT
Make sure that you can describe the hinge joint (using knee and elbow examples) and the ball and socket joint (using shoulder and hip joints) in particular, because these are identified in the Specification. You need to be able to give examples of each and describe movements that are associated with the use of each of these two joints – for example, the biceps curl for the elbow, the squat movement for the knee, the bowling action for the shoulder and the sit-up action for the hip.

athlete throwing a javelin. An example of a physical activity that uses the hip joint is a sit-up training exercise.

The articulating bones for the shoulder joint are the:
- humerus
- scapula.

The articulating bones for the hip joint are the:
- pelvis
- femur.

Types of movement at hinge joints and ball and socket joints

There are different types of movement associated with the joints in our bodies.

The types of movement at hinge joints are:
- flexion
- extension.

The types of movement at ball and socket joints are:
- flexion
- extension
- rotation
- abduction
- adduction
- circumduction.

Movement at hinge joints

Flexion is a decrease in the angle around a joint.
- **At the knee**: for example, bending your leg at the knee when preparing to make a pass in football.
- **At the elbow**: bending your arm at the elbow and touching your shoulder with your hand – for example, when a badminton player prepares to hit an overhead clear, the arm shows flexion at the elbow (Figure 1.1.5).

? Extend your knowledge

Other types of joint:
- **Pivot joint**: this allows rotation only and is therefore also uniaxial, e.g. axis and atlas of the cervical vertebrae. An example of a physical activity that uses this joint is turning the head to find a fellow player to pass to in hockey.
- **Gliding joint**: this is when two flat surfaces glide over one another and can permit movement in most directions, although mainly biaxial, e.g. the carpal bones in the wrist. An example of a physical activity that uses this joint is dribbling the ball by moving the hockey stick over and back.
- **Saddle joint**: this is when a concave surface meets a convex surface and is biaxial, e.g. carpal–metacarpal joint of the thumb. An example of a physical activity that uses this joint is gripping a tennis racket with the thumb.

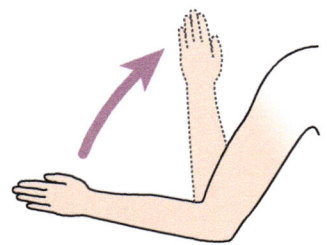

▲ Figure 1.1.5 Flexion at the elbow

Section 1 Applied Anatomy and Physiology

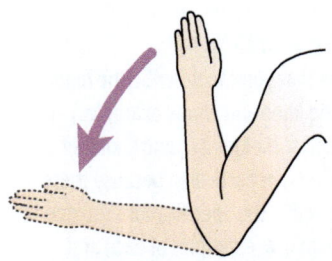

▲ Figure 1.1.6 Extension at the elbow

Extension is when the angle of the bones that are moving (articulating bones) is increased.

- **At the knee**: from a stooped or squat position you then stand up. The angle between your femur and tibia (upper and lower leg) increases, thus extension has taken place – for example, when a basketball player drives up to the basket from bent legs to straight, extension occurs at the knee joint.
- **At the elbow**: straightening your arm at the elbow joint. The angle between the humerus and the radius/ulna (upper and lower arm) is increased, thus extension takes place – for example, when making a basketball set shot, the bent arm moves to a straight arm as you release the ball and extension occurs at the elbow joint (Figure 1.1.6).

Movement at ball and socket joints

Flexion:

- **At the shoulder**: involves movement of the arm forwards and up overhead – for example, lifting the arms out of the water during the backstroke in swimming.
- **At the hip**: describes the bending motion that brings your thigh toward your chest – for example, in hockey, bending down to ensure that your hockey stick is flat on the floor and can stop the ball.

▲ Figure 1.1.7 A ballet dancer moves into first position and rotates the hip joint laterally

Extension:

- **At the shoulder**: is the lowering of the arm from in front and taking it back behind you – for example, the execution of a serve in tennis, when the player takes the arm back before throwing the ball up.
- **At the hip**: moving the leg backwards towards the posterior side of the body – for example, a rugby player extends the hip in preparation for kicking through the ball, to get maximum power.

Rotation:

Rotation is when the bone turns about its longitudinal axis within the joint. Rotation towards the body is called internal or medial rotation; rotation away from the body is called external or lateral rotation. For example:

- **Hip**: a ballet dancer moves into first position and rotates the hip joint laterally (Figure 1.1.7).
- **Shoulder**: a tennis player uses external rotation at the shoulder joint during the backswing of the serve (Figure 1.1.8).

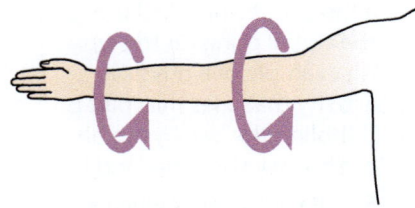

▲ Figure 1.1.8 Rotation at the shoulder

Abduction:

Abduction is the movement of the body away from the middle or the midline of the body – for example:

- **Shoulder**: a swimmer lifts the arms out to the side during the butterfly stroke (Figure 1.1.9).
- **Hip**: a gymnast with her leg lifted to the side of her body shows abduction (Figure 1.1.10).

Adduction:

Adduction is the opposite of abduction and is the movement towards the midline of the body, e.g. lowering your lifted leg that you have abducted towards the middle of your body – for example:

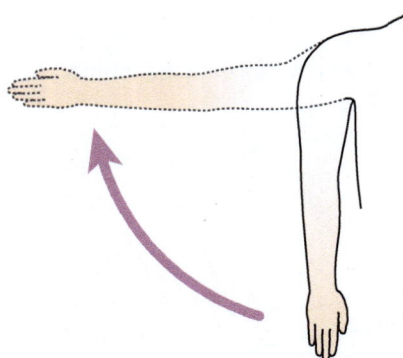

▲ Figure 1.1.9 Abduction at the shoulder

6

Chapter 1.1 The structure and function of the skeletal system

- **Shoulder**: a rugby player tackling another player will hold on to the player by adducting her arms as she tackles (Figure 1.1.11).
- **Hip**: in swimming the recovery of the legs from the breaststroke leg kick involves adduction (Figure 1.1.12).

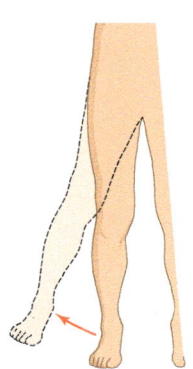

▲ Figure 1.1.10 Abduction of the leg at the hip

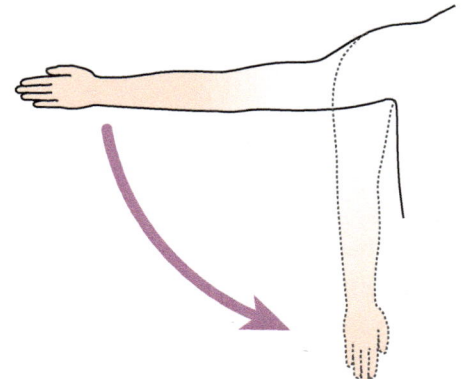

▲ Figure 1.1.11 Adduction at the shoulder

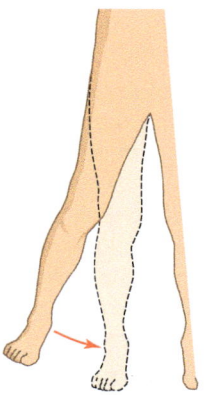

▲ Figure 1.1.12 Adduction at the hip

Circumduction:
Circumduction is a combination of abduction, adduction, extension or flexion and rotation. It describes a continuous circular movement of a limb around a joint:

- **Hip**: a gymnast on the beam takes her back leg off the beam and moves it out and round to place her foot ahead of her front foot (Figure 1.1.13).
- **Shoulder**: a swimmer during the front crawl will take their arm out and round and back into the water, showing circumduction at the shoulder joint.

Other components of joints

Besides articulating bones, there are three other main components of joints that it is helpful for budding athletes to know about. These are:

- ligaments
- cartilage
- tendons.

In the same way that joints link the various bones in our body, these tissue-based components help to reduce wear and tear in a variety of ways, for example, by absorbing shock or reducing friction.

Ligaments

These are found between bones and attach bone to bone. They are bands of connective tissue that are very tough and resilient.

- **Function**: the role of ligaments is to help join bones together and keep the joints stable during movement.

Some ligaments lie within the synovial capsule, others are outside the capsule. The ligaments prevent movements that are extreme and help stop dislocation.

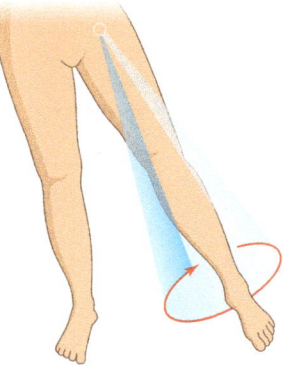

▲ Figure 1.1.13 Circumduction at the hip

Activity

1. Sketch a simple diagram of the knee joint and label the bones that move around this joint.
2. Name a specific skill that involves both flexion and extension of the knee joint.
3. Draw the hip joint and label the bones that move around this joint.
4. Describe a skill in a physical activity that involves both abduction and adduction of the hip joint.

Section 1 Applied Anatomy and Physiology

> **? Extend your knowledge**
>
> There are three basic types of cartilage:
> - **Yellow elastic cartilage:** flexible tissue, e.g. part of the ear lobe.
> - **Hyaline or blue articular cartilage:** found on the articulating surfaces of bones, it protects and allows movement between bones with limited friction and therefore more flexibility. Hyaline cartilage can thicken as a result of exercise.
> - **White fibro-cartilage:** consists of tough tissue that acts as a shock absorber. It is found in parts of the body where there is a great amount of stress, for example, the semi-lunar cartilage in the knee joint. It also allows bones to fit together properly; for example, as discs between the vertebrae.

Key term

Meniscus cartilage In the knee, these are areas of cartilage tissue that act like shock absorbers in the joint.

Cartilage

This is soft connective tissue.
- **Function:** the role of cartilage is to reduce friction and act as a shock absorber for the joint.

Newly born babies have a skeleton consisting of cartilage and as they get older this cartilage is mostly replaced by bone, a process known as ossification. Bones have a blood supply, but cartilage has no blood supply.

You may tear a cartilage with a forceful knee movement. For example, a footballer may twist the knee while their foot is still on the ground, perhaps while dribbling round a defender. Or a tennis player may twist to hit a ball hard but keep their foot in the same position.

Sometimes a tear develops due to repeated small injuries to the cartilage, or to degeneration ('wear and tear') of the **meniscus cartilage** in older people. In severe injuries, other parts of the knee may be damaged in addition to a meniscus tear – for example, you may also sprain or tear a ligament.

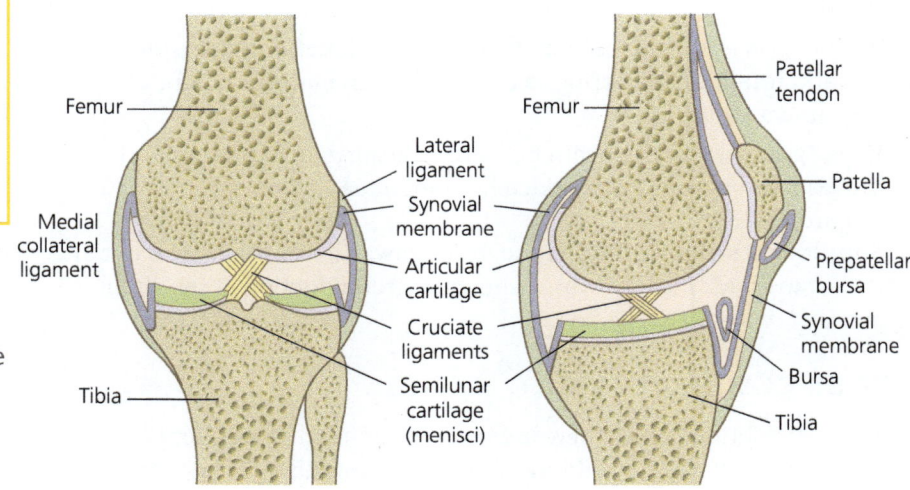

▲ Figure 1.1.14 (a) The knee joint viewed from the rear   ▲ Figure 1.1.14 (b) The knee joint viewed from the side

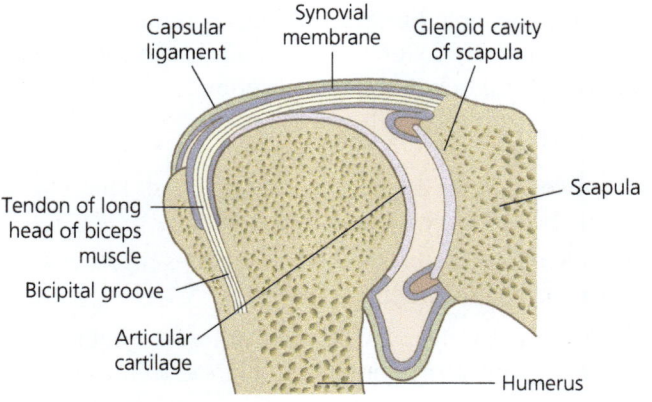

▲ Figure 1.1.14 (c) The shoulder joint

Chapter 1.1 The structure and function of the skeletal system

The cartilage does not heal very well once it is torn. This is mainly because it does not have a good blood supply. So, some small outer tears may heal in time, but larger tears, or a tear in the middle of the knee cartilage, tend not to heal properly.

IN THE NEWS
The benefits of running

Many people, including some health professionals, agree that running can damage knee joints. However, exercise supplies our joints with important nutrients and is important to maintain healthy cartilage. Research also shows that recreational runners actually experience lower rates of knee osteoarthritis compared to non-runners.

The other benefit is that you can run outdoors, and alone if you prefer, which makes it a great way to exercise during a pandemic, such as the COVID-19 pandemic that started in 2020.

? Extend your knowledge

Severs disease is common in children and can cause pain around the heel bone of the foot – called the calcaneus. This condition (it is not actually a disease) affects children during an adolescent growth spurt – especially those who are physically active with lots of running and jumping. It is caused by inflammation as a result of over-use, or excessive force on, the growth plate.

Tendons

Muscles are attached to bones via tendons. These are strong and can be a little flexible.

- **Function**: as well as their attachment role, they help to transmit the power needed to move bones. When a muscle shortens, it pulls on the tendons; this pulls on the bones to which the tendons are attached and causes movement.

? Extend your knowledge

Osgood-Schlatter's disease is often found in adolescents, especially those who are regular sports participants.

It is a disease that causes pain and swelling below the knee and is associated with overuse. It is often treated through the application of ice and resting the leg. The pain associated with Osgood-Schlatter's disease goes away when bone growth is finished.

An active, healthy lifestyle that is balanced in the amount and type of exercise undertaken can limit the damage that may be caused to tendons. Exercise can strengthen tendons and make them less prone to injury.

Section 1 Applied Anatomy and Physiology

> **SUMMARY**
> - The main functions of the skeleton are to give shape and support to the body, to allow movement of the body, to give protection to the internal organs, to produce blood cells and to store minerals.
> - Muscles are attached to bones via tendons. As well as their attachment role, they help to transmit the power needed to move bones.
> - The role of ligaments is to help join bones together and keep the joints stable during movement. The role of cartilage is to reduce friction and act as a shock absorber for the joint.
> - The articulating bones for the knee joint are the femur and the tibia. The articulating bones for the elbow joint are the humerus, the radius and the ulna. The articulating bones for the shoulder joint are the humerus and the scapula.
> - A synovial joint is a freely movable joint in which the bony surfaces are covered by articular cartilage and connected by a fibrous connective tissue capsule lined with a synovial membrane.
> - Flexion is a decrease in the angle around a joint. Extension is when the angle of the bones that are moving (articulating bones) is increased. Rotation is when the bone turns about its longitudinal axis within the joint.
> - Abduction is the movement of the body away from the middle or the midline of the body. Adduction is the opposite of abduction and is the movement towards the midline of the body.
> - Circumduction is a combination of abduction, adduction, extension or flexion and rotation. It describes a continuous circular movement of a limb around a joint.

Practice questions

1. Which one of the following is an articulating bone in the knee joint? **(1 mark)**
   a. ulna
   b. radius
   c. tibia
   d. fibula

2. Describe how the skeleton performs four of its main functions. **(4 marks)**

3. Which one of the following statements is false? **(1 mark)**
   a. The movement at the knee joint during a leg curl is an example of flexion and extension.
   b. The movement at the shoulder joint during a bicep curl is an example of abduction.
   c. Most of the lever systems that provide movement in sport are examples of third class levers.
   d. An example of a second-class lever is a badminton player using their ankle joint during a smash.

4. A Gaelic football player will use their elbow joint when catching the ball. Name the two articulating bones in the elbow joint that are at risk of injury during the catch in a Gaelic football game. **(2 marks)**

Chapter 1.2
The structure and function of the muscular system

Understanding the Specification

This topic area will teach you the name and location of the main muscle groups in the human body and you will be able to apply them to examples from physical activity/sport. You will need to know the definitions and roles of the:

- agonist
- antagonist
- fixator
- antagonistic muscle action.

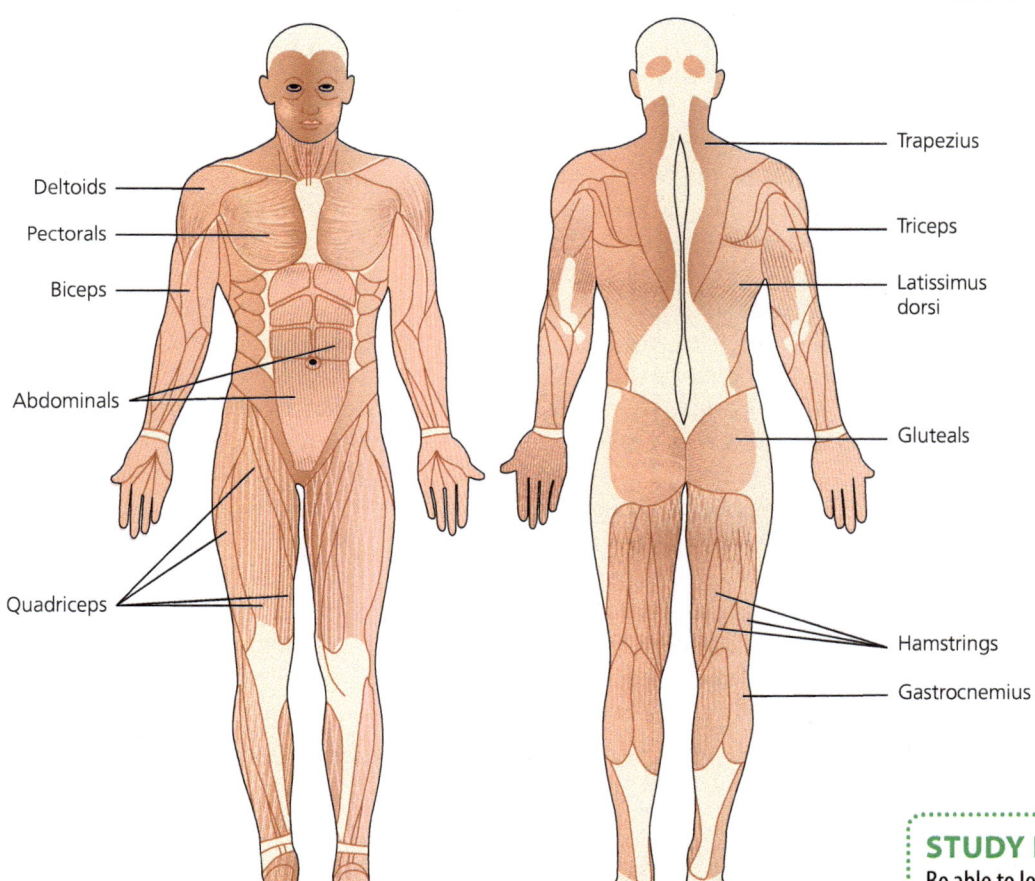

▲ Figure 1.2.1 The main muscle groups in the human body

Muscles are made up of soft muscle tissue and skeletal muscle enables us to move. In sport, the study of muscle and how it works gives us a good insight into how we might make our sports skills and activities even more effective and efficient.

> **STUDY HINT**
> Be able to locate each of these major muscle groups and label an appropriate diagram showing the position of each muscle group. Also know the main role of each of these groups by using an example from sport. For example, the quadriceps extends the leg at the knee joint – an action used when kicking a football.

Section 1 Applied Anatomy and Physiology

The location of major muscle groups

The following muscles are named in the specification:

- **Deltoid** – this is used in all movements of the arms. Its most important function is to lift the arm straight out to the side and up (abduction at shoulder joint), e.g. to make a block in volleyball with arms straight above the head.
- **Trapezius** – this causes extension at the neck, e.g a rugby forward in a scrum will use the trapezius to bind into the opponents.
- **Latissimus dorsi** – this is the broad back muscle. It causes adduction at the shoulder joint. It will swing the arm backwards and rotate it inwards. For example, a tennis player who swings their arm back to hit the ball when serving is using the latissimus dorsi.
- **Pectorals** – there are two sets of chest muscles: pectoralis major (greater chest muscle) and pectoralis minor (lesser chest muscle). This causes adduction and flexion at the shoulder joint in the horizontal plane. These help to adduct the arm and rotate it inwards as well as lowering the shoulder blades. For example, a rugby player making a tackle would hold on to their opponent using the pectoral muscles.
- **Biceps** (biceps brachii) – this causes flexion at the elbow. Its function is to swing the upper arm forward and to turn the forearm so that the palm of the hand points upwards (supination), e.g. biceps curl in weight training.
- **Triceps** (triceps brachii) – this causes extension at the elbow. Its function is to straighten the elbow and to swing the arm backwards, e.g. backhand in table tennis.
- **Abdominals** – these bend the body forwards at the hips causing flexion of vertebral column and help to turn the upper body. For example, performing a sit-up exercise will use the abdominals.
- **Quadriceps** – this provides stability to the knee joint and extends or straightens the knee joint. For example, a long jumper when driving off the board will straighten the knee joint at take-off using the quadriceps.
- **Hamstrings** – these muscles will straighten the hip and cause flexion at the knee joint. They will also bend the knee and rotate it outwards. For example, a hockey player running across the pitch will be using her hamstrings in the running action to bend the knees.

Activity

1. Write the names of the major muscle groups on sticky notes
2. With a partner, place the sticky notes on each other's body showing that you know the location of the muscle groups. Or use a diagram and identify the major muscle groups.
3. You could make giant posters for the classroom walls to help you to remember the locations of these muscle groups.

❓ Extend your knowledge

There are three types of muscle:
- Involuntary muscle – or smooth muscle, which is found in the body's internal organs. This is involuntary muscle because it is not under our conscious control.
- Cardiac muscle – this is found in the heart only and is also involuntary.
- Skeletal or voluntary muscle – this is under our conscious control and is used primarily for movement, e.g. the biceps muscle in our arms.

▲ Figure 1.2.2 A hockey player will use her hamstrings to bend the knees when she runs

12

Chapter 1.2 The structure and function of the muscular system

- **Gluteals** – these are the muscles in your buttocks. They cause extension at the hip joint and adduct the hip, rotate the thigh outwards and help to straighten the knee. For example, a sprinter will use the gluteals in the leg action of sprinting down the track.
- **Gastrocnemius** – this muscle is used to bend the knee and to straighten or plantarflex the ankle. For example, a swimmer doing front crawl will point their toes in the leg action using the gastrocnemius.

The roles of muscles in movement

Pairs of muscles

There is a vast range of movements that can be made by the human body. To produce these movements, muscles either shorten, lengthen or remain the same length when they contract. Muscles work in pairs: as one muscle contracts, the other relaxes. Muscles that work together like this are called **antagonistic pairs**. This type of action enables the body to move with stability and control.

Examples of antagonistic pairs are:

- **Biceps and triceps** – at the elbow joint. As the biceps bends or flexes the elbow joint by contracting, the triceps relaxes. As the arm straightens, the opposite occurs.
- **Hamstrings and quadriceps** – at the knee joint. The hamstrings contract and the quadriceps relax and the knee joint flexes. As the knee joint extends, the quadriceps (quads) contract and the hamstrings relax.

Agonist

This is the working muscle that produces or controls the desired joint movement. It is also known as the **prime mover**. For example, the biceps brachii is the muscle that produces the flexion movement at the elbow.

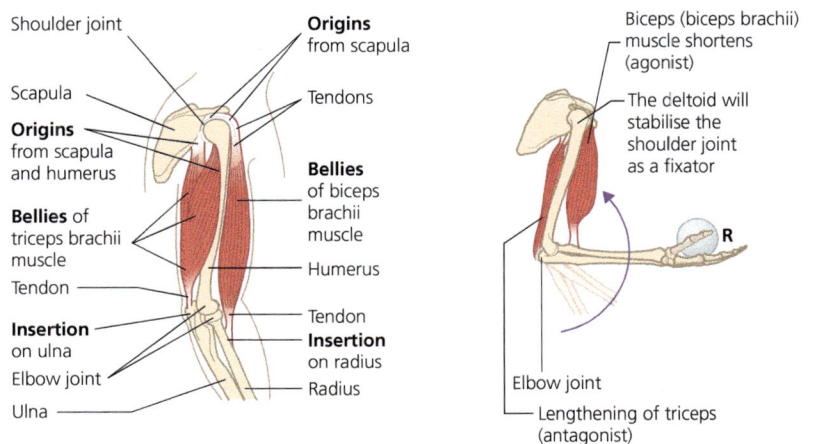

▲ Figure 1.2.3 Flexion at the elbow with agonist labelled

Key terms

Agonist This is the muscle that initiates a movement. It is also called the prime mover.

Antagonistic pair This is a pair of muscles that work together: as one muscle contracts then the other muscle relaxes.

Prime mover This is the muscle that initiates the movement and is also often called the agonist. A prime mover does not act alone – it acts simultaneously with other muscles to perform a specific movement.

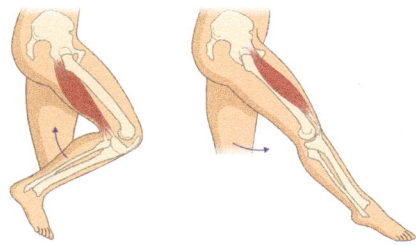

▲ Figure 1.2.4 Antagonistic pairs at the knee joint

Key terms

Origin This is the end of the muscle attached to a bone that is stable, e.g. the scapula. The point of origin remains still when contraction occurs.

Insertion This is the end of the muscle attached to the bone that actively moves, e.g. the biceps insertion is on the radius.

13

Section 1 Applied Anatomy and Physiology

> **? Extend your knowledge**
>
> **Synergists**
> These refer to muscles that are actively helping the prime mover or agonist to produce the desired movement. They are sometimes called **neutralisers** because they prevent any undesired movements. Sometimes the fixator and the synergist are the same muscle, e.g. the brachialis acts as a synergist when the elbow is bent and the forearm moves upwards. For example, the arm action when a volleyball player is setting the ball.

Antagonist

For movement to be co-ordinated, muscles work in pairs so that control is maintained. The movement caused by the agonist is countered by the action of the opposing muscle, called the antagonist. For example, the flexion at the elbow caused by the biceps shortening is opposed by the lengthening of the triceps, which acts as the antagonist, which is the relaxing muscle.

Fixator

This is a muscle that works with others to stabilise the origin of the prime mover. For example, the trapezius contracts to stabilise the origin of the biceps.

Some muscles have two or more origins. For example, the biceps muscle has two heads that pull on the one insertion to lift the lower arm.

> **SUMMARY**
> - The agonist, also known as the prime mover, is the working muscle and produces the desired joint movement, e.g. the biceps produces flexion at the elbow.
> - The role of the antagonist is to counter or oppose the action of the agonist.
> - The fixator works with others to stabilise the joint.
> - Antagonistic muscle action is when muscles work in pairs. As one muscle contracts, the other relaxes.

Practice questions

1. Which one of the following statements is false? **(1 mark)**
   a. Fixators help to stabilise a joint.
   b. An example of a first-class lever is a gymnast standing on tip toes.
   c. A common hazard in rugby league is concussion.
   d. Circuit training involves repetition of several different activities.

2. Which one of the following muscles is the odd one out in relation to location in the human body? **(1 mark)**
   a. deltoid
   b. trapezius
   c. gastrocnemius
   d. pectorals

3. Identify the two different types of movement that can take place at the elbow joint. **(2 marks)**

4. The knee is an example of a synovial joint. Complete the table below for the knee joint. **(3 marks)**

Type of joint (other than synovial)	Articulating bones	Movements available
i.	Femur and ii.	iii. and extension

14

Chapter 1.3
Movement analysis

Understanding the Specification

This topic area will teach you the three classes of lever and you will be able to apply examples from physical activity/sport to each class.

You will need to know the planes of movement and axes of rotation and be able to apply examples from physical activity/sport to each class of lever.

Lever systems

Levers are important in movement because they allow efficiency and force to be applied to the body's movements.

Many bones and muscles act together to form levers. A lever is a rigid structure, a length of bone that turns about a pivot – the joint.

Levers are used to make a small amount of force into a much bigger force. This is known as gaining **mechanical advantage**.

There are four parts to a lever: lever arm, pivot, effort and load.

- Bones act as lever arms.
- Joints act as pivots.
- Muscles provide the effort to move loads.
- Load forces are often the weight of the body parts that are moved or forces needed to lift, push or pull things.

Levers can also be used to increase the force of movement. For example, when throwing a javelin, small contractions of arm and back muscles produce a much greater force of movement at the end of the arm.

Key term

Mechanical advantage Some levers (first class and second class) provide mechanical advantage. This means that they allow you to move a large output load with a smaller effort. Load and effort are forces and are measured in Newtons (N). Mechanical advantage is calculated as follows:

Mechanical advantage = Load ÷ Effort

For example, where the load = 500 N and the effort = 100 N, the mechanical advantage would be:

$$500 \text{ N} \div 100 \text{ N} = 5$$

▲ Figure 1.3.1 Levers can be used to increase the force of movement

Section 1 Applied Anatomy and Physiology

> **STUDY HINT**
> Make sure you can define each class of lever and that you can use the following joints in appropriate practical examples: neck; ankle; elbow.

IN THE NEWS

Using high-speed cameras to evaluate movement

At the 2017 IAAF World Championships in London, there were 49 high-speed and HD cameras. Their recordings were analysed to evaluate the movements of the world's top athletes, such as Usain Bolt, Mo Farah and Allyson Felix. Analysing the Men's 100 metres included measuring the angles at which various parts of the eight finalists' bodies were positioned at touchdown and toe off (that is, when their foot was in contact with the ground and when that same foot was in the air). The analysis showed that Bolt's left foot was in contact with the ground for a longer period of time than his right – this could have been a contributory factor to a persistent left leg injury. (This issue with his technique and the leg injury can be attributed to the extreme scoliosis he suffers as a result of his poor technique when running the bend as a junior.)

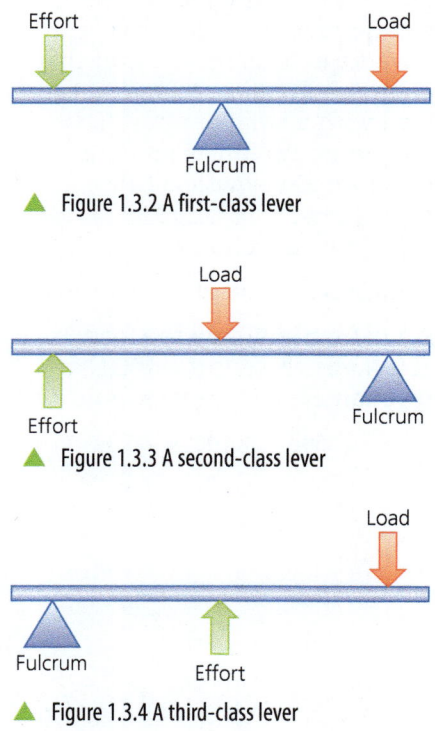

▲ Figure 1.3.2 A first-class lever

▲ Figure 1.3.3 A second-class lever

▲ Figure 1.3.4 A third-class lever

There are three classes or types of lever. Some levers operate differently to others.

1. **First-class levers** – the fulcrum (sometimes called the pivot) is located between the effort force and the load force on the lever arm. First class levers can increase both the effects of the effort and the speed of a body. An example of this type of lever is the neck joint.
   - **Practical example**: At the neck – heading a ball in football is an example of a first-class lever. Extending the arm when shooting in basketball is another example.
2. **Second-class levers** – this is when the load or resistance is between the fulcrum and the effort. Second class levers tend only to increase the effect of the effort force. If you raise up on your toes or plantarflex at the ankle, the second-class lever comes into operation.
   - **Practical example**: At the ankle – standing on tip toes when reaching for a smash in badminton.
3. **Third-class levers** – this is when the effort is between the fulcrum and the load or resistance. Third class levers can be used to increase the speed of a body. This is the most common form of lever in the human body.
   - **Practical example**: At the elbow – the action of the biceps and the triceps at the elbow joint when performing a biceps curl.
   - At the knee – the action of the hamstrings and the quadriceps at the knee joint when leaping up to catch a basketball.

> **STUDY HINT**
> One way to remember the different types of levers is:
> EFL the ELF FEL
> (EFL = first-class lever; ELF = second-class lever; FEL = third-class lever)

Planes of movement

To be able to explain how the body moves, it is useful to see the body as having imaginary lines or planes running through it. These planes divide the body in three ways:
- frontal plane
- transverse plane
- sagittal plane.

Chapter 1.3 Movement analysis

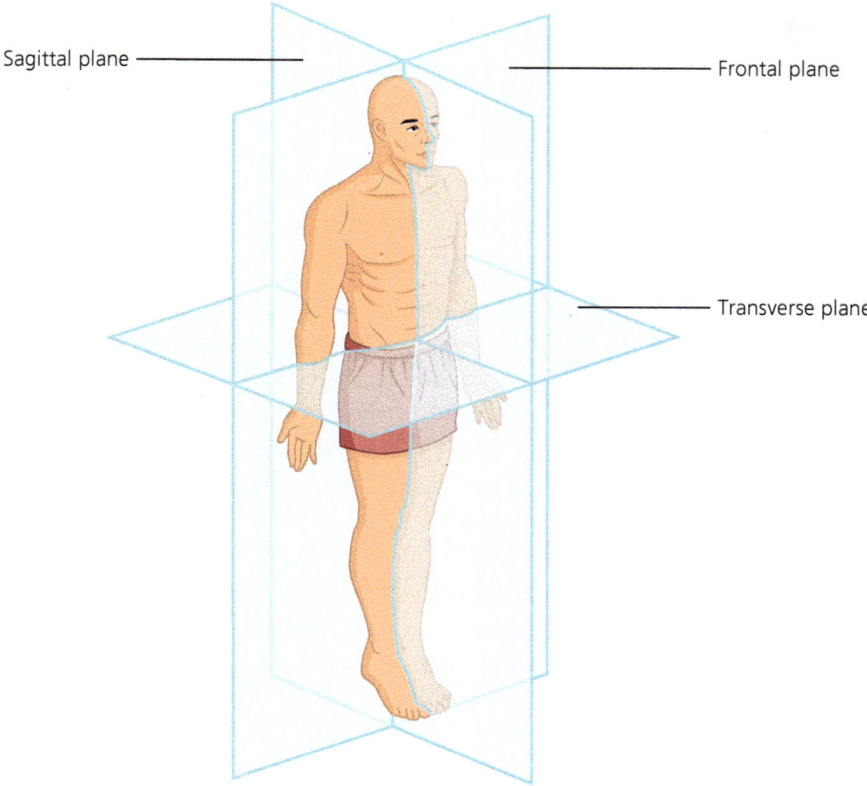

▲ Figure 1.3.5 The planes of movement

Frontal plane

The frontal plane runs vertically and divides the body in sections, between front (anterior) and back (posterior). Movements in this plane are sideways movements of abduction and adduction.
- **Practical example**: abduction and adduction of the legs at the hip joint, e.g. performing 'jumping jack' type exercises, or action at the hip during the breast stroke leg action in swimming.

Transverse plane

The transverse plane divides the body into upper or superior section and lower or inferior section. Movements in this plane are rotational.
- **Practical example**: arm action (circumduction) when bowling in cricket with rotation at the shoulder joint.

Sagittal plane

The sagittal plane splits the body vertically into left and right sides. Movements in this plane are the up and down movements of flexion and extension.
- **Practical example**: leg action in running takes place in a sagittal plane.

> **? Extend your knowledge**
>
> Multi-planar movement is the body working in all planes and can be a good full-body workout. A dancer can spin and leap in a multi-planar activity. Many movements in sports activities involve movements that are multi-planar.

17

Section 1 Applied Anatomy and Physiology

Axes of rotation

Key term

Axes of rotation The centre around which something rotates.

An axis is a straight line around which an object rotates. The movement at a joint takes place in a plane about an axis.

There are three **axes of rotation**:
- frontal axis
- transverse axis
- longitudinal axis.

The frontal axis runs horizontally from the front of the body to the back of the body and is formed by the intersection (crossing over) of the sagittal and transverse planes. A practical example of an activity showing the frontal axis of rotation is when a gymnast performs a cartwheel.

The transverse axis of rotation passes horizontally from the left of the body to the right of the body and is formed by the intersection of the frontal and transverse planes. A practical example of an activity showing the transverse axis of rotation is a trampolinist performing a somersault.

The longitudinal axis of rotation passes vertically from the top of the body to the bottom of the body and is formed by the intersection of the sagittal and frontal planes. A practical example of an activity showing the longitudinal axis of rotation is when a figure skater performs a full 360° turn.

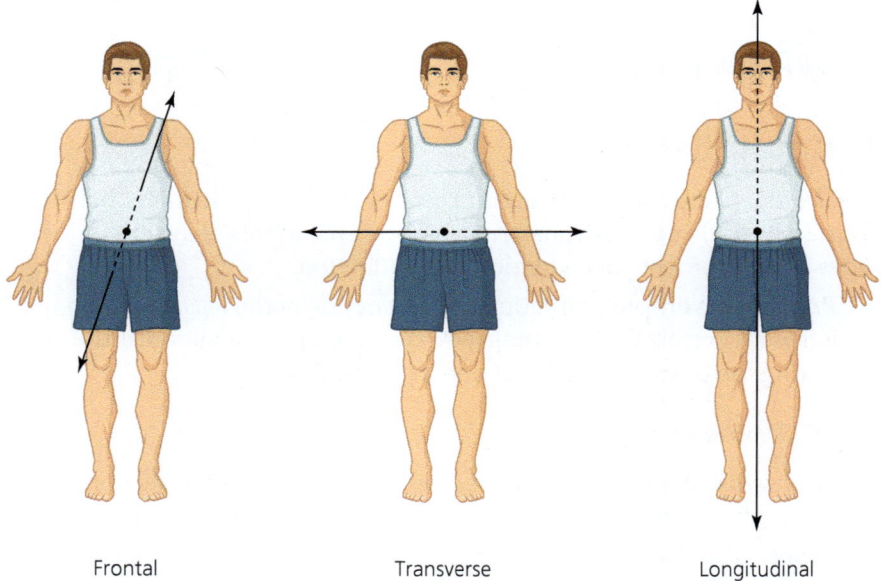

Frontal   Transverse   Longitudinal

▲ Figure 1.3.6 The axes of rotation

? Extend your knowledge

The frontal plane is sometimes called the coronal plane.
The transverse plane is also known as an axial plane or cross-section.

▼ Table 1.3.1a Movements with their dominant planes

Plane	Movement
Frontal	Adduction/abduction
Transverse	Rotation
Saggital	Flexion/extension

18

Chapter 1.3 Movement analysis

▼ Table 1.3.1b Activity examples with their axes of rotation

Axis	Example
Transverse (side to side)	Somersault
Longitudinal (top to bottom)	Pirouette in dance
Frontal (back to front)	Cartwheel

> **STUDY HINT**
> Link a plane of movement to an axis of rotation for a variety of activities other than those shown in Table 1.3.1b. Examination questions may ask for locations of each axis and for a practical example for each. Use diagrams for each axis to help you to remember.

SUMMARY

- Levers are important in movement because they allow efficiency and force to be applied to the body's movements.
- First class and second class levers can both provide mechanical advantage.
- First-class levers – the fulcrum is located between the effort force and the load force.
- Second-class levers – this is when the load or resistance is between the fulcrum and the effort.
- Third-class levers – this is when the effort is between the fulcrum and the load or resistance.
- The frontal plane runs vertically and divides the body in sections, between front (anterior) and back (posterior). Movements in the frontal plane are abduction and adduction.
- The transverse plane divides the body into upper or superior section and lower or inferior section. Movements in the transverse plane are rotational.
- The sagittal plane splits the body vertically into left and right sides. Movements in the sagittal plane are the up and down movements of flexion and extension.
- An axis is a straight line around which an object rotates. There are three axes of rotation:
  - frontal (front to back) axis
  - transverse (side to side) axis
  - longitudinal (top to bottom) axis.

Practice questions

1. Which class of lever will a football player be using in their neck when heading a ball? **(1 mark)**
2. Identify the main plane of movement for the arm action during bowling in cricket. **(1 mark)**
3. Using practical examples, explain the difference between the frontal and longitudinal axes of rotation. **(3 marks)**
4. Explain the differences between a second-class and a third-class lever system. **(3 marks)**

Chapter 1.4
The cardiovascular and respiratory systems

Understanding the Specification

In this large topic area you will learn about the structure and function of the cardiovascular system, including:
- the double circulatory system (systemic and pulmonary)
- the different types of blood vessels
- the pathway of blood through the heart.

You will know the definitions of heart rate, stroke volume and cardiac output as well as learning about the role of red blood cells. This topic area also covers the structure and function of the respiratory system and you will understand:

- the pathway of air through the respiratory system
- the role of respiratory muscles in breathing.

You will need to understand the definitions of:
- breathing rate
- tidal volume
- minute ventilation.

You will need to understand about alveoli as the site of gaseous exchange.

This topic area includes the definitions of aerobic and anaerobic exercise and you should be able to apply practical examples of aerobic and anaerobic activities in relation to intensity and duration.

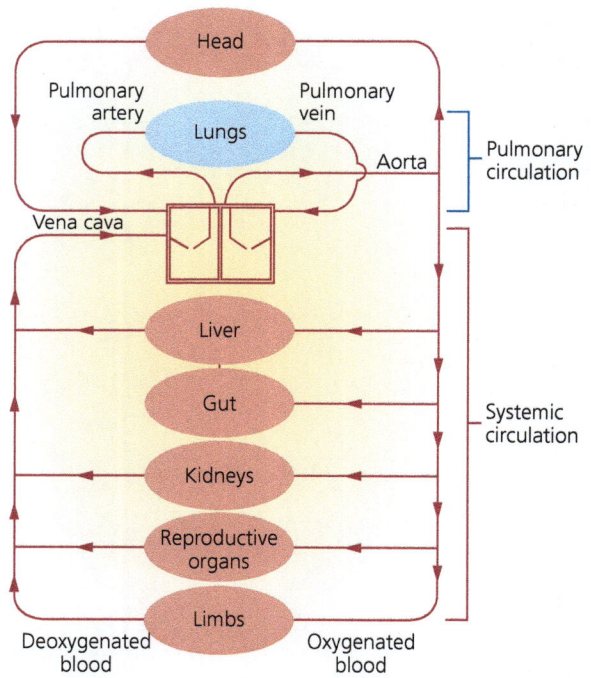

▲ Figure 1.4.1 The double circulatory system

Structure and function of the cardiovascular system

Both the heart and the blood vessels are crucial for anyone who wishes to improve their fitness for sport. A good working knowledge of these will enable an athlete to identify how the body can be helped to work harder and for longer.

The double circulatory system

Blood in the body continuously flows through a network of blood vessels that forms a double circuit. This circuit connects the heart to the lungs and then the heart to the other organs in the body. This double circuit involves pulmonary circulation and systemic circulation.

The pulmonary system

This involves the transportation of blood between the lungs and the heart. The pulmonary artery takes deoxygenated blood from the right ventricle of the heart to the lungs. In the lungs the blood becomes oxygenated and off-loads carbon dioxide. The pulmonary vein then takes the oxygenated blood back to the left atrium of the heart.

The systemic system

The blood is pumped from the left ventricle of the heart into the aorta. The blood is then transported to the rest of the body via arteries. Veins return

Chapter 1.4 The cardiovascular and respiratory systems

the blood, which is low in oxygen and high in carbon dioxide, to the heart. The blood then enters the right atrium via the vena cava.

> **STUDY HINT**
> Be able to draw a simple diagram of the double circulatory system and describe the pulmonary and systemic elements of this double system. See Figure 1.4.2.
>
>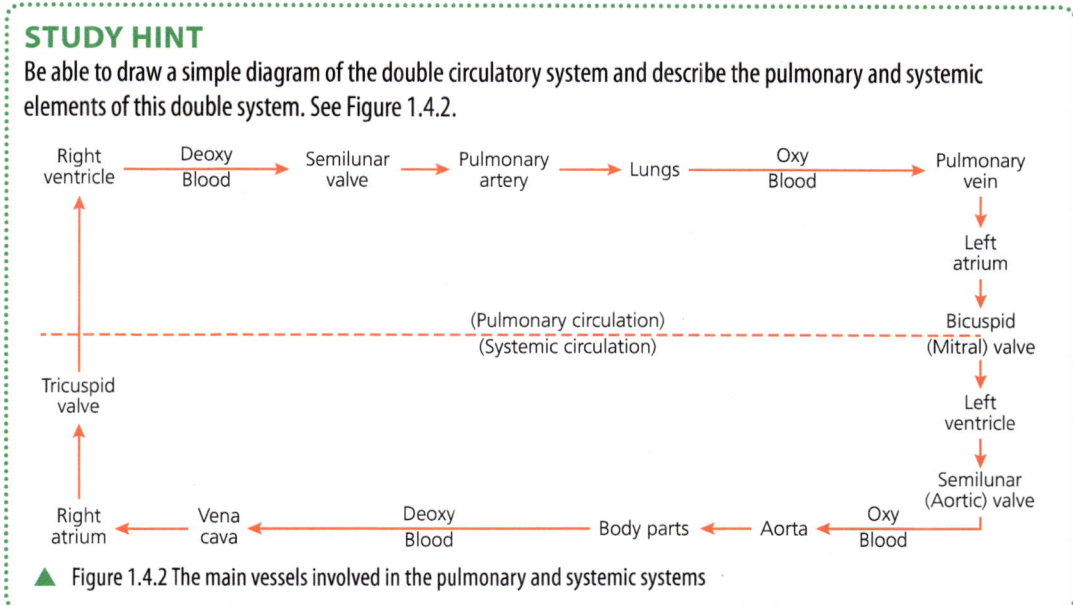
>
> ▲ Figure 1.4.2 The main vessels involved in the pulmonary and systemic systems

Blood and blood vessels

Blood vessels are an integral part of the **cardiovascular** system and are essential for the transportation of material around the body. During exercise, most of the blood goes to the working muscles so that oxygen can be delivered and carbon dioxide taken away efficiently and effectively, which is important when the body is exercising.

Blood consists of cells and is surrounded by a liquid called plasma. The total blood volume in the average male is five to six litres and the blood volume in the average female is four to five litres. Blood also consists of erythrocytes, which are red corpuscles (cells) containing **haemoglobin**.

Blood also consists of leucocytes, which are white blood cells that combat infection, and thrombocytes (platelets), which are important in the process of blood clotting.

The vascular system includes blood vessels called:
- arteries
- arterioles
- capillaries
- veins
- venules.

The role of red blood cells

Red blood cells, or erythrocytes, are the most abundant blood cells. The primary function of red blood cells is to transport oxygen to cells around the body and to deliver carbon dioxide to the lungs.

Arteries

These are blood vessels that carry blood at high pressure from the heart to the body tissues. The largest artery is called the aorta, which leaves the heart and subdivides into smaller vessels. The smaller of these are called arterioles and have a very small diameter. The walls of arteries

Key terms

Cardiovascular Cardio means heart, vascular means circulatory networks of the blood vessels.

Haemoglobin This is iron-rich protein found in red blood cells and transports oxygen in the blood. The more concentrated the haemoglobin, the more oxygen can be carried. This concentration can be increased through endurance training.

> **❓ Extend your knowledge**
>
> The University of Delaware in the USA has investigated the measurement of haemoglobin. The concentration of haemoglobin affects sports performance. The concentration of haemoglobin can be affected by altitude training and exercise intensity. Endurance athletes such as long-distance track runners often get their haemoglobin concentration tested as part of their training to check how effective their training has been.

Section 1 Applied Anatomy and Physiology

Key terms

Vasodilation This occurs when the artery walls increase their diameter.

Vasoconstriction This occurs when the artery walls decrease their diameter.

contain smooth muscle tissue, which enables the vessels to increase (**vasodilation**) or decrease their diameter (**vasoconstriction**). This then controls the blood flow and therefore the amount of oxygen that is delivered to body tissues.

By increasing and decreasing their diameter, the vessels in arteries can therefore help to change the pressure of the blood, which is especially important during exercise. Normally during exercise, the blood pressure increases to ensure the flow of blood with much needed oxygen throughout the body.

Veins

These carry blood at low pressure and return the blood to the heart. Their walls are less muscular but gradually increase in thickness as they approach the heart. The vena cava is the largest vein, which enters the heart through the right atrium. The smallest veins are called venules and these transport the blood from the capillaries. Veins contain pocket valves that prevent the backflow of blood. The pulmonary vein carries oxygenated blood from the lungs to the left atrium of the heart.

Capillaries

These have only a single layer of cells in their walls. This makes them thin enough for nutrients and waste products to pass through them. Capillaries occur in large quantities around the muscles and this enables effective exchange of gases.

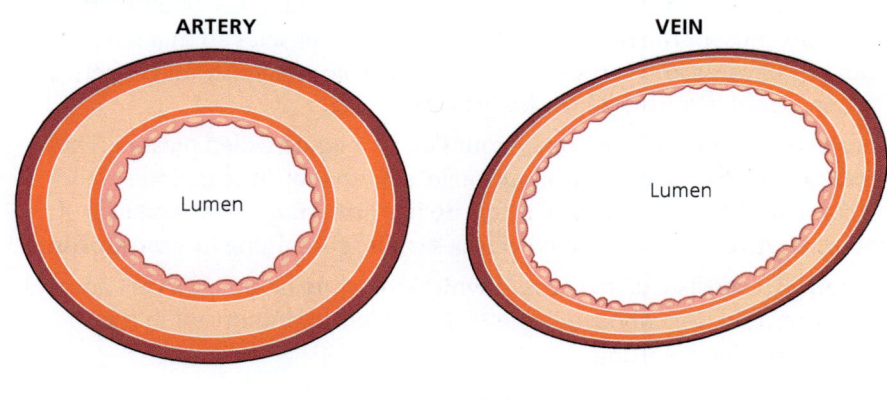

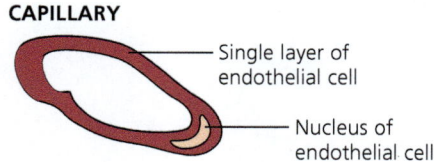

▲ Figure 1.4.3 The three main types of blood vessels – arteries, veins, and capillaries

❓ Extend your knowledge

The muscular wall of the heart is called the myocardium and is found between the inner endocardium and the outer membrane called the pericardium.
The two chambers at the superior (top) part of the heart are called **atria**. The two inferior (lower) chambers are called **ventricles**.

The heart and the pathway of blood

The heart is part of the cardiovascular system. About the size of a closed fist, it consists of four chambers and is made up almost entirely of cardiac muscle. The heart can be seen as incorporating two separate pumps, whose main function is to pump blood around the body. The right-side pump sends deoxygenated blood to the lungs, while the left-side pump sends oxygenated blood to the body's muscles. A muscular wall called a septum separates these two pump systems.

Chapter 1.4 The cardiovascular and respiratory systems

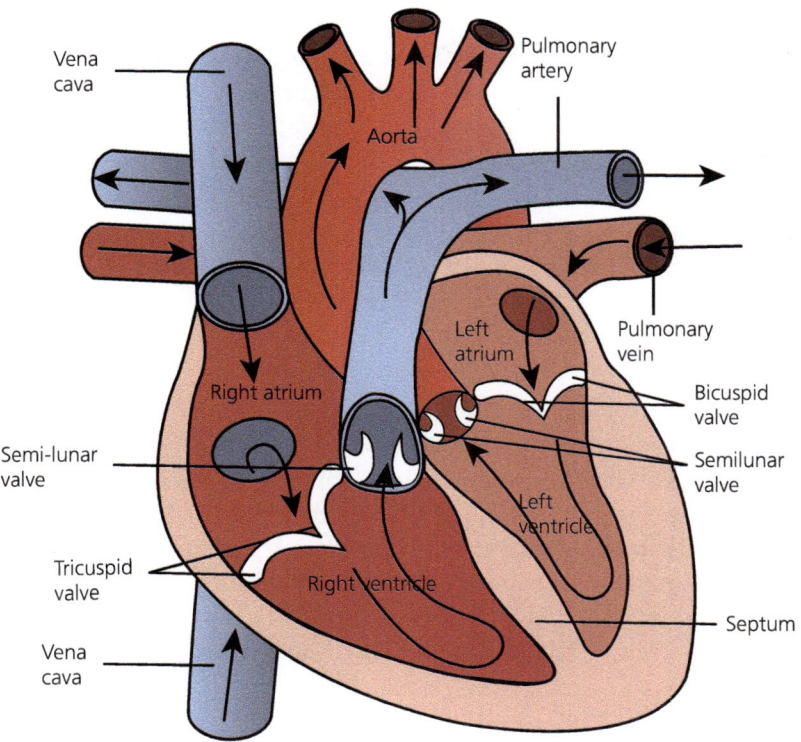

▲ Figure 1.4.4 The structure of the heart

> **STUDY HINT**
> The specification requires you to know the following structures and vessels associated with the heart. Make sure you know where they are and what they do:
> - ✔ atria
> - ✔ ventricles
> - ✔ bicuspid, tricuspid and semilunar valves
> - ✔ septum and major blood vessels:
>   - ✔ aorta
>   - ✔ pulmonary artery
>   - ✔ vena cava
>   - ✔ pulmonary vein.

There are many blood vessels associated with the heart. The inferior and superior venae cavae bring deoxygenated blood from the body to the right atrium. The pulmonary veins bring oxygenated blood from the lungs to the left atrium. The pulmonary artery takes deoxygenated blood from the right ventricle to the lungs. The aorta takes oxygenated blood from the left ventricle to the rest of the body.

IN THE NEWS

Athletic heart syndrome and COVID-19

Athletic heart syndrome is a heart condition that may occur in people who train most days for at least an hour at a time. The heart is a muscle, and therefore the heart gets stronger and bigger with exercise. A person with athletic heart syndrome may also have a very slow resting heart rate – between 35 to 50 beats per minute. Athletic heart syndrome as such is not dangerous and does not require treatment, but it is important to diagnose it so that other heart conditions can be ruled out.

An enlarged heart, however, could be dangerous for the 'average' person. In 2020, a number of studies suggested that many COVID-19 survivors experienced heart damage, even if they did not have underlying heart disease.

Key term

Heart rate (HR) This refers to the speed at which the heart beats (contractions of the ventricles) and is measured by beats per minute (bpm).

23

Like other muscles, the heart muscle (myocardium) requires a blood supply and this is transported to the heart muscle via the coronary artery giving oxygenated blood to the heart muscle via capillaries. Deoxygenated blood is taken away from the heart and into the right atrium through the coronary sinus.

The heart also consists of valves, which ensure that the blood can flow in one direction only. There are four valves within the heart: two that separate the atria from the ventricles and two in the arteries carrying blood from the ventricles. To stop the backflow of blood, the valves work one way only. The blood, which flows from the atria to the ventricles, pushes the valves open; the valves are then closed due to blood pressure.

Atrioventricular valves is a collective term for all the valves between atria and ventricles. The locations of the valves are as follows:

- **tricuspid valve**: valve between the right atrium and the right ventricle
- **bicuspid valve**: valve between the left atrium and the left ventricle
- **aortic valve**: valve between the left ventricle and the aorta
- **pulmonary valve**: valve between the right ventricle and the pulmonary artery
- **semilunar valves**: collective term for aortic and pulmonary valves.

Heart rate (HR)

The heart contracts and relaxes in a rhythm, which produces a heartbeat. This is started by an electrical impulse from the sino-atrial (SA) node, which is the 'pacemaker' of the heart.

> **STUDY HINT**
> Remember: the right-side pump sends deoxygenated blood to the lungs and the pump on the left-hand side sends oxygenated blood to the body's muscles.

IN THE NEWS

COVID-19 and its implications for athletes

Findings from studies into the effects of COVID-19 had implications for the sports world. Research indicated that athletes who recovered from COVID-19 could face extreme or lasting heart complications. Because of this, medical experts urged athletes who contracted the virus to be screened before they returned to play. Two high-level athletes suffered heart issues after recovering from COVID-19; one of them was a member of the Boston Red Sox baseball team.

IN THE NEWS

Athletes' resting heart rates

- The cyclist Miguel Indurain (a retired Spanish road race cyclist) was reported to have a resting heart rate of just 28 bpm.
- Cyclist Chris Froome's resting heart rate is reported as 32 bpm.
- Mo Farah has a resting heart rate of 33 bpm.

Heart rate is measured by beats per minute. The average resting HR is 75 bpm.

Measurement of heart rate = beats per minute (HR = bpm)

A decrease in resting heart rate is a good indicator of fitness. A trained athlete's resting heart rate falls below 60 bpm. This is known as bradycardia.

Stroke volume (SV)

This is the volume of blood that is pumped out of the heart by each ventricle during one contraction. Stroke volume varies depending on the:
- amount of blood returning to the heart (venous return)
- elasticity of the ventricles
- contractility of the ventricles
- blood pressure in the arteries leading from the heart.

Measurement of stroke volume (SV) = millilitres per beat (ml per beat)

Cardiac output (Q)

This refers to the volume of blood ejected from the left ventricle in one minute. The cardiac output is equal to the stroke volume × the heart rate:

Cardiac output (Q) = Stroke volume (SV) × Heart rate (HR)

Measurement of Q = litres/minute

If an athlete's resting heart rate falls below 60 bpm, to produce the same cardiac output, the stroke volume has to increase to compensate for the drop in heart rate. This is caused by an increase in the size of the heart (myocardial hypertrophy). The higher the cardiac output, the more oxygen can be delivered to the muscles and the longer and harder the athlete can work.

▲ Figure 1.4.5 The more oxygen can be delivered to the muscles, the longer and harder the athlete can work

Section 1 Applied Anatomy and Physiology

> ### ❓ Extend your knowledge
>
> #### Blood pressure (BP)
> This is the force of blood applied to the blood vessel walls. It is the pressure needed to pump the blood around the body. It is measured by blood flow multiplied by the resistance to that flow. An instrument called a sphygmomanometer often takes blood pressure.
>
> > Measurement of blood pressure = millimetres of mercury (mmHg)
>
> **Systolic blood pressure** is measured when the heart forcibly ejects blood.
> **Diastolic blood pressure** is measured when the heart relaxes.
> The average blood pressure reading for an adult is 120/80 mmHg. The first number is the systolic blood pressure and the second number is the diastolic blood pressure. With regular exercise resting blood pressure can be reduced. Other factors affecting blood pressure are age, stress and diet.
>
>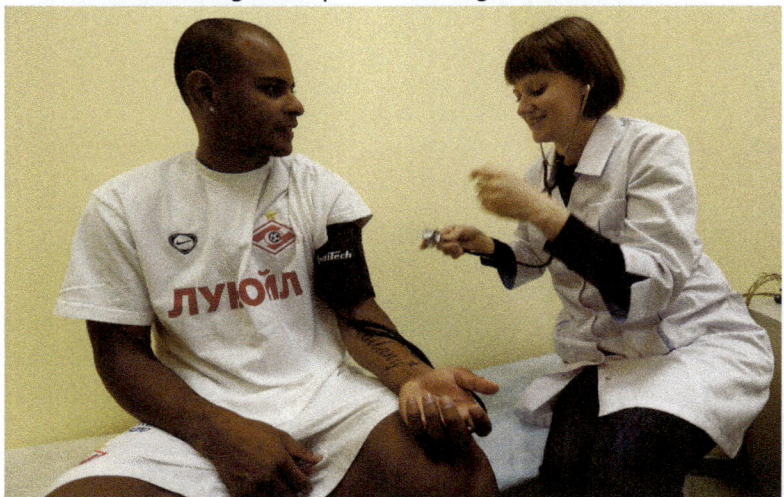
>
> ▲ Figure 1.4.6 With regular exercise resting BP can be reduced

Activity

1. Draw and label each type of blood vessel.
2. Write an account of the journey of blood from the heart and back to the heart. Describe what happens along this journey.

✔ Check your understanding

The cardiovascular system

1. Name the two elements of the double circulatory system.
2. What are the differences between arteries, capillaries and veins?
3. List the vessels showing the pathway of blood into and out of the heart.
4. What is meant by the following terms?
   - Heart rate
   - Stroke volume
   - Cardiac output
5. What is the main role of red blood cells?

Structure and function of the respiratory system

The respiratory system is important to study in combination with the cardiovascular system because the two systems work closely together to maintain a supply of oxygen to the working muscles, which is so crucial in sport. The external respiratory system involves the exchange of gases between the lungs and the blood. The internal respiratory system involves the exchange of gases between the blood and the cells.

The pathway of air through the respiratory system

Nasal passages

The air enters the body by being drawn in through the nose and mouth. The nasal cavity is divided by a cartilaginous septum that forms the nasal passages. Here the mucus membranes, or damp walls, warm and moisten the air and the hair filters and traps dust.

The pharynx and the larynx

The throat has both the respiratory and alimentary tract, so both food and air pass through. The pharynx is the passage to the digestive system and to the larynx. Air passes over the vocal cords of the larynx and into the **trachea** or windpipe. Swallowing draws the larynx upwards against the **epiglottis** and prevents the entry of food. Any food is sent down the oesophagus (foodpipe).

The bronchi and bronchioles

The trachea divides into two bronchi. The right bronchus goes into the right lung and the left bronchus goes into the left lung. The bronchi then divide up into smaller bronchioles. The bronchioles enable the air to pass into the alveoli, where gaseous exchange takes place.

Alveoli

These are responsible for gaseous exchange between the lungs and the blood. They are tiny air-filled sacs and there are millions of them in the lungs, providing an enormous surface area (estimated as the size of a tennis court). The walls of the alveoli are extremely thin and are lined by a thin film of water, which allows the dissolving of oxygen from air as it is breathed into the lungs (inspired).

Gaseous exchange

Within the alveoli, an exchange of gases takes place between the gases inside the alveoli and the blood.

Blood arriving in the alveoli has a higher carbon dioxide concentration, which is produced by the body's cells. The air in the alveoli has a much lower concentration of carbon dioxide, which allows carbon dioxide to diffuse from the blood and into the alveoli.

Blood arriving in the alveoli has a lower oxygen concentration (as it has been used for respiration by the body's cells), while the air in the alveoli has

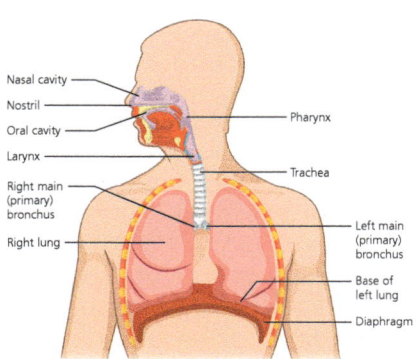

▲ Figure 1.4.7 Structure of the respiratory system

Key terms

Trachea This is sometimes called the windpipe. It has 18 rings of cartilage, which are lined with a mucous membrane and ciliated cells, which trap dust. The trachea goes from the larynx to the primary bronchi.

Epiglottis The main function of this flap of tissue is to close over the windpipe (trachea) while you are eating, to prevent food entering your airways.

Section 1 Applied Anatomy and Physiology

Key terms

Oxyhaemoglobin Haemoglobin combines with oxygen in the lungs to form a bright red chemical called oxyhaemoglobin. When the blood gets to places where oxygen is being used up, oxyhaemoglobin releases the oxygen and turns back into haemoglobin.

Breathing rate Sometimes called the respiratory rate or ventilation rate, it is the frequency of breathing measured in breaths per minute. Normal breathing rate at rest is approximately 12 breaths per minute.

❓ Extend your knowledge

Breathing patterns for most people are irregular, with often shallow and inefficient breathing. It is possible to improve lung capacity through more efficient and effective breathing patterns. If you concentrate on your breathing patterns at rest by breathing slowly and deeply via your nose, and using your diaphragm to breathe rather than just your chest in a regular pattern, then breathing will be more effective in utilising your lung capacity. Activities such as yoga are also effective in training your breathing.

❓ Extend your knowledge

During exercise, a healthy young adult takes around 35 to 45 breaths per minute. In some endurance sports athletes may breathe 60 to 70 times a minute. As people get older, they tend to breathe more shallowly, and therefore more often, to get enough oxygen in the blood.

❓ Extend your knowledge

During exercise the sternocleidomastoid muscle lifts the sternum; the scalenes and the pectoralis minor both elevate the ribs. These actions help to increase the size of the thoracic cavity.

a higher oxygen concentration. Therefore, oxygen moves into the blood, again by diffusion, and combines with the haemoglobin in red blood cells to form **oxyhaemoglobin**.

Athletes who are involved with endurance events have a greater ability to diffuse oxygen because of an increase in cardiac output and in the surface area of the alveoli. The exchange of oxygen is illustrated in Figure 1.4.8.

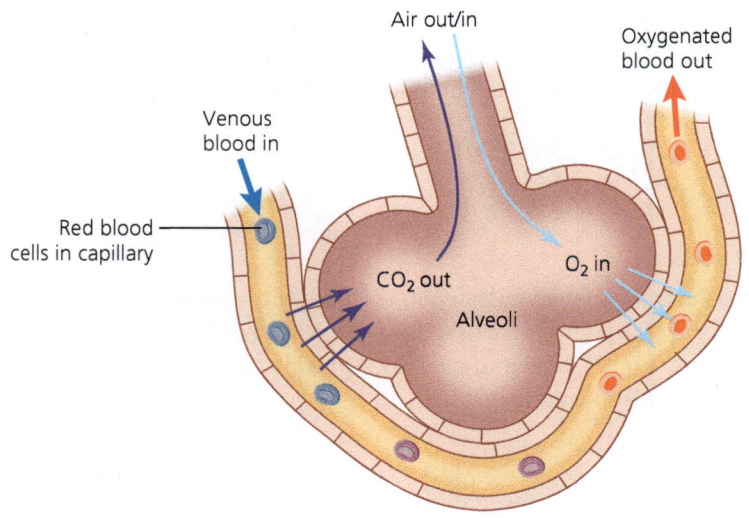

▲ Figure 1.4.8 Gaseous exchange at the alveoli

The role of respiratory muscles in breathing

Inspiration (breathing in)

The respiratory muscles contract. These include the external intercostal muscles and the diaphragm. The external intercostal muscles are attached to the ribs and when they contract, the ribs move upwards and outwards. The diaphragm contracts downwards and thus the area of the thoracic cavity is increased. The lungs are pulled outwards through surface tension along with the chest walls, which causes the space within the lungs to increase. The pressure within the lungs decreases and becomes less than the pressure outside the body. Gases move from areas of high pressure into areas of low pressure and so air is inspired into the lungs.

Expiration (breathing out)

This is more of a passive process than inspiration and is caused by the relaxation of the respiratory muscles. When the external intercostal muscles relax, the ribs are lowered and the diaphragm relaxes. The area of the lungs decreases and the pressure within the lungs becomes greater than the pressure outside the body. Air is now forced out to equalise this pressure and expiration takes place. The frequency of breathing is called the **breathing rate**.

Tidal volume

The volume of air that is inspired or expired per breath is known as tidal volume.

Chapter 1.4 The cardiovascular and respiratory systems

Minute ventilation

The volume of air that is inspired or expired in one minute is called minute ventilation. This is calculated by multiplying tidal volume by the number of breaths per minute:

$$VE = TV \times f$$

where VE is minute ventilation (l/minute)

TV is tidal volume (ml)

f = number of breaths per minute.

> ### ✓ Check your understanding
> 1. Describe the structure of the respiratory system, the mechanisms of breathing, and respiratory volumes.
> 2. Explain the function of the respiratory system, including the mechanism of breathing.

Aerobic and anaerobic exercise

Many types of sports and exercise involve both aerobic and anaerobic aspects, but some are predominantly one or the other.

Aerobic exercise

Aerobic fitness is the ability to continuously exercise without tiring. The more oxygen that can be transported around the body and the more the muscles can utilise this oxygen determines the level of aerobic endurance you have. The level of endurance fitness is indicated by an individual's VO_2 max, which is the maximum amount of oxygen an individual can take in and use in one minute.

For most people, low to moderate exercise or exertion is generally aerobic. With aerobic exercise, oxygen is carried through your breath to the muscles, helping them to provide the energy needed to sustain effort.

When we exercise aerobically our bodies use glycogen (carbohydrates) and fat as fuel. This low to moderate level of exertion (e.g. light jogging) can be sustained over long periods. As you breathe more heavily with exercise, carbon dioxide is expelled from your body. **Lactic acid** is not produced as it is with anaerobic exercise.

Activities that rely heavily on aerobic endurance are long-distance running in athletics, some activities in invasion games and outdoor activities such as hiking and rock climbing. Aerobic exercise also includes simply running at a comfortable pace (where you are able to talk comfortably while running); swimming and cycling.

Aerobic training should be carried out at a steady rate or with low intensity – between 20 minutes and 2 hours. This type of training ensures that there is not the build-up of lactate associated with anaerobic training.

> **STUDY HINT**
> For training the aerobic system, there should be intervals of low intensity or easier work, which is suitable for sports such as athletics and swimming and for team games such as hockey and football.

> **STUDY HINT**
> Remember the respiratory muscles include the external intercostal muscles and the diaphragm.

> **? Extend your knowledge**
> The lungs can never get rid of all the air completely and approximately 1 200 ml remains in the alveoli. This is called the reserve or residual volume.

> **STUDY HINT**
> The exchange of gases between the lungs and the blood is called the external respiratory system. The internal respiratory system involves the exchange of gases between the blood and the muscle cells.

> **Activity**
> 1. Construct a 'guide to breathing' and describe the mechanisms of breathing.
> 2. Make a list of the respiratory volumes.

Key term

Lactic acid With the absence of oxygen, lactic acid is formed in the working muscles. Lactic acid causes muscle pain and fatigue. It often leads us to stop or reduce the activity we are doing.

Section 1 Applied Anatomy and Physiology

▲ Figure 1.4.9 Athletes rely on high levels of aerobic endurance

Anaerobic exercise

Anaerobic fitness is being able to exercise without the use of oxygen; instead we use glycogen within the muscles as a fuel. Anaerobic energy produces short-term bursts of energy and does not require oxygen. During anaerobic exercise the body produces lactic acid. Anaerobic exercise is high intensity or at your maximum level of work. Examples include sprinting and weight lifting.

For training the anaerobic system, there should be shorter intervals of more intense training. The work interval should be up to 30 seconds at high intensity for anaerobic exercise.

The intensity of the work interval should be 90–100 per cent of maximum intensity for anaerobic exercise.

> **? Extend your knowledge**
>
> Physical activity has been significantly affected by the COVID-19 pandemic. Research cited in the *British Journal of Sports Medicine* shows that there was a massive increase in data related to online queries about exercise. In the UK, Australia and the USA, community interest in exercise surged immediately following the lockdown, peaked within the first two weeks and then declined, but remained at a higher level than before the lockdown.

IN THE NEWS

Pandemic 'lockdown' exercise trends

During 2020 and 2021, the fitness industry had to evolve in response to the demands of those who wished to carry out exercise programmes remotely. Throughout the COVID-19 pandemic, media sources and government scientists often highlighted the need to keep fit and healthy.

Home-based exercise saw a dramatic rise in popularity. In April 2020, a survey carried out in Great Britain found that since the lockdown had been imposed as a result of the coronavirus pandemic, 61 per cent of women and 50 per cent of men were walking more often than previously. In addition, 15 per cent of men and 13 per cent of women were running and jogging more in the lockdown period.

(Research from Sport England, April 2020)

STUDY HINT

Table 1.4.1 Differences between aerobic and anaerobic

Aerobic	Anaerobic
Stimulates your heart rate and breathing to increase and you can sustain the activity for more than a few minutes	You get out of breath in just a few moments, such as when you lift weights for improving strength, when you sprint, or when you climb a long flight of stairs
With oxygen	Without oxygen
Low intensity with long duration	High intensity with short duration

Chapter 1.4 The cardiovascular and respiratory systems

> **SUMMARY**
> - Blood in the body continuously flows through a network of blood vessels that forms a double circuit. This circuit connects the heart to the lungs and then the heart to the other organs in the body. This double circuit involves pulmonary circulation and systemic circulation.
> - Arteries are blood vessels that carry blood at high pressure from the heart to the body tissues.
> - Veins carry blood at low pressure and return the blood to the heart.
> - Capillaries have a single layer of cells in their walls and occur in large quantities around the muscles and this enables effective exchange of gases.
> - The average resting heart rate (HR) is between 60–100 beats per minute (bpm), depending on physical fitness and age (source: NHS). Athletes can have a resting heart rate of 40–60 bpm, or lower.
> - Stroke volume (SV) is the volume of blood that is pumped out of the heart by each ventricle during one contraction.
> - Cardiac output (Q) refers to the volume of blood ejected from the left ventricle in one minute. The cardiac output is equal to the stroke volume × the heart rate.
> - The primary function of red blood cells is to transport oxygen to cells around the body and to return carbon dioxide to the lungs.
> - Gases move from areas of high pressure into areas of low pressure and so air is inspired into the lungs.
> - Within the alveoli, an exchange of gases takes place between the gases inside the alveoli and the blood.
> - Breathing rate is the frequency of breathing measured in breaths per minute.
> - Tidal volume is the volume of air that is inspired or expired per breath.
> - Minute ventilation is the volume of air that is inspired or expired in one minute.
> - Aerobic exercise uses oxygen.
> - Aerobic training should be carried out at a steady rate or at low intensity.
> - Anaerobic fitness is being able to exercise without the use of oxygen.
> - During anaerobic exercise the body produces lactic acid.

Section 1 Applied Anatomy and Physiology

✔ Check your understanding

1. Which of the following activities would be best described as both aerobic *and* anaerobic?
   a. Sprinting
   b. Long jump
   c. Weight lifting
   d. Tennis
2. Natalie has decided to take up cross-country running. Which type of training would be most suitable for this activity?
   a. Circuit training
   b. Weight training
   c. Continuous training
   d. Flexibility training
3. Explain the difference between aerobic and anaerobic exercise.

Practice questions

1. Describe the role of red blood cells during exercise. **(2 marks)**
2. Describe how the double circulatory system pumps blood around the body. **(4 marks)**
3. Two long-distance athletes are preparing just before a race.

   Athlete A is sitting on the floor performing static stretching. Athlete B is gently striding out along the track.
   i. Describe how the changes in blood flow for athlete B will be different to those for athlete A. **(3 marks)**
   ii. Compare the changes in the respiratory system of athlete A to athlete B. **(3 marks)**
4. Explain the function of the alveoli located in the lungs. **(2 marks)**
5. Describe the role of the diaphragm during inspiration and expiration of a squash player while they are playing in a competitive game. **(2 marks)**
6. Give a practical example of where anaerobic exercise is important in sport. **(1 mark)**
7. Using practical examples, show the differences in intensity and duration between aerobic and anaerobic activities. **(4 marks)**

Chapter 1.5
The effects of exercise on the body systems

Understanding the Specification

You should understand the short-term effects of exercise on the cardiovascular and muscular systems and be able to apply the effects to examples from physical activity/sport. You will need to collect and use data relating to short-term effects of exercise.

You should understand the long-term effects of exercise on bones, muscles and the cardiovascular system and be able to apply the effects to examples from physical activity/sport. You will be able to collect and use data relating to the long-term effects of exercise.

Short-term effects of exercise on the body systems

The following section looks at the short-term effects of exercise on the muscular, respiratory and cardiovascular systems. It is important that athletes have an understanding of this because they will be able to recognise their body's reaction to exercise and thus take suitable rests or identify areas of fitness they may need to improve.

Muscular system

The immediate effects of exercise on the muscular system involve an increase in the temperature of muscles and metabolic activity or **metabolism**. There is also an increase in the production of lactic acid in the muscles depending on the type of exercise. This increase in the production of lactic acid is a result of prolonged high-intensity exercise when there is a lack of oxygen in the muscles.

Effects of lactic acid

Lactic acid produced in the muscles results in muscular pain and fatigue and often leads to the activity being stopped or curtailed. Therefore the build-up of lactic acid has a negative effect on our ability to keep exercising. During recovery, the intake of oxygen helps to convert lactic acid into waste products such as water and carbon dioxide (CO_2).

> **❓ Extend your knowledge**
>
> Lactic acid is still regarded as the source of the burning sensation experienced during intense exercise, but new research has shown that delayed onset of muscle soreness (DOMS) is caused by microscopic tears in the muscle fibres. It is now thought that, by training at a high intensity (lactate threshold training), the body is able to convert lactic acid into energy. Therefore, lactic acid can be a source of energy for those training at high levels of intensity.

Key term

Metabolism This involves the many continuous chemical processes inside the body that are essential for living, moving and growing. The number of kilojoules the body burns is regulated by the rate of metabolism.

Section 1 Applied Anatomy and Physiology

Key terms

Anticipatory rise This is the raising of the heart rate before exercise begins. It is caused through the release of adrenaline, which is a hormone.

Adrenaline This is a hormone released from the adrenal glands and its major action is to prepare the body for 'fight or flight'.

Key term

Redistribution of blood (vascular shunts) occur when more blood is distributed to the working muscles and less to the non-essential organs. The vascular shunt mechanism involves two processes:

- The arterioles (smaller arteries) that supply muscle tissue experience vasodilation (diameter increases) and this increases the blood flow to the muscles. Vasoconstriction (diameter decreases) of the arterioles that supply other organs such as the liver means that blood flow is lessened to these organs that do not require as much blood supply.
- In the capillaries that supply the skeletal muscles the precapillary sphincters (valves) open up and blood flow is again increased. In the capillaries that supply other organs, the precapillary sphincters close, thus decreasing the blood flow.

The result of these processes is to significantly increase the supply of oxygen to the working muscles during exercise.

The cardiovascular system

In the short term, the heart rate is raised just before exercise and will increase during exercise to ensure that there is enough supply of oxygen to the working muscles and that waste products, such as carbon dioxide, are removed. The raising of the heart rate before exercise is called the **anticipatory rise**.

▲ Figure 1.5.1 When the heart rate rises before exercise, this is called the anticipatory rise

When exercise begins, the heart rate will rise rapidly. As exercise continues, the heart muscle also becomes warmer. When exercise ceases, the heart rate will fall rapidly and the level of **adrenaline** falls, along with a drop in temperature of the heart. The heart rate then returns to around its pre-exercise rate.

During exercise, the working skeletal muscles require more and more oxygen. The increase in stroke volume, cardiac output and heart rate enables more oxygen to be delivered, but this is often not enough and therefore the **redistribution of blood** or vascular shunt mechanism takes effect.

> **STUDY HINT**
> The main short-term effect of exercise on the cardiovascular system is an increase in:
> ✓ heart rate (beats per minute)
> ✓ stroke volume (the volume of blood that is pumped out of the heart by each ventricle during one contraction)
> ✓ cardiac output (the volume of blood ejected from the left ventricle in one minute. The cardiac output is equal to the stroke volume × the heart rate).

The respiratory system

The short-term response of the respiratory system to exercise includes a rise in the breathing rate (respiratory rate) due to the body's demands for more oxygen.

Tidal volume (TV) also increases during exercise. This is the volume of air either inspired **or** expired per breath.

Minute ventilation also increases during exercise. This is the volume of air that is inspired **and** expired in one minute.

Chapter 1.5 The effects of exercise on the body systems

> **Activity**
>
> **Collecting and using data relating to short-term effects of exercise**
>
> Analyse how the cardiovascular system responds to exercise.
> 1. Record your resting pulse rate.
> 2. Using a treadmill or an exercise bike, exercise with moderate effort for 20 minutes.
> 3. Record your pulse rate every 4 minutes and then finally at the end.
> 4. After you have finished exercising, record your pulse rate after every 4 minutes.
> 5. Record how you feel before the exercise and then after the 20 minutes are up.
> 6. Draw a graph showing your pulse rate before, during and after exercise.
>
> Describe what has happened to the cardiovascular system during your run/ride.
>
> Explain these effects – e.g. why has your heart rate increased just before exercise? How do you account for any changes in your feelings?
>
> Analyse the possible long-term effects of exercise on the cardiovascular system if you continued with this training three times a week, increasing the effort over a period of eight weeks.

> **? Extend your knowledge**
>
> - Inspiratory reserve volume (IRV) – this is the maximal volume inspired in addition to the tidal volume. This decreases during exercise
> - Expiratory reserve volume (ERV) – this is the maximal volume expired in addition to the tidal volume. This decreases slightly during exercise.
> - Reserve or residual volume (RV) – this is the amount of air left in the lungs after maximal expiration. This increases slightly during exercise.
> - Vital capacity (VC) – this is the maximum amount of air that can be forcibly exhaled after maximal inspiration. This decreases slightly during exercise.
> - Total lung capacity (TLC) – this is the vital capacity plus the reserve or residual volume and is the volume at the end of maximal inspiration. This decreases slightly during exercise.

Applying the short-term effects of exercise to examples from physical activities

- When sculling, a rower will experience a rise in muscle temperature.
- Over the first few metres in a race, a BMX cyclist's heart rate will increase.
- A volleyball player performing shuttles in training will have a raised stroke volume.
- A water polo player will have a higher cardiac output when swimming over the ball during a competition.
- A 400-metre athlete (when running) will experience a redistribution of blood away from the body's organs and to the working muscles (vascular shunt).
- During a competitive rally, a table tennis player's respiratory rate will increase.
- A wheelchair rugby player's tidal volume increases as they intercept the ball.
- A handball player's minute ventilation increases as they run into space during competition.
- A basketball player's oxygen being supplied to the working muscles will increase when running up the court during a competitive match.
- As a figure skater progresses during a routine, their levels of lactic acid production will increase.

Section 1 Applied Anatomy and Physiology

▲ Figure 1.5.2 Muscular strength and muscle size can increase with a programme of weight or resistance training

Key terms

Tendons Muscles are attached to bones by tendons. These tendons help to 'pull' the muscle to the bone and help with the power of muscle contractions. Tendons are attached to the periosteum (a membrane that covers the outer surface of bones) of the bone through tough tissue called Sharpey's fibres.

Muscular endurance This is the ability of the muscle or group of muscles to repeatedly contract or keep going without rest.

Hypertrophy This term means that there is an increase in the size or the mass of an organ in the body or a muscle. Hypertrophy often occurs as a result of regular training or exercise and can lead to an increase in muscular strength and power.

Long-term effects of exercise on the body systems

This section explores the long-term effects of exercise on these systems. It is important that athletes have an understanding of both the short-term and the long-term effects, so that they can identify which areas require improvement and are aware of their body's reactions to exercise.

Muscular system

The long-term responses to exercise of the muscular system depend on the amount and the intensity of the exercise undertaken. Muscular strength and muscle size can increase with a programme of weight or resistance (against weights or body weight) training.

Following resistance training, there is an increase in the thickness of the muscle fibres due to greater muscle protein. Muscle strength will therefore be increased along with strength of **tendons**.

Following flexibility training, there is often an increase in the range of movement possible around a joint.

Following endurance (stamina) training, **muscular endurance** increases. During stamina activities, the slow twitch muscle fibres will get larger by up to around 20 per cent. This means that there is greater potential for energy production. Endurance training will also increase the capacity to carry oxygen and the athlete will become aerobically fitter.

Following training of high intensity, often called anaerobic training, the fast twitch fibres will increase in size – this is called **hypertrophy**. Muscles will also be able to work for longer and the athlete's muscle fatigue or tiredness will be delayed following this type of training.

IN THE NEWS

'All round fitness' achieved via a blend of endurance and power training

Researchers at Manchester Metropolitan University claim that team sport players have muscular endurance to match that of long-distance runners and are as powerful as hammer throwers. Their studies suggest that, to achieve all-round fitness, sportspeople need to combine strength and endurance training. All-round fitness can be achieved via cycling, running or swimming. Also, climbing stairs or carrying out 'energetic' chores can prove to be a big boost.

Chapter 1.5 The effects of exercise on the body systems

▲ Figure 1.5.3 Leg strength training will help with jumping to head the ball

The cardiovascular system

The long-term effects of exercise and training depend on the duration and intensity of the training, but with most training programmes the heart will become stronger and will increase in size. This increase in size is known as cardiac hypertrophy. This will occur particularly with endurance-type exercise or training. The wall of the left ventricle becomes thicker, thus increasing the strength of contractions in the heart. This increase in contractions will ensure more blood is delivered to the working muscles.

More blood is pumped from the heart per beat of the heart and therefore stroke volume will increase. Cardiac output will also therefore increase during high or maximal levels of exercise.

The resting heart rate will also fall as a long-term consequence of exercise and training. This reduces how hard the heart needs to work and the heart rate returns to normal more quickly following exercise. Resting stroke volume also increases. When the resting heart rate falls below 60 beats per minute this is known as bradycardia.

IN THE NEWS

Keeping active during COVID-19 restrictions

During the COVID-19 restrictions of 2020, people became creative and kept themselves active via activities as diverse as dance, window bingo and even garden boot camps.

Plenty of fitness classes and sports groups could also be found online, helping people to get active and stay in touch with others.

Parents also reported that coronavirus restrictions gave them a chance to spend quality time as a family.

Activity

Using the information from this chapter, briefly list the short-term and the long-term effects of exercise on the muscular system.

Now give reasons for why these responses or adaptations have taken place.

❓ Extend your knowledge

Hypertrophy is a term that means an increase in size. Cardiac hypertrophy is where the ventricle wall of the heart thickens because of exercise. The muscle wall of the left ventricle increases in size and is able to pump out more blood during each contraction. This increases the stroke volume.

STUDY HINT

The vascular shunt mechanism is important because during exercise, the working skeletal muscles require more and more oxygen. The increase in stroke volume and heart rate enables more oxygen to be delivered, but this is not enough.

Activity

The cyclist Chris Froome's resting heart rate has been recorded as low as 29 beats per minute.
1. What has caused bradycardia in this cyclist?
2. How does the cyclist's cardiovascular system adapt in the short term just before and just after the race has begun?
3. Other than bradycardia, name one other long-term effect of exercise on the cardiovascular system of such a cyclist.

37

Section 1 Applied Anatomy and Physiology

▲ Figure 1.5.4 The effect of endurance training is to lower the resting heart rate

Other long-term effects of exercise on the cardiovascular system include the following:
- There is increased capillarisation of muscles, meaning new capillaries may develop. This enables more blood to flow and therefore more oxygen to reach the muscle tissues. Existing capillaries also become more efficient with similar effects.
- Blood vessels become more efficient with the vascular shunt mechanism.
- Blood pressure, if previously high, decreases at rest. This is because the cardiovascular system has become more efficient.
- There is an increase in the number of red blood cells. This will also mean that haemoglobin content is higher and therefore more oxygen can be delivered to muscles.
- There is a decrease in **blood viscosity** that again makes oxygen carriage more effective and can reduce blood pressure.

✔ Check your understanding

1. Describe the cardiovascular system.
2. Explain the function of the cardiovascular system and how it responds to exercise.

The respiratory system

The long-term effects of exercise, or adaptations, on the respiratory system are as follows:
- There is an increase in capillary density, which increases the efficiency of oxygen uptake for energy.
- There is a slight increase in vital capacity, which means more air can be inspired, and also a slight increase in tidal volume, which means again more oxygen can enter the lungs.
- There is greater intercostal muscle strength, allowing more air to be breathed in and out, and a reduction in resting respiratory rate, which makes the body more efficient.
- The exchange of gases at the alveoli (pulmonary diffusion) becomes more efficient and therefore the body can work harder and longer due to the increased surface area of the alveoli. An increase in capillarisation again leads to more effective uptake of oxygen and more effective removal of carbon dioxide.

Key term

Blood viscosity This refers to the thickness of the blood and how resistant the blood is to flow freely. The more viscous the blood, the more it resists free flow. The amount of plasma or water content of the blood affects the viscosity. Therefore to ensure fast blood flow, the plasma level needs also to be high.

Chapter 1.5 The effects of exercise on the body systems

✔ Check your understanding

A student who recently joined a rugby club has started to train twice a week. Training involves stamina or endurance running. Immediately after the training session the student's breathing is very rapid. After about eight weeks, they are less out of breath after training, and on match days they seem to be able to keep running for longer without getting out of breath.

Questions

1. Why does the student get out of breath immediately after training?
2. What other short-term effects might there be related to the respiratory system?
3. Why is the student now less out of breath during a rugby match?

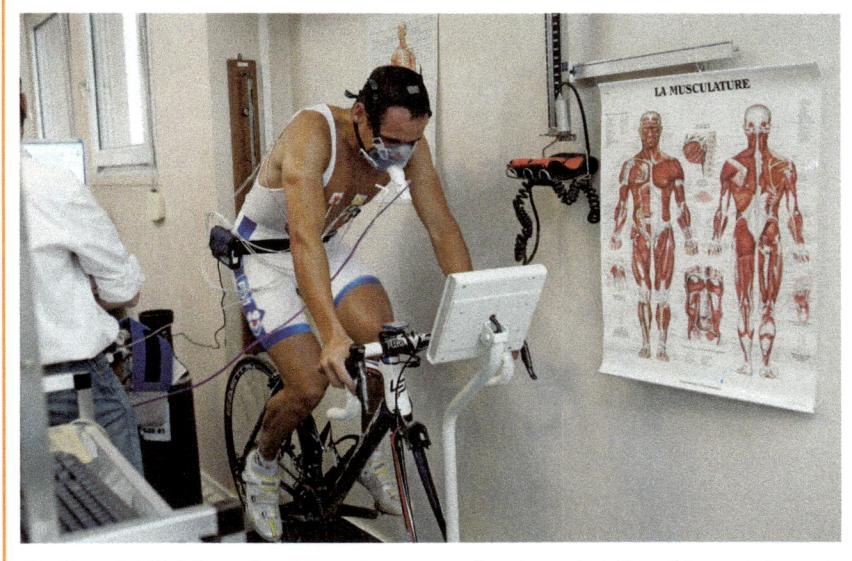

▲ Figure 1.5.5 Training and regular exercise can ensure long-term adaptations of the respiratory system

Applying the long-term effects of exercise to examples from physical activities

Regular exercise or training about three times per week for six weeks will lead to the adaptation of the body systems that are used or trained during exercise.

For example:
- A tennis player will experience an increase in bone density.
- An amateur boxer will have hypertrophy of muscle.
- A skier will experience an increase in muscular strength.
- A cross-country runner will have an increase in muscular endurance.
- A swimmer will have more resistance to fatigue.
- A marathon runner will have hypertrophy of the heart.
- An inline roller hockey player will have a lower resting heart rate and resting stroke volume.

Section 1 Applied Anatomy and Physiology

- A netball player will have an increased cardiac output.
- A gaelic football player will increase their rate of recovery.
- An ice hockey player's aerobic capacity will increase.
- A football player's respiratory muscles (internal and external intercostals and diaphragm) will increase in strength.
- A rugby league player's tidal volume and minute volume will both increase.
- A rock climber's capilliarisation of the lungs and muscles will increase.

Activity

Draw out the grid shown below. In the first column name both the short-term and the long-term adaptations of the respiratory system as a result of exercise. In the second column analyse these effects by explaining what happens as a result of these adaptations.

	Adaptations	Effects of these adaptations on the body
Short-term effects of exercise on the respiratory system		
Long-term effects of exercise on the respiratory system		

Other long-term effects of exercise

In the longer term, and with more persistent exercise, the connective tissue around the skeleton becomes more flexible. Over a period of time the short-term improvement in the range of movement becomes more sustained.

Skeletal bone increases in its density as a result of exercise. This makes the bones stronger and can help to offset the effects of bone disease such as **osteoporosis**.

Hyaline cartilage also thickens with exercise, which helps to cushion the joint, therefore preventing damage to the bone. Tendons thicken and the ligaments have a greater stretch potential, again helping to protect the body from injury.

The bone mineral content of calcium and phosphate has been shown to be significantly higher in those that participate in regular exercise for all ages than those who do not. This is a compelling reason for regular exercise for all, including the elderly.

Key term

Osteoporosis This is a disease in which bones become fragile and more likely to break. If not prevented or if left untreated, osteoporosis can progress painlessly until a bone breaks. These broken bones, also known as fractures, occur typically in the hip, spine and wrist.

Chapter 1.5 The effects of exercise on the body systems

Activity

Collecting and using data relating to long-term effects of exercise

1. Before an exercise programme, carry out a cardiovascular endurance test, such as the multi-stage fitness test, and a flexibility test, such as the sit and reach test.
2. Record your results (data).
3. Follow a training programme for six to eight weeks, such as the training described in the earlier activity related to short-term effects. You should train three times a week and increase the intensity over a period of eight weeks.
4. Repeat the tests and record your results in a data table.
5. Draw graphs to show the changes in scores for cardiovascular endurance and flexibility.
6. Using your results data and the graphs you have drawn, analyse the possible long-term effects of exercise on the cardiovascular system if you continued with the training described.

Extend your knowledge

Osteoporosis occurs when the body may fail to form enough new bone, or too much old bone may be reabsorbed, or both. Two essential minerals for normal bone formation are calcium and phosphate. The leading cause of osteoporosis is a lack of certain hormones, particularly oestrogen in women. Women, especially those older than 60 years, are frequently diagnosed with the disease. Other factors that may contribute to bone loss in this age group include inadequate intake of calcium and vitamin D and a lack of weight-bearing exercise.

SUMMARY

Short-term effects of exercise

- The immediate effects of exercise on the muscular system involve an increase in the temperature of muscles and metabolic activity or metabolism.
- In the short term, the heart rate is raised just before exercise and will increase during exercise to ensure that there is enough supply of oxygen to the working muscles.
- The increase in the heart rate before exercise is called the anticipatory rise.
- The short-term response of the respiratory system to exercise includes a rise in the respiratory rate (breathing rate) due to the body's demands for more oxygen.
- Tidal volume (TV) also increases during exercise. This is the volume of air either inspired or expired per breath.
- Minute ventilation also increases during exercise. This is the volume of air that is inspired and expired in one minute.

Long-term effects of exercise

- The long-term responses to exercise of the muscular system depend on the amount and the intensity of the exercise.
- Following resistance training, there is an increase in the thickness of the muscle fibres due to greater muscle protein.
- Endurance training will also increase the capacity to take in, carry and use oxygen and the athlete will become aerobically fitter.
- The long-term effects of exercise and training depend on the duration and intensity of the training.
- Skeletal bone increases in its density as a result of exercise. This makes the bones stronger and can help to offset the effects of bone disease such as osteoporosis.

Section 1 Applied Anatomy and Physiology

✔ Check your understanding

1. What are the short- and long-term effects of exercise on the cardiovascular system?
2. What are the short- and long-term effects of exercise on the muscular system?
3. What are the short- and long-term effects of exercise on the respiratory system?
4. What happens to bones after a long-term training programme?
5. What is meant by hypertrophy?

Practice questions

1. Which main waste product causes muscular fatigue during exercise? **(1 mark)**
2. Analyse the effects that lactic acid could have on the recovery of netball players. **(3 marks)**
3. Explain the short-term effects on the heart and the blood of an athlete performing a 100-metre sprint. **(5 marks)**
4. *Evaluate how the long-term effects of exercise on the muscular system could be beneficial to a football player. **(6 marks)**
5. A rower who trains for six months will experience muscular hypertrophy.
   i. What is meant by the term 'muscular hypertrophy'? **(1 mark)**
   ii. Describe other muscular benefits which the six-month training might have for the rower. **(4 marks)**
6. *Describe the long-term effects of exercise on the respiratory system and describe how these effects may benefit a road race cyclist. **(6 marks)**

These questions include an assessment of the quality of your written communication.

Section 2
Physical Training

2.1 Components of fitness
2.2 Applying the principles of training
2.3 Preventing injury in physical activity and training

Chapter 2.1
Components of fitness

Understanding the Specification

On completion of this topic you should know the definition of each of the following components of fitness, know a suitable test for each component and be able to give practical examples where each component is particularly important:

- cardiovascular endurance/stamina
- muscular endurance
- speed
- strength
- power
- flexibility
- agility
- balance
- co-ordination
- reaction time.

You should also be able to collect and use data relating to the components of fitness.

Fitness can be seen as a group of components that, if trained, will enable the body to do more work and for longer, as well as be more skilful in sports activities. Fitness is often referred to as one aspect. However, it is not and different components of fitness need to be trained for different types of activities. For example, if you were to run a marathon, although all aspects of fitness are important, you would probably work more on your cardiovascular endurance fitness. If you are a gymnast, then you might work more on your strength and flexibility.

Fitness testing for each component of fitness is important if you want to find out your current standard of fitness as well as assessing the effectiveness of any fitness programme you undertake. For any fitness test and retest to be valid and accurate, the tests must take place in a consistent environment – the same time of day and the same place, for example, for the retest as for the test. The test procedures (called protocols) must be strictly followed, for example measurements to be taken accurately.

It is important that for every test you are fit and healthy enough to withstand the rigour and physical demands of that test. If there are any doubts about being healthy enough to take the test or if there are any underlying health conditions, then you should consult a doctor before any fitness tests are undertaken.

Key term

VO_2 max The maximum amount of oxygen an individual can take in and use in 1 minute.

Cardiovascular endurance/stamina

This is sometimes called aerobic endurance. Cardiovascular endurance is the ability to continuously exercise without tiring. The more oxygen that can be transported around the body and the more the muscles can utilise or use this oxygen, the more cardiovascular endurance you have. The level of endurance fitness is indicated by an individual's **VO_2 max**.

Chapter 2.1 Components of fitness

▲ Figure 2.1.1 Athletes such as long-distance swimmers rely on high levels of cardiovascular endurance

> **? Extend your knowledge**
>
> Completing 15 minutes of moderate exercise three times a week will help to improve your cardiovascular endurance fitness component. (You can find more information on this in Chapter 2.2: Applying the principles of training.)

The body adapts to endurance training and aerobic adaptations occur. The more aerobic endurance you have, the more the onset of fatigue can be delayed, or in other words the less tired you get. High levels of cardiovascular endurance can ensure that the body has the ability to exercise whole muscle groups over an extended period of time at moderate intensity, using or utilising aerobic energy. Your aerobic system uses oxygen to break down carbohydrates and convert them into energy that lasts.

Activities that rely heavily on cardiovascular endurance are long-distance running in athletics, invasion games and outdoor activities.

The cardiovascular system involves transporting oxygen around the body. The cardiovascular system includes:

- the heart
- the network of blood vessels
- the blood that transports essential material around the body.

Examples of activities where cardiovascular endurance is particularly important:

- running
- aerobics
- swimming
- fast walking
- cross-country skiing
- treadmill 15–20 minutes – light jog to run
- cardio bike 15–20 minutes – medium to quick pace
- skipping rope 10–15 minutes – fast pace.

Suitable tests for cardiovascular endurance

The level of endurance fitness is indicated by an individual's VO_2 max (that is, the maximum amount of oxygen an individual can take in and utilise in one minute). The potential VO_2 max of an individual can be predicted via tests such as the Cooper 12-minute run/walk test and the multi-stage fitness test.

Cooper 12-minute run/walk test

The 12-minute run/walk fitness test was developed from the work of Dr Ken Cooper in 1968 as a simple method to measure aerobic endurance and provide an estimate of VO_2 max.

> **? Extend your knowledge**
>
> With a healthy balanced lifestyle the cardiovascular system can lead to:
>
> - healthy capillaries and through exercise an increase in capillary density – they become more efficient and lead to greater oxygen uptake
> - a healthy heart that is less likely to suffer from disease and eventually, through exercise, a lower resting heart rate
> - good blood circulation – with exercise, this can increase the amount of blood pumped by the heart both at rest and during exercise
> - healthy blood pressure and with exercise a decrease in resting blood pressure
> - feeling energetic because of the uptake of oxygen by the body – with exercise, there may be an increase in haemoglobin, which helps carry oxygen, along with an increase in red blood cells
> - not being too tired during the day to complete tasks, both physically and mentally.

45

Section 2 Physical Training

IN THE NEWS

Exercise on prescription to improve mental health

Many doctors from around the UK are now prescribing exercise as a treatment for a range of conditions, including for mental health and to help combat the effects of depression.

Depression can make people feel low in energy and that in turn can put them off being active. However, exercising regularly can be a mood-booster and it is particularly helpful for anyone who has mild to moderate depression. The key is to find a form of exercise that you enjoy, so that you are more likely to feel motivated to do it regularly.

❓ Extend your knowledge

Walking

Some volunteers were asked to complete three 50-minute sessions a week of moderate physical activity, such as walking, for 24 weeks. Others were asked not to increase their exercise levels.

At the end of the study, the people in the exercise group achieved better scores in tests of their cognitive function and lower scores in tests to determine signs of dementia. Follow-up showed that the benefits persisted for at least another 12 months after the exercise programme was stopped. Exercise is known to help keep the cardiovascular system healthy and may help boost cognitive function by boosting blood supply to the brain.

Dr Cooper found that there was a very high correlation or relationship between the distance someone could run or walk in 12 minutes and their VO_2 max, which measures the efficiency with which someone can use oxygen while exercising.

The Cooper 12-minute run/walk test requires the person being tested to run or walk as far as possible in a 12-minute period. The objective is to measure the maximum distance they can cover during 12 minutes. The test is usually carried out on a running track by placing cones at various points to measure the distance. A stopwatch is required to ensure the individual runs for the correct length of time.

Safety

This can be a strenuous fitness test and you should have your doctor's permission to carry it out, particularly if you have any underlying medical conditions such as asthma.

The test

- Perform a short 10–15 minute warm-up before performing the test.
- When you are warmed up, run or walk as far as you can in 12 minutes.
- Record the total number of metres you have travelled in 12 minutes.

To calculate your estimated VO_2 max results (in ml/kg/min) use either of these formulas:

- in miles: VO_2 max = $(35.97 \times \text{miles}) - 11.29$

- in kilometres: VO_2 max = $(22.351 \times kilometres) - 11.288$

Compare your 12-minute run fitness test results

After you complete the test, you can compare your results to the norms and recommendations for your age and gender in Table 2.1.1. The norms are based on 20–29 year olds, but these will give you some idea of your own level of cardiovascular fitness. The distance in Table 2.1.1 is measured in metres.

▼ Table 2.1.1 12-minute run fitness test results interpretation

	Excellent	Above average	Average	Below average	Poor
Male 20–29	>2 800 m	2 400–2 800 m	2 200–2 399 m	1 600–2 199 m	<1 600 m
Females 20–29	>2 700 m	2 200–2 700 m	1 800–2 199 m	1 500–1 799 m	<1 500 m

Multi-stage fitness test

Sometimes called the 'bleep' or 'beep' test, this test involves a shuttle run that gets progressively more difficult. The test is published by what was the National Coaching Foundation and is in the form of a CD (there are now mobile phone apps that do a similar thing).

The test

Subjects are required to run a 20-metre shuttle as many times as possible but ensuring that they turn at each end of the run in time with the 'bleep' on the CD. The time lapse between each bleep sound on the CD gets progressively shorter and so the shuttle run has to be completed progressively quicker. At the point when the subject cannot keep up with the bleeps, they are deemed to have reached their optimum level. That level is recorded and used as a baseline for future tests or can be compared with national norms.

Safety

- A person experiencing shortness of breath, chest pains, palpitations or light-headedness should stop exercising immediately and be sensitively advised to seek advice from a general practitioner.
- Teachers or coaches should observe participants continuously while the test is taking place, keeping a particular eye on pupils known to be physically less fit.

Table 2.1.2 shows national team average scores on the multi-stage fitness test.

▼ Table 2.1.2 National team scores on the multi-stage fitness test

Sport	Male	Female
Basketball	L11–S5	L9–S6
Hockey	L13–S9	L12–S7
Rugby league	L13–S1	
Netball		L9–S7
Squash	L13–S13	

L = level, S = shuttle

Section 2 Physical Training

The multi-stage fitness test includes predictions of VO_2 max for individuals. Tables 2.1.3 and 2.1.4 outline norms for VO_2 max for different age groups.

▼ Table 2.1.3 Maximal oxygen uptake norms for men (ml/kg/minute)

	18–25 years old	26–35 years old	36–45 years old	46–55 years old	56–65 years old	65+ years old
Excellent	>60	>56	>51	>45	>41	>37
Good	52–60	49–56	43–51	39–45	36–41	33–37
Above average	47–51	43–48	39–42	35–38	32–35	29–32
Average	42–46	40–42	35–38	32–35	30–31	26–28
Below average	37–41	35–39	31–34	29–31	26–29	22–25
Poor	30–36	30–34	26–30	25–28	22–25	20–21
Very poor	<30	<30	<26	<25	<22	<20

▼ Table 2.1.4 Maximal oxygen uptake norms for women (ml/kg/minute)

	18–25 years old	26–35 years old	36–45 years old	46–55 years old	56–65 years old	65+ years old
Excellent	>60	>56	>51	>45	>41	>37
Good	52–60	49–56	43–51	39–45	36–41	33–37
Above average	47–51	43–48	39–42	35–38	32–35	29–32
Average	42–46	40–42	35–38	32–35	30–31	26–28
Below average	37–41	35–39	31–34	29–31	26–29	22–25
Poor	30–36	30–34	26–30	25–28	22–25	20–21
Very poor	<30	<30	<26	<25	<22	<20

STUDY HINT
Make sure you:
- ✓ learn the definition of cardiovascular endurance or stamina
- ✓ have clear, practical examples of activities that are predominantly aerobic
- ✓ know the two tests for cardiovascular (VO_2) fitness.

IN THE NEWS
The Bronco test

The Bronco test has been developed in New Zealand as a rugby fitness test. This is an alternative to the multi-stage fitness test and measures aerobic endurance. It has been performed by some of the top All Blacks players. It is a shuttle run to achieve a total time with cones placed at 20-, 40- and 60-metre intervals. One set involves each player performing shuttles to each cone and back. This is then repeated five times with no rest in between each set.

Standards recorded in 2019 were:
- rugby (male) backs: 4.23–4.40 minutes
- rugby (male) forwards: 4.35–5.00 minutes.

Muscular endurance

This is the ability of the muscle or group of muscles in the body to repeatedly contract or keep going without rest. For example, the number of press-ups you can perform depends on the muscular endurance of your pectorals, deltoids and triceps. You can target one or a few muscle groups when building muscular endurance, and you can build endurance using weight training or your body's resistance.

With a healthy, balanced lifestyle the muscular system can keep going because of greater aerobic potential. Activities such as swimming or running can enlarge slow twitch fibres, which gives greater potential for energy production. The onset of fatigue is delayed (you get tired less quickly) because of higher maximum oxygen uptake (VO$_2$ max).

With a healthy lifestyle muscles can keep going during repetitive tasks that are found in work and in sport and exercise, for example finishing an exercise routine or keeping up with your friends when walking home from school.

By exercising, the size and number of **mitochondria** in muscles are increased. Also with exercise there is an increase in **myoglobin** content within the muscle cell.

Activities such as sprinting or weight lifting can cause hypertrophy or the build-up of **fast twitch muscle fibres**.

Key terms
Mitochondria These are parts of each muscle cell and places where energy is produced – sometimes referred to as 'powerhouses' of muscle cells. Those who exercise regularly and participate in endurance activities such as long-distance cycling often have more mitochondria.

Myoglobin This is related to haemoglobin and is found in muscle cells that transport oxygen to the mitochondria to provide energy. Those who are more active – especially those who exercise regularly for endurance events such as marathon running – have higher levels of myoglobin.

Fast twitch muscle fibres Sometimes called type 2 fibres. These are used to generate short bursts of speed or strength but these fibres fatigue very quickly.

▲ Figure 2.1.2 Muscular endurance in the shoulders is very important to the canoeist

Examples of activities where muscular endurance is particularly important:
- cross-country running
- long-distance cycling
- long-distance swimming
- rugby, football and hockey (full matches)
- step machine 15–20 minutes – quick pace
- tuck jumps 15–25 reps.

Suitable tests for muscular endurance

Testing the endurance of one particular muscle group can assess an individual's muscular endurance.

Section 2 Physical Training

The press-up test
- Lie on the mat, hands shoulder width apart, and fully extend the arms.
- Lower the body until the elbows reach 90°.
- Return to the starting position with the arms fully extended.
- Do not hold the feet.
- Make the push-up action continuous, with no rest.
- Complete as many press-ups as possible.
- Record the total number of full-body press-ups.

Weaker athletes can use the modified press-up position to assess their upper body strength. The test is then performed as follows:
- Lie on the mat, hands shoulder width apart, bent knee position, and fully extend the arms.
- Lower the upper body until the elbows reach 90°.
- Return to the starting position with the arms fully extended.
- Do not hold the feet.
- Make the push-up action continuous, with no rest.
- Complete as many modified press-ups as possible.
- Record the total number of modified press-ups.

▲ Figure 2.1.3 Weaker athletes can use the modified press-up position to assess their upper body strength

▼ Normative data for the press-up tests
▼ Table 2.1.5 Full-body press-up

Age	Excellent	Good	Average	Fair	Poor
20–29	>54	45–54	35–44	20–34	<20
30–39	>44	35–44	25–34	15–24	<15
40–49	>39	30–39	20–29	12–19	<12
50–59	>34	25–34	15–24	8–14	<8
60+	>29	20–29	10–19	5–9	<5

Chapter 2.1 Components of fitness

▼ Table 2.1.6 Modified press-ups

Age	Excellent	Good	Average	Fair	Poor
20–29	>48	34–38	17–33	6–16	<6
30–39	>39	25–39	12–24	4–11	<4
40–49	>34	20–34	8–19	3–7	<3
50–59	>29	15–29	6–14	2–5	<2
60+	>19	5–19	3–4	1–2	<1

This test is easy, quick to perform and requires no equipment. The subject's motivation level rather than their fitness can be the deciding factor. Poor technique can also invalidate the results and could lead to injury.

The sit-up test

This tests the endurance of the abdominal muscle group by measuring the number of sit-ups (curl-ups) an individual can perform by keeping to a 'bleep' indicated on the recording/app. When the individual cannot complete any more sit-ups in time with the bleep, they are deemed to have reached their optimum level. Again this test can be used as a benchmark for training or used for comparison with national norms.

If you are suffering from any injury or illness, you should consult a doctor before doing this test.

▼ Table 2.1.7 Normative scores

Stage	Number of sit-ups cumulative	Standard male	Standard female
1	20	Poor	Poor
2	42	Poor	Fair
3	64	Fair	Fair
4	89	Fair	Good
5	116	Good	Good
6	146	Good	Very good
7	180	Excellent	Excellent
8	217	Excellent	Excellent

The test must be conducted by using the standardised instructions. The individual's level of motivation to perform the test can affect the results. This test is simple and quick to perform, requiring minimal equipment, and large groups may be tested at once.

The subject's technique can affect the results, e.g., a curl-up with the feet held increases the involvement of the hip flexor muscles, making the test less valid as a measure of abdominal strength.

> **STUDY HINT**
> It is important that you can:
> ✔ define muscular endurance
> ✔ name activities that predominantly use muscular endurance
> ✔ describe the tests for muscular endurance.

Section 2 Physical Training

Speed

This is the ability of the body to move quickly. The movements may be the whole body or parts of the body, for example, arm speed in cricket bowling. Speed can be seen as the maximum rate that a person can move over a specific distance or speed of specific body parts such as the legs. Genetics influence how quick you are, but training can improve your rate or speed of movement. The amount of fast twitch muscle fibres also influences speed.

Examples of activities where speed is particularly important include:
- athletics, e.g. a 200-m sprint race
- swimming, e.g. a 50-m freestyle race
- squash, e.g. running to the front of the court to retrieve a drop shot
- football, e.g. the attacking player quickly pressing a defender with the ball.

▲ Figure 2.1.4 Speed is important for a fast bowler

If you are fit and healthy your speed is helped because:
- your heart and lungs are more efficient
- your muscles can move quicker because they have more energy available
- the energy available is greater because your muscles are more efficient in producing energy
- your joints are more healthy and therefore they can help you to move more effectively.

Suitable test for speed

The 30-metre sprint test

This should be on a flat, non-slippery surface to prevent accidents. The sprint should be from a flying start back from the beginning of the marked-out stretch of running surface. The time is taken from the beginning of the 30 m stretch to the end.

Before you do the test, you should have an appropriate warm-up and a practice sprint, You should be given some encouragement to continue running hard through the finish line (but this encouragement should be standardised to ensure validity).

Approximate norms for intermediate-level team players (30-m sprints) are shown in Table 2.1.8.

▼ Table 2.1.8 Approximate norms for 30 m sprints

Rating	Male	Female
Very good	<4.80 seconds	<5.30 seconds
Good	4.80–5.09	5.30–5.59
Average	5.10–5.29	5.60–5.89
Fair	5.30–5.60	5.90–6.20
Poor	>5.60	>6.20

▲ Figure 2.1.5 Speed is important in a lot of different sports activities

The test is easy to administer and no specialist equipment is required. However, the conditions must remain similar for each test. The appropriate warm-up should also be replicated. Sprint technique may affect times and the level of motivation may invalidate results. The timing procedure should be standardised and this is probably the weakest part of the test. The timer should be the same person for each subject's test.

Timing can be unreliable and the activity could be dangerous without appropriate warm-up and if the surface is slippery. It is important for subjects to have appropriate footwear to avoid injury. Weather conditions can also affect the results if the test takes place outdoors.

Strength

This is the ability of a muscle to exert force for a short period of time. The amount of force that can be exerted by a muscle depends on the size and number of muscles involved, as well as the type of muscle fibres used and the co-ordination of the muscles. Sports such as cycling can enlarge **slow twitch fibres**, thus giving greater potential for energy production. When training for an increase in speed, the size and number of mitochondria increases, as does the myoglobin content in the muscle cells. There are **anaerobic** benefits to muscle with activities like sprinting because the muscles get bigger and stronger (hypertrophy).

Key term

Slow twitch fibres (sometimes called type 1 muscle fibres) These are muscle fibres that can produce energy over a long period of time. They have high levels of myoglobin and mitochondria and are used for mainly aerobic activities.

Anaerobic This is when the body is working without the presence of oxygen, for example, lifting something quickly off the floor or doing an activity such as sprinting for a ball. This type of activity can be carried out only for a short amount of time because of the lack of oxygen and the build-up of lactic acid.

Section 2 Physical Training

Examples of activities where strength is particularly important:
- sprinting, e.g. the strong arm action in the 100-m sprint
- rugby, e.g. driving forward in the scrum
- cycling, e.g. the strong leg action required or sprinting
- rowing, e.g. arm action in each rowing stroke.

Suitable tests for strength

The grip strength dynamometer test

This test is an objective measure of strength using the handgrip dynamometer, which measures the strength of the handgrip. It is generally accepted that there is a strong correlation or link between handgrip strength and overall strength.

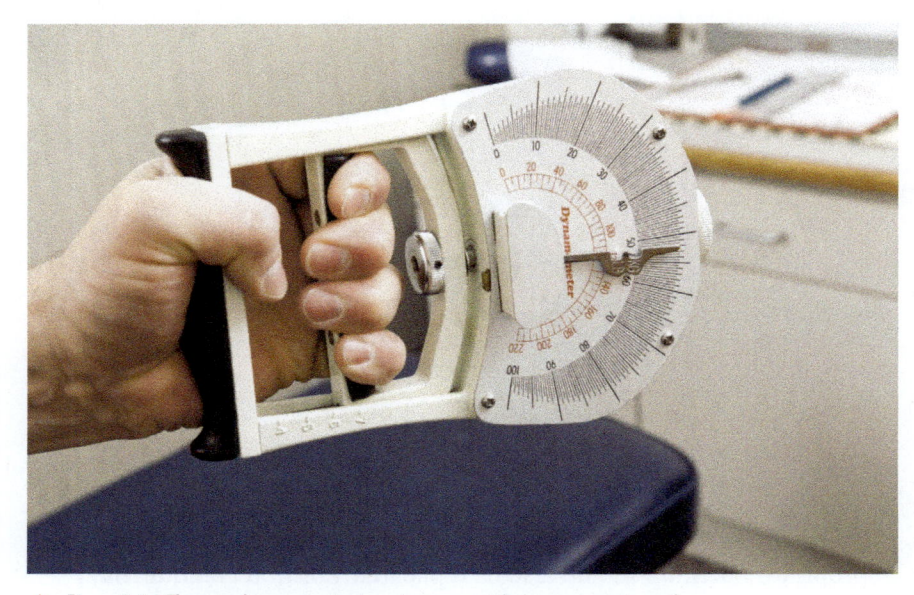

▲ Figure 2.1.6 The grip dynamometer is an instrument that measures strength

Make sure that the handgrip is adjusted to fit the subject's hand. The subject should stand, holding the dynamometer parallel to the side of the body, with the dial facing away from the body. They should squeeze the handle as hard as possible without moving the arm. Three attempts are recommended, with a one-minute rest between each attempt.

Table 2.1.9 outlines national norms for 16–19 year olds, showing the average from the three attempts with the favoured hand.

▼ Table 2.1.9 National norms for grip strength (favoured hand) for 16–19 year olds

Gender	Excellent	Good	Average	Fair	Poor
Male	>56 kg	51–56	45–50	39–44	<39
Female	>36 kg	31–36	25–30	19–24	<19

Another method of scoring is by recording the better of two attempts for each hand. Table 2.1.10 shows the average of the best scores of each hand (norms are in kilograms for adults).

▼ Table 2.1.10 National norms for grip strength (average of both hands) for 16–19 year olds

Rating*	Males (kg)	Females (kg)
Excellent	>64	>38
Very good	56–64	34–38
Above average	52–56	30–34
Average	48–52	26–30
Below average	44–48	22–26
Poor	40–44	20–22
Very poor	<40	<20

The validity of this test as a measure of general strength has been questioned, as the strength of the forearm muscles does not necessarily always represent the strength of other muscle groups.

This is a simple and easily used test indicating general strength level. It is relatively safe and quick to administer. There is no need for specific facilities – the only equipment required is the dynamometer. However, the dynamometer must be adjusted properly for the athlete's hand size. If this is not done accurately, the test lacks validity.

Take into consideration that the non-dominant hand usually scores about 10 per cent lower than the dominant hand. It is important for the validity of the test to use the same hand or an average score of both.

One repetition maximum test (1RM)

This test measures the maximum strength of muscle groups and is based on the maximum weight that can be moved a distance for one repetition (one rep max). The bench press for one rep max can be carried out as a test for upper body strength.

The participant should warm up with about ten reps of a light weight, followed by a minute's rest. They should then perform two warm-up sets of two to five reps with slightly heavier weights, with a two-minute rest between sets. Following a two-minute rest, the test is performed by doing the 1RM attempt with correct bench press technique.

▲ Figure 2.1.7 A 1RM test is often carried out using the bench press technique

Section 2 Physical Training

If the lift is successful, there should follow a rest for another 2 minutes. The load is then increased by 10 per cent and the subject then attempts another lift. If there is a failed attempt to perform the lift using the correct technique, the subject should rest for 2 minutes and then try again with a weight about 5 per cent lower. The weights should either increase or decrease until a maximum lift is performed. The starting weight is important because the maximum weight should be lifted within five attempts.

Good 1RM scores are mostly agreed to be:
- males 1.25 × body weight
- females 0.8 × body weight.

▼ Table 2.1.11 Rep max bench press table (weight lifted per body weight) for adults

Rating	Score (per body weight)
Excellent	>1.60
Good	1.30–1.60
Average	1.15–1.29
Below average	1.00–1.14
Poor	0.91–0.99
Very poor	<0.90

For those with less experience of lifting weights results can be variable due to technique rather than strength. Those performing this test must be taught the correct technique, otherwise it can be very dangerous. Variations in technique may also affect the score, as could the level of motivation, so it is best for the subject to motivate themselves.

The muscle energy systems also vary when reps are changed, which again will affect the score. Therefore the test may become invalid.

The equipment required is found in most gyms and health clubs. The test is simple to perform and does not require a great deal of technical expertise.

The squat is considered the most convenient leg strength test in predicting sprinting and jumping ability.

Good 1RM scores are mostly agreed to be:
- males to squat carrying twice their body weight
- females to squat carrying one and half times their body weight.

For hamstrings and quadriceps strength:
- Record the one repetition maximum (1RM) for the leg curl and the same for the leg extension exercise.
- Divide the leg curl score by the leg curl extension to find the ratio for each leg.
- For each leg, the curl score should be at least 80 per cent of the extension score and at least 75 per cent to reduce the chance of injury.

Chapter 2.1 Components of fitness

Power

Power is an important component of fitness that is used in many dynamic sports activities. In basketball, the legs must be powerful to enable the player to jump for rebounds; a gymnast needs power for vaulting; and a rugby player needs to use power to run through a tackle.

Power is often referred to as fast strength.

Examples of activities where power is particularly important:
- triple jump in athletics
- games activities such as rugby
- sprinting
- throwing events in athletics.

Key term

Power This is a combination of strength and speed.

▲ Figure 2.1.8 Strength and power are very important to the hammer thrower

Suitable test for power

Vertical jump test

Power can be assessed by using the vertical jump test, often called the sargent jump test. There are commercial jump test boards that can be fixed to the wall, which makes standardised measurement easier. The subject jumps vertically, using both feet, and then touches the calibrated scale on the board with one hand. The position of the touch is noted. The test is completed three times and the maximum height attained is recorded. If there is no test board, the subject stands next to a wall (side on) and stretches up with the hand closest to the wall. With the feet still flat on the ground, the point of the fingertips on the wall is marked with chalk. The subject then stands slightly away from the wall, jumps vertically as high as possible and touches the wall at the highest point of the jump.

The difference in distance between the static reach height and the jump height becomes the score. The best of three attempts is recorded. There are other mechanisms that can test for power, for example force plates and vertical jump meters.

Section 2 Physical Training

Table 2.1.12 Norms for 16–19 year olds for vertical jump test

Gender	Excellent	Above average	Average	Below average	Poor
Male	>65 cm	50–65 cm	40–49 cm	30–39 cm	<30 cm
Female	>58 cm	47–58 cm	36–46 cm	26–35 cm	<26 cm

Standing jump test

This test measures the explosive strength of the leg muscles. The subject stands behind a line marked on the ground, with feet slightly apart. A two-foot take-off and landing is used, with swinging of the arms and bending of the knees to drive forward. The subject attempts to jump up and forward as far as possible, landing on both feet. The jump is measured from the take-off line to the nearest point of contact on the landing. The longest distance jumped is recorded after three attempts.

This is a simple test that does not take long to carry out. The technique of the jump can obscure the results, making the test invalid, unless the test and re-test technique are identical.

The norms in Table 2.1.13 are approximate for adults.

Table 2.1.13 Norms for standing jump test (adults)

Rating	Males (cm)	Females (cm)
Excellent	>250	>200
Very good	241–250	191–200
Above average	231–240	181–190
Average	221–230	171–180
Below average	211–220	161–170
Poor	191–210	141–160
Very poor	<191	<141

Activity

1. Look at the data in the table.
   - What is the percentage difference between males and females in the 'excellent' category?
   - What are the reasons for this difference?
2. Carry out the test to assess your power.
   - Within which category do your results fall?
   - What are the possible problems with this test in assessing power as a component of fitness?

Flexibility

This is the amount or range of movement that you can have around a joint.

The structure of the joint restricts movement as well as the muscles, tendons and ligaments. As part of a healthy lifestyle or to perform sports safely and effectively, it is important to have flexibility or suppleness to prevent strains and it enables us to move quicker. If we are flexible then when we exercise, we are less likely to be injured and as we go about our daily routines, we can reach for objects more effectively. It also prevents stresses and strains to our muscles and joints.

Chapter 2.1 Components of fitness

▲ Figure 2.1.9 It is important to have flexibility or suppleness to prevent strains and to move quicker and more effectively

When we are flexible:
- our ligaments and supporting tissues can stretch further
- the blood flow to our muscles is improved and this helps with flexibility (also, the rise in muscle temperature can help the muscle to be more flexible)
- the body is used to stretching and it is easier to stretch further.

Examples of activities where flexibility is particularly important:
- gymnastics, e.g. to achieve the splits in a floor routine
- dance, e.g. to make a lunge in a dance performance
- hockey, e.g. to stretch forward to tackle another player
- table tennis, e.g. to perform an effective smash
- tennis, e.g. to perform a sliced serve.

Ballistic stretching uses the momentum (a tendency for the body to keep moving) of a moving body or a limb in an attempt to force it beyond its normal range of motion. This is different from dynamic stretching, which involves controlled gradual stretching up to but not beyond the normal range of movement.

Suitable test for flexibility

The sit and reach test

The objective of this test is to measure the athlete's lower back and hamstring flexibility. The subject sits on the floor with legs outstretched in a straight position. They reach as far forward as possible but keeping the legs straight and in contact with the floor. The distance that the ends of the fingers are from the feet (pointing upwards) is measured. Using a 'sit and reach' box ensures more accurate measurements.

Once again this test can provide measurements that can be used in assessing any future training and also for the subject to compare performance with national norms.

Table 2.1.14 shows the national norms for 16–19 year olds.

? Extend your knowledge

Flexibility and health

Everyone, not just sportspeople, can derive physical and mental benefits from stretching exercises. Increased flexibility helps to lengthen muscles, which in turn means more mobility in everyday life.

The ideal way to perform flexibility, or stretching exercises, is to combine several different types of exercise:

- static stretching: stretching a muscle to its furthest point and then holding that position
- dynamic stretching: a series of controlled movements (such as swinging the leg from front to back) to increase the range of movement in a specific part of the body
- isometric stretching: a type of static stretching which uses isometric contractions or tensing of the stretched muscles
- active stretching: holding a stretch with no assistance other than the strength of the opposing muscles
- passive stretching: using another person or an object to help you to bring a joint from a relaxed position through the full range of motion.

Overstretched muscles are more prone to injury, so it is advisable to stick to lighter stretching before and during exercise, leaving intense stretching for training sessions. This avoids your muscles being stretched to their limits without enough time to recover before being put under further stress during training. Stretching should not be painful: stretching to the furthest point should still be within the athlete's pain threshold in order to avoid injury. It is generally regarded to be good practice to warm up before stretching.

59

Section 2 Physical Training

Table 2.1.14 National norms for sit and reach test for 16–19 year olds

Gender	Excellent	Above average	Average	Below average	Poor
Male	>14	11–14	7–10	4–6	<4
Female	>15	12–15	7–11	4–6	<4

The validity or accuracy of the test depends on how strictly the test is conducted and the individual's level of motivation. There are published tables to relate results to potential level of fitness and the correlation is high. This test measures the flexibility of the lower back and hamstrings only and is a valid measure of this. The reliability depends on the amount of warm-up allowed and whether the same procedures are followed each time.

The test is simple and quick to administer and perform, but the variations in arm and leg length can obscure the results.

Most norms are based on no previous warm-up, though the best results will be achieved after a warm-up or if the test is preceded by a test such as the endurance test. There is therefore a need for a consistent method of administrating the test.

IN THE NEWS

Core exercises to help balance and cope with the coronavirus pandemic

'Most people have had a sedentary lifestyle,' Shannon Johnson, centre manager of the Prince George Family YMCA, said.
'Covid has provided an even playing ground so we're all having to start over again. People who have had positive experiences in the past know how to do it and some of us never really had those positive experiences so it's a bit more of a challenge and maybe even feel defeated or a bit overwhelmed. I think it's important for people to realise that everybody has an opportunity to restart and make new choices on how they want to move forward in the new normal and what that means for them. We have to take care of ourselves. Nobody is going to do that for us.'

Fall prevention is a big movement in the fitness industry for seniors.
'…give people an opportunity to engage their core,' Johnson said.
'By engaging your core you are using the deep muscles in your pelvic floor and the transverse abdominal muscles and those stabilise your hip alignment as well as your lower back and provide a good base for any movement that you make so you have better balance.'

Source: www.princegeorgecitizen.com/news/local-news/exercise-essential-to-healthy-aging-1.24198963

Agility

Agility is how quickly you can change direction under control and maintaining speed, balance and power, for example, a netball centre changing direction quickly to receive a pass or a gymnast changing direction in a floor routine.

There are three main components of agility:
- Core strength – this will allow the performer in sport to transfer power from the feet and legs to the upper body and transfer that energy from the upper body back down to the lower body. This will help make changes of direction go more smoothly.
- Balance – the sports performer must be in control of their body at all times in order to make the right moves for their sport.
- Flexibility – the sports performer will move their body in an efficient manner through the required range of motion. Flexibility training directly improves the flow of movement by loosening up tight muscles and developing the range of movement in the joints.

Examples of activities where flexibility is particularly important:
- trampolining and gymnastics – to perform a sequence of moves
- netball – to pass the ball when leaping in the air
- volleyball – to jump quickly and in a timely fashion to block the ball at the net
- basketball – to perform a lay-up shot under pressure.

▲ Figure 2.1.10 Agility is an important skill-related fitness component in netball

Suitable test for agility

The Illinois agility test

The purpose of this is to test running agility.

You need a non-slip surface, a stopwatch, measuring tape and marking cones. The length of the course is 10 metres and the width (distance between the start and finish points) is 5 metres. Four cones are used to mark the start, the finish and the two turning points. Another four cones are placed down the centre, spaced 3.3 metres apart.

Subjects for the test should lie on their front (head to the start line) and hands by their shoulders. On the 'Go' command, the stopwatch is started and the athlete gets up as quickly as possible and runs around the course in the direction indicated, without knocking the cones over, to the finish line, at which the timing is stopped. An excellent score is approximately under 15.2 seconds for a male and approximately less than 17 seconds for a female.

This is a simple test to administer, requiring little equipment. It establishes the players' ability to turn in different directions and at different angles. The choice of footwear and surface of the running area can affect times greatly, so these should be consistent when re-testing.

Section 2 Physical Training

> **Activity**
>
> 1. Make a table with all the fitness components down one side. Choose three different sporting activities and label these at the top of the table. Now tick which components are the most important with each activity. Then present your findings.
> 2. Using the table you have constructed, explain these physical fitness- and skill-related fitness components to a novice performer for each of your chosen activities.
> 3. Write a report comparing and contrasting six physical fitness- and skill-related fitness requirements for all three of your activities.

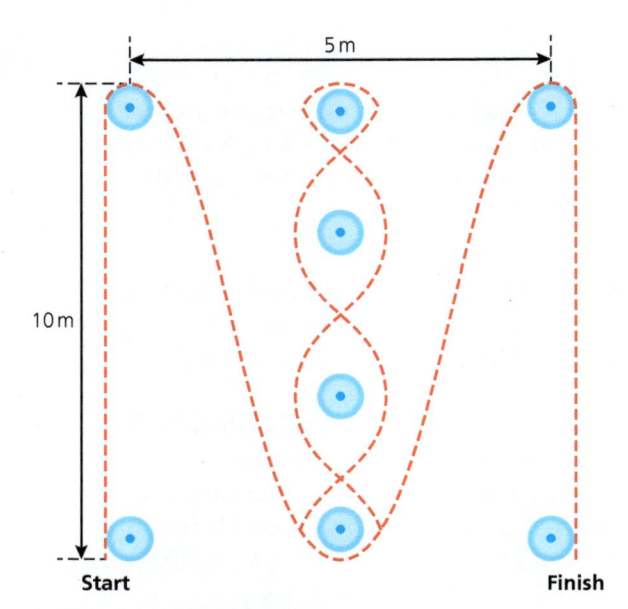

▲ Figure 2.1.11 The Illinois agility test

Balance

This is the ability to keep your body mass or centre of mass over a base of support, e.g. a gymnast performing a handstand on a balance beam. Balance can be static (still) or dynamic (moving but in control).

Balance is a crucial component of fitness for many different activities. It can help co-ordination and fluency in movement as well as protecting the body and keeping the athlete safe in physical activities.

Examples of activities where balance is particularly important:

- gymnastics – to perform a somersault on the beam
- hockey – to maintain balance when taking a penalty flick
- pole vault – to keep your balance on the upward phase of the vault
- dance – to hold an arabesque position.

Suitable test for balance

Stork stand test

Before the test, you warm up for approximately 10 minutes. Stand upright with legs about shoulder width apart and with your hands on your hips. Lift the right leg and place the sole of the right foot against the side of the left knee. The timer shouts 'Start' and you raise the heel of your left foot to stand on your toes.

You should try to hold the balanced position for as long as possible. The timer is stopped when the left heel touches the ground or the right foot loses contact with the knee. The time is then recorded and you rest for 3 minutes. Then the test is repeated but this time the left leg is lifted instead of the right. The same procedure is followed but with opposing legs.

Table 2.1.15 shows norms for 16–19 year olds.

▼ Table 2.1.15 Norms for stork stand test for 16–19 year olds

Rating	Males	Females
Excellent	>50 seconds	>30 seconds
Above average	41–50	23–30
Average	31–40	16–22
Below average	20–30	10–15
Poor	<20	<10

Co-ordination

Another important component of fitness is **co-ordination**, which is used widely in many different physical activities and sport. We often associate good co-ordination with the ability to move different limbs at different times or to do more than one task at a time effectively, for example, running and then passing a ball in rugby. A sports performer who makes a decision and then puts it into action effectively is showing good co-ordination.

Examples of activities where co-ordination is particularly important:
- dance
- tennis and other racket sports
- gymnastics
- team games such as football and netball
- outdoor adventure sports such as rock climbing.

Key term

Co-ordination This is the ability to repeat a pattern or sequence of movements with fluency and accuracy.

Suitable test for co-ordination

Wall throw test

This is often referred to as the 'alternate hand wall toss test'. A mark or line is placed on the floor 2 metres from the wall. You then stand behind the line and face the wall. You throw a tennis ball against the wall with one hand in an underarm action and you attempt to catch it with the opposite hand. The ball is then thrown back against the wall and caught with the initial hand. The test continues for 30 seconds and the number of completed catches is recorded.

Table 2.1.16 shows the norms for 16–19 year olds.

▼ Table 2.1.16 Norms for wall throw test for 16–19 year olds

Rating	Score (in 30 seconds)
Excellent	>35
Good	30–35
Average	20–29
Fair	15–19
Poor	<15

Section 2 Physical Training

Key term

Reaction time This is the time it takes for you to initiate an action or movement, or the time it takes someone to make a decision to move, for example how quickly a sprinter reacts to the gun and decides to drive off the blocks.

> **❓ Extend your knowledge**
>
> **Reaction time** is the time between the onset of the stimulus and the initiation of the response (hearing the gun in a sprint race and making the decision to drive off the blocks).
> **Movement time** is the time it takes to move (driving from the blocks to finishing the race).
> **Response time** is the time between the onset of the stimulus to the completion of the movement (from hearing the gun to finishing the race).

Reaction time

The ability to react quickly in sports situations is crucial if you are to outwit your opponent or out-sprint another athlete.

▲ Figure 2.1.12 Good reaction time is important for a sprinter to get a good start

Examples of activities where reaction time is particularly important:
- sprint start in athletics
- receiving a serve in tennis or squash
- team games such as basketball and hockey
- football, e.g. a goalkeeper saving a penalty.

IN THE NEWS

Improving speed of reactions by training your eyes

A series of eye exercises, called the 'EyeGym' workout, has been helping elite athletes to improve their reactions, peripheral and special awareness, eye–hand co-ordination and tactical decisions. Among those who have benefited are England's 2019 World Cup finalists rugby team, British skier Chemmy Alcott and India's professional squash player Saurav Ghosal.

The exercises include matching pulsating colour patterns, recalling six-digit numbers that flash up on the screen for milliseconds and tracking fast bouncing objects.

Suitable test for reaction time

Ruler drop test

This is an activity, done in pairs, to show individual differences in the speed of reactions. Each pair of subjects should use a metre rule. One student, playing the role of the 'tester', places the rule vertically against the wall so that the 100-cm mark is in line with a mark on the wall just above their eye level and holds the rule against the wall with their thumb at the 95-cm mark.

The second subject must stand in front of the rule and place a hand flat against the wall with their thumb over (but not touching) the 5-cm mark and focus on the 15-cm mark of the rule.

The tester then lets the rule fall and the subject must try to trap the rule by pressing their thumb on it. The point at which the thumb presses is marked and the distance the rule has dropped is measured.

Table 2.1.17 enables you to convert distance on the ruler to reaction time. For example, if you catch the ruler at the 30.5-cm mark, your reaction time is 0.25 seconds.

▼ Table 2.1.17

Distance on the ruler (centimetres)	Reaction time (seconds)
5	0.10
10	0.14
15	0.17
20	0.20
25.5	0.23
30.5	0.25
43	0.30
61	0.35
79	0.40
99	0.45

> **STUDY HINT**
> For all the components of fitness, the examiner may ask you to use data relating to all the above components. So be prepared for some simple calculations, e.g. percentage increase, and be aware of the main norms for each test result. Every examination paper will have questions related to some data – usually in a table or a graph. Practise using data to formulate conclusions – there are often questions that ask for reasons behind a set of data.

Section 2 Physical Training

> **SUMMARY**
> - Cardiovascular endurance is the ability to exercise continuously without tiring.
> - Tests for cardiovascular endurance include the Cooper 12-minute run/walk test and the multi-stage fitness test.
> - Muscular endurance is the ability of the muscle or group of muscles in the body to repeatedly contract or keep going without rest. The tests for muscular endurance are the press-up test and the sit-up test.
> - Speed is the maximum rate that a person can move over a specific distance or the speed of specific body parts. Tests for speed include the 30-metre sprint test.
> - Strength is the ability of a muscle to exert force for a short period of time. Tests for strength include the grip strength dynamometer test and the 1RM test.
> - Flexibility is the amount or range of movement that you can have around a joint. A test for flexibility is the sit and reach test.
> - Agility is how quickly you can change direction under control and maintaining speed, balance and power. A test for agility is the Illinois agility test.
> - A test for balance is the stork stand test.
> - A test for co-ordination is the alternate wall toss test.
> - A test for power is the vertical jump test.
> - A test for reaction time is the ruler drop test.

Practice questions

1. Identify a suitable test that can be used to assess the power of a diver. **(1 mark)**
2. Which one of the following is the best practical example of agility? **(1 mark)**
   a. An athlete running a 400-metre race
   b. A netball player running into space to receive the ball
   c. A tennis player who sprints to return a lob
   d. A hockey player dribbling around an opponent to score a goal
3. Which one of the following shows the correct distances for the multi-stage fitness test? **(1 mark)**
   a. 10 metres   c. 25 metres
   b. 20 metres   d. 30 metres
4. i. Define the fitness components of stamina and muscular endurance.
   ii. Explain their importance to a cross-country runner. **(4 marks)**
5. Name the fitness component that can be measured using the 'stork stand' test. **(1 mark)**
6. Using a suitable diagram, describe the Illinois agility test. **(5 marks)**

Chapter 2.2
Applying the principles of training

> ## Understanding the Specification
>
> In studying this section you should get to know the following definitions of principles of training and be able to apply them to personal exercise and training programmes:
> - specificity
> - overload
> - progression
> - reversibility.
>
> You should also know the definition of the elements of FITT (frequency, intensity, time, type) and be able to apply these elements to personal exercise and training programmes.
> You should know the different types of training and understand the key components and benefits of a warm-up and cool-down and be able to apply examples.

Principles of training

For training to be effective and to ensure that the person training gets the most out of demanding exercise sessions, there needs to be a set of guidelines or rules to follow. The main principles for you to understand are specificity, overload, progression and reversibility.

1. Specificity

This principle indicates that the training undertaken should be relevant to the activity or the type of sport. For instance, a sprinter would carry out more anaerobic training because the event is mostly anaerobic in nature. It is not just energy systems that have to be specific – muscle groups and actions involved in the training also have to be as specific as possible. There is, however, a consensus that a good general fitness is required before any high degree of specificity can be applied.

2. Overload

This principle underpins the need to work the body harder than normal so that there is some stress and discomfort. Adaptation and progress will follow overload because the body will respond by adapting to the stress. For instance, in weight training, the lifter will eventually attempt heavier weights or an increase in repetitions, thus overloading the body. Overload can be achieved by increasing the frequency, the intensity and the duration of the activity.

3. Progression

Not only has overload got to occur, it should become increasingly more difficult. Once adaptations have occurred, the performer should make even more demands on the body. It is important that progression does not mean 'overdoing it'. Training must be sensibly progressive and realistic if it

Section 2 Physical Training

❓ Extend your knowledge

Variance and periodisation

These are extra principles that are not stated in the OCR GCSE PE Specification, but should be taken into consideration to make training as effective as possible. Variance states that there should be variety in training methods. If training is too predictable, performers can become demotivated and bored. Over-use injuries are also common when training is too repetitive with one muscle group or part of the body, therefore variance can also help prevent injury.

Periodisation is another additional training principle that is often used to optimise training. This principle is not on the OCR GCSE PE Specification, but it is often used to construct training programmes in sport. Periodisation is a planned, structural variation in training over time with a constant recycling of the training variables (activity, rest, frequency, intensity and duration) within a daily, weekly and monthly training programme. This avoids overtraining leading to injury and excessive fatigue. Periodisation often involves the training cycles called microcycles, mesocycles and macrocycles.

Microcycle: typically a week's training block

Mesocycle: usually three to six weeks in length and with a specifically targeted outcome such as improving strength

Macrocycle: long-term training plan, often a year long

---

is to be effective, otherwise injury may occur and there will be regression instead of progression.

4. Reversibility

This principle states that performance can deteriorate if training stops or decreases in intensity for any length of time. If training is stopped, then the fitness gained will be largely lost. For instance, VO_2 max and muscle strength can decrease.

Optimising training

To be able to maximise or to get the very best out of each training session or programme of sessions, a further principle should be considered. We call this the FITT principle – frequency, intensity, time and type.

The FITT principle

The FITT method ensures that athletes adhere to the principles of training. FITT stands for:

- F = frequency of training (number of training sessions each week). This will depend on the performer's level of ability and fitness. The elite athlete will train every day, whereas the lower-level club player may train only once per week. The type of training also dictates the frequency – aerobic training can be followed five or six times per week. With strength training, however, you may train only three or four times per week. How frequently you exercise or train depends on your ability and fitness level. You should also bear in mind the progression and overload principles. Too much training can be as harmful as not enough.
- I = intensity of the exercise undertaken (how hard the athlete is training). This will again take into account the individual differences of the performer and the type of training being undertaken. A 'training zone' is often created for aerobic training where heart rate ranges dictate the intensity of training. It is suggested that there should be a training intensity of 60–75 per cent of maximal heart rate reserve for the average athlete.
- T = time or duration that the training takes up. If aerobic training is required, this should be a minimum of 20 minutes or so. The duration of the training must take into account the intensity of training to be effective.
- T = type of training to be considered that fulfils specific needs. The methods of training are described earlier in this chapter and the type of sport or your role in that sport will dictate what type of training you follow. A triathlete, for example, will train all areas of fitness but pay particular attention to aerobic and muscular endurance because of the nature of the sport. For sprinting in athletics, the type of training might include muscular endurance to keep muscles steady during the sprint start.

> **STUDY HINT**
> The Specification demands that you know what FITT stands for and that you can give a practical example for each element. You should be able to apply examples to constructing a personal exercise and training programme.

Example of applying training principles

The programme below illustrates two days of a week's training programme for a Premier League football player, illustrating the FITT principle:
- Frequency = (how often?), e.g. twice a week.
- Intensity = (how hard?), e.g. ten sprints.
- Time = (how long?), e.g. 10 minutes' 'keep up' football skills.
- Type = (what type?), e.g. stretching.

Monday
- **Prehabiliation** (Prehab) work such as massage and physiotherapy.
- 30 minutes – own programme of core exercises and warm-up.
- 10 minutes – run at moderate pace followed by **ballistic stretching**.
- 20 minutes – interval work with 'ladder' training for quick footwork. Ten sprints followed by stretching.
- 10 minutes – 'keep ball' in small grids.
- 10 minutes – further grid work including 4 v 1 and 3 v 2.
- 20 minutes – defenders and attackers separate drills, e.g. forwards shooting drills.
- 30 minutes – all involved in link-up play.
- 10 minutes – warm-down and further rehab where necessary.

Tuesday
- Rehab work and physiotherapy where required.
- 30 minutes – own programme of core exercises and warm-up, including ballistic stretching and ending in short sprints.
- 30 minutes – 'keep ball' and 2 teams 9 v 9 possession game with restrictions to improve quick passing and control.
- 30 minutes – grid work from 1 v 1 through to 4 v 4.
- 10 minutes – five a side with two touch restrictions.
- 20 minutes – short run intervals with 100 per cent intensity.
- 20 minutes – circuit training.
- 10 minutes – warm-down.
- 1 hour's rest.
- 10 minutes – warm-up.
- 60 minutes – weight training for strength and power.
- 10 minutes – warm-down and further rehab if necessary.

Types of training

Training or exercise routines have a purpose, for example, to improve cardiovascular endurance or flexibility. The type of training you choose can work on one or a number of components of fitness depending on your needs.

Continuous training

Continuous training activities seek to maintain and improve cardiovascular endurance. Running, cycling or swimming can be very beneficial for cardiovascular endurance. Cardiovascular adaptations can arise from continuous training, for example, the heart will get bigger and stronger and the heart will not have to work so hard because each beat will force more blood around the body, therefore achieving an increase in stroke volume.

Activity
1. Write a plan to outline a six-week programme and justify your activities by referring to all the principles of training listed in Extend your knowledge and in the Optimising training section.
2. Plan an hour of exercise and include the principles of overload and specificity.

Key terms

Prehabilitation This term is not explicit in the OCR GCSE PE Specification, but nevertheless is often used in the context of physical preparation in sport. It is a term used to describe exercises before medical surgery but has been adopted by sports trainers to describe strength and conditioning exercises for specific muscles that help to reduce injury risks, before an injury occurs.

Ballistic stretching This uses the momentum (a tendency for the body to keep moving) of a moving body or a limb in an attempt to force it beyond its normal range of motion. This is different from dynamic stretching, which involves controlled gradual stretching up to but not beyond the normal range of movement.

Section 2 Physical Training

This training is related to rhythmic exercise that stresses the aerobic system. This should be carried out at a steady rate or with low intensity – between 20–30 minutes and 2 hours. This type of training ensures that there is not the build-up of lactate associated with anaerobic training.

▲ Figure 2.2.1 Aerobic capacity can be improved through continuous training

IN THE NEWS
Using unilateral movements

'When progress slows down or even comes to a halt, we often make the mistake of simply trying to push harder in an attempt to get ourselves back on track.'

According to conditioning coach and former sprinter, Courtney Fearon, training can be tweaked by using unilateral work. 'Unilateral movements are ones where you work one side at a time. Running is all about being on one leg at a time, so including strength exercises that reflect this is going to strengthen your body optimally. Single-leg work also boosts balance, stability and co-ordination.'

Source: www.runnersworld.com/uk/training/beginners/a33482259/beginners-guide-to-running-stronger/

> **? Extend your knowledge**
>
> Fartlek training can be adapted to treadmill running – which was especially convenient during the COVID-19 pandemic with home-based treadmills. Intervals of training can be varied, such as eight sets of 1 minute of 'hard' training, followed by 2 minutes of 'easy' training.
>
> Example of a Fartlek interval workout:
> - 2 minutes hard, 1 minute easy
> - 1 minute hard, 1 minute easy
> - 30 seconds hard, 2 minutes easy.
>
> Repeat the above circuits three times.

Fartlek

Fartlek is also known as 'speed play' and is often used to maintain and improve aerobic endurance. Throughout the exercise, the speed and intensity of the training are varied. In a 1-hour session, for instance, there may be walking activity (which is low in intensity) and fast sprinting (which is high in intensity). This training is good for aerobic fitness because it is an endurance activity. It is good for anaerobic fitness because of the speed activities over a short period of time.

Cross-country running with sprint activities every now and again is a simplistic but reasonable way of describing fartlek; it could also be incorporated into road running. Fartlek has the added benefit of a more varied and enjoyable way of endurance training. It helps to train both the aerobic and the anaerobic energy systems and is ideal for many team sports that include intermittent sprinting and long periods of moderate activity.

Fartlek sessions need to achieve two main aims:

- to give a session that benefits the athlete's development
- to provide an environment that is varied and a worthwhile training session that encourages a high degree of effort.

✔ Check your understanding

1. Why do fartlek rather than track running?
2. Which component/s of fitness can be improved via fartlek training?
3. What do you need to do to vary such training sessions?

Interval training

Interval training is one of the most popular types of training for aerobic endurance. It is adaptable to individual needs and sports. Interval training can, however, improve both aerobic and anaerobic fitness. It is called interval training because there are intervals of work and intervals of rest.

For training the aerobic system, there should be intervals of slower work, which is suitable for sports such as athletics and swimming and for team games such as hockey and football.

IN THE NEWS

'SIT' Training

SIT – or sprint interval training – is another form of training. This type of aerobic training is often used for fat loss. The exercise is intense and helps to burn calories. It consists of 'all out' sprints using 100 per cent effort, followed by rest intervals – for example:

- four to six 30-second sprints at an intensity of 10
- rest for 2 to 4 minutes after each sprint
- REST period consists of either fully resting (intensity of 0) or low-intensity active recovery such as walking (intensity of 1).

Repeat this workout two to three times per week.

Section 2 Physical Training

> **STUDY HINT**
> For examination purposes, you will need to be able to name the following types of training:
> - ✓ continuous
> - ✓ fartlek
> - ✓ interval (including circuit, weight training plyometrics and HIIT (high-intensity interval training)).
>
> Make sure you can describe each of these types and which components of fitness they seek to improve.

For training, the anaerobic system in athletics and swimming, there should be shorter intervals of more intense training.

The following factors should be taken into account before the design of a training session:

- **Duration** of the work interval. The work interval should be 3–10 seconds at high intensity for anaerobic and 7–8 minutes for aerobic exercise.
- **Speed** (intensity) of the work interval. This should be high (90–100 per cent of maximum intensity) for anaerobic and moderate (70–80 per cent of your maximum heart rate) for aerobic exercise.
- **Number of repetitions**. This depends on the length of the work period (the length of the training session). If the work period is short, then up to 50 repetitions is appropriate for anaerobic. For aerobic with a long work period, 3–4 repetitions are more appropriate.
- **Number of sets** of repetitions. Repetitions can be divided into sets. For example, 50 repetitions could be divided into sets of 5.
- **Duration of the rest interval**. The rest period is the length of time that the heart rate falls to about 150 bpm. Aerobic training will require a shorter rest interval for effective training.
- **Type** of activity during the rest interval. If the energy system is aerobic, then only light stretching is needed. For anaerobic activity, some light jogging may help to disperse lactic acid.

Circuit training

This involves a series of exercises arranged in a particular way called a circuit because the training involves repetition of each activity. The resistance that is used in circuits relates mainly to body weight and each exercise in the circuit is designed to work on a particular muscle group.

For effective training, different muscle groups should be worked at each station, with no two consecutive stations working the same muscle groups. For instance, an activity that uses the main muscle groups in the arms should be followed by an exercise involving the muscle groups in the legs. The types of exercises that are involved in circuit training are press-ups, star jumps, dips and squat thrusts.

Circuit training can also incorporate skills in the activities. A circuit for footballers, for instance, may include dribbling activities, throw-ins, shuttle runs and shooting activities.

The duration and intensity depend on the types of activities incorporated. An example would be a circuit with one minute's worth of activity, followed by one minute's worth of rest. The whole circuit could then be repeated three times. The score at the end of the circuit may be related to time or repetitions and is a good way of motivating in training. It is also easy to see progression in fitness as more repetitions can be attempted or times improved as the weeks go by.

Typical circuit exercises:
- running, skipping, bounding, step-ups
- press-ups, tricep dips, burpees or squat thrusts, chin-ups
- crunchies, trunk twists, dorsal raises
- squats, standing jumps, leg raises, sprints.

> **Activity**
> 1. Describe the circuit training method by drawing out a proposed circuit designed to improve muscular endurance. Present your findings.
> 2. Write a thorough explanation (two or three paragraphs) of how the circuit training method can improve muscular endurance.

Weight training

In circuit training, it is the body weight that is used as resistance to enable the body to work hard and to physiologically adapt to the training stresses. For strength to be developed, more resistance can be used – in the form of weights or against other types of resistance, such as the use of pulleys.

Weight training involves a number of repetitions and sets, depending on the type of strength that needs to be developed. For throwing events in athletics, for example, training methods must involve very high resistance and low repetition. For strength endurance needed in swimming or cycling, more repetitions need to be involved, with lighter weights.

If maximum strength is required as a result of training (e.g. for athletic throwing events), include a high resistance activity (high percentage of your maximum), with low number of repetitions (number of times you repeat the movement), e.g. 80 per cent maximum strength with three sets of five repetitions. If strength endurance is required then higher reps and lower resistance is best – 3 sets of 20 reps at 55 per cent max strength.

Plyometrics

Plyometrics is a form of training exercise that involves rapid and repeated stretching and contracting of the muscles, designed to increase strength and power. This type of training is specifically intended to improve dynamic strength. Plyometrics improves the speed with which muscles contract and therefore affects power.

If muscles have previously been stretched, they tend to generate more force when contracted. Any sport that involves sprinting, throwing and jumping will benefit from this type of training.

Plyometrics involves bounding, hopping and jumping, when muscles have to work concentrically (jumping up) and eccentrically (landing).

One type of jumping used in this training method is called in-depth jumping, which is when the athlete jumps on to and off boxes. This type of training is strenuous on the muscles and joints and the athlete must be reasonably fit before attempting it. As usual, it is important that the muscles are warmed and stretched before beginning. Footballers often do plyometrics for increasing the power in their legs.

> **Extend your knowledge**
>
> Weight training is potentially dangerous – never train alone and ensure that you train within your capabilities, and do not forget to regularly re-hydrate. Poor technique can do lasting damage – weights that are too heavy for you may cause you to use poor technique; better to go lighter and perform each lift correctly.

IN THE NEWS

Weight training for golf

Bryson DeChambeau, who won the 2020 US PGA Golf Championship, prepared by adopting more strength training and he increased his protein intake. He gained 19 kilos in nine months and can now out-drive many of his opponents. He added 9 kilos during the three-month COVID-19 lockdown to return with a drastically bigger physique. His strength training included weight training that activated all of his muscles so they could tolerate greater amounts of force, before adding weight to make sure that, muscle by muscle, his movements became stronger.

Section 2 Physical Training

IN THE NEWS

Preparing for the Wimbledon Tennis Championships with a 'donkey-kick press-up'

The British tennis player Andy Murray was seen preparing for his Wimbledon matches with a modified press-up activity – this is an example of plyometrics. Some call it the 'donkey-kick press-up', which is an explosive-type movement, much more intense and dynamic than a normal press-up. You do the kick when you are down, then push up as your legs are coming back down to the ground.

The pectorals, triceps and core muscles, such as the rectus abdominus and the obliques, are worked hard in this activity, which involves shortening and lengthening the muscles at speed to generate power and create more force.

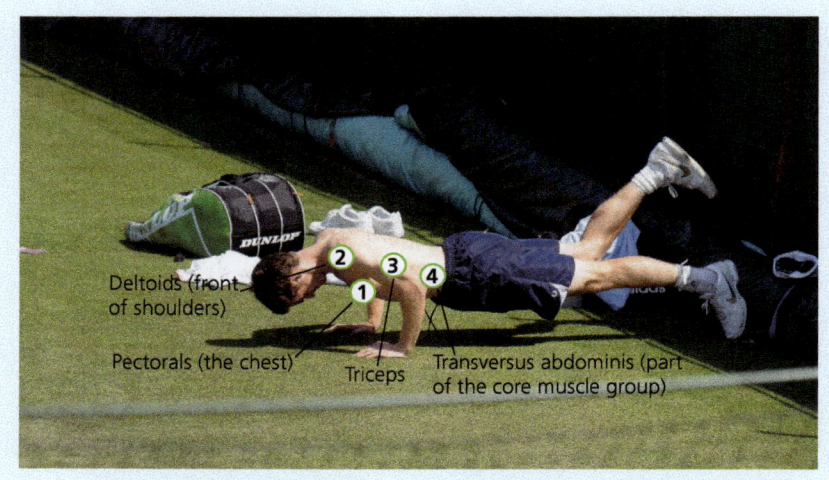

▲ Figure 2.2.2 Murray kicks his legs up in the air and, as they fall to the ground, he pushes his upper body off the ground. Although you cannot see it, the serratus anterior under the armpit is also being worked

High-intensity interval training (HIIT)

High-intensity interval training is a cardiorespiratory training technique that alternates brief speed and recovery intervals to increase the overall intensity of a workout.

Most endurance workouts, such as walking, running or stair climbing, are performed at a moderate intensity, or an exertion level of 5–6 on a scale of 0–10. High-intensity intervals are done at an exertion level of 7 or higher and are typically sustained for between 30 seconds and 3 minutes, although they can be as short as 8–10 seconds or as long as 5 minutes – the higher the intensity, the shorter the speed interval. Recovery intervals are equal to or longer than the speed intervals.

Chapter 2.2 Applying the principles of training

HIIT training not only helps performance, it also improves the ability of the muscles to burn fat. A typical HIIT training session usually lasts about 20–30 minutes.

▲ Figure 2.2.3 HIIT is a cardiorespiratory training technique that alternates brief speed and recovery intervals to increase the overall intensity of a workout

> **? Extend your knowledge**
>
> Some typical HIIT sessions:
>
> - **On a track**. Warm up with five laps at an easy pace. Gradually speed up so that you end up running briskly. Then do 200 metres at maximal sprint effort followed by 400 metres gentle jog. Repeat six times.
> - **On a treadmill**. Set the incline to 1 per cent. Warm up by running gently, gradually building speed, for 10 minutes. On an effort scale of 1–10, you should be at 5–6 by the end. Run 30 seconds at close to maximal speed; jog gently for 3 minutes. Repeat 4–6 times.
> - **On a bike**. Following a short warm-up, try 4–6 bouts of maximal sprint efforts, each lasting for 30 seconds, and follow with 4 minutes of easy spinning recovery.

IN THE NEWS

An Olympic gymnast's high-intensity interval training (HIIT) routine

Max Whitlock, GB's Olympic gymnast, likes to exercise by using a high-intensity interval training (HIIT) routine. It features six exercises that give a whole-body workout.

The HIIT routine includes two sets of the following six exercises – 30 seconds for each:
1. rebound jumps
2. three hops
3. dish rocks
4. arch ups
5. front support climbs
6. front support to back support.

Other HIIT-type training activities typically involve 60 seconds of exercise near your maximum effort, followed by a recovery period of the same amount, repeated for 20 minutes, three times a week. Your peak effort is around 80–90 per cent of your maximum heart rate.

You can do HIIT on a bike, running, swimming, on gym equipment like a cross trainer, or by sprinting up and down the stairs.

Section 2 Physical Training

IN THE NEWS
Static stretching may make little difference

Surprisingly, while it is thought that static stretching will reduce the risk of injury during physical activity or exercise, or soreness the next day, there is not much evidence or recent research to support this. However, it is still advised to incorporate dynamic stretching into your aerobic warm-up.

The warm-up

The key components of a warm-up are as follows.

1. **Pulse raising**. This includes exercises that slowly increase heart rate and gradually increase body temperature, for example, jogging, cycling, skipping or gentle running.
2. **Mobility**. Exercises that take the joints through their full range of movement (ROM), for example, arm swings, hip circles, high-knees activities.
3. **Stretching**. This can include developmental stretches, gradually increasing the difficulty of each stretch or dynamic stretches that include more ballistic movements (e.g., lunges). Examples of stretches include open and close the gate, and groin walk for more dynamic exercises. Most modern research suggests that static stretching should not be included in the warm-up as it is counterproductive due to the reduction in explosive power associated with it.
4. **Dynamic movements**. This involves movements that show a change of speed and direction, for example, shuttle runs.
5. **Skill rehearsal**. This involves practising or rehearsing common movement patterns and skills that will be used in the activity, for example, dribbling drills for football or passing drills for netball.

▲ Figure 2.2.4 Whatever the level of the sport, whether it is serious competition or recreational play, you should be prepared for the activity by carrying out an effective warm-up

Chapter 2.2 Applying the principles of training

> **? Extend your knowledge**
>
> ### Warm-up for wheelchair rugby players
>
> The warm-up described in 'Physical benefits of a warm up' will help to prepare wheelchair rugby players to perform well and to reduce their chance of injury. The warm-up should be about 10 to 20 minutes long and should start with low intensity, moving up to a higher intensity as the warm-up progresses.
>
> The International Wheelchair Rugby Federation suggests the following:
>
> 1. Start with some movement/fun activities: slow wheeling is a good start, followed by upper body stretches of the shoulders, neck, wrists, hands and fingers, including low-impact arm swings, shoulder circles, rolls and back slaps.
> 2. Increase the level of intensity and focus more on transit movements that require each player to travel a greater distance.
> 3. Prepare the players for the session by developing their skills as part of the warm-up. To achieve this, the coach can integrate a technical element into the warm-up which relates to the focus of the session.

> **STUDY HINT**
>
> It may be helpful to learn a summary of the benefits of a warm-up:
> - ✔ Gradually raises body temperature and heart rate
> - ✔ Improves flexibility/pliability of muscle fibres
> - ✔ Increases pliability of ligaments and tendons
> - ✔ Increases the blood flow and the amount of oxygen to the muscles
> - ✔ Increases the speed of muscle contractions
>
> It is also helpful if you can construct a warm-up using pulse raiser, mobility, stretching, dynamic movements and skill rehearsal.

Physical benefits of a warm-up

The warm-up enables the body to prepare for exercise and decreases the likelihood of injury and muscle soreness. There is also a release of adrenaline that will start the process of speeding up the delivery of oxygen to the working muscles. An increase in muscle temperature will help to ensure that there is a ready supply of energy and that the muscle becomes more flexible to prevent injury.

It is crucial that all performers in physical activities and sport take appropriate steps to prepare for vigorous activity through an effective warm-up and, following the activity, a cool-down. This applies to all physical activities at all levels. If you are a beginner, it is just as important to warm up properly.

> **? Extend your knowledge**
>
> Factors to be taken into consideration before planning a warm-up/cool-down:
>
> - Size of group – large/small
> - Age of participants – young/old
> - Sex of participants – gender/whether group is mixed sex
> - Experience of participants – novice or expert/skill level
> - Individual fitness levels – trained/unfit/previous injury/flexibility/size/weight
> - Medical conditions – asthma/diabetes/other named conditions
> - Disability

Section 2 Physical Training

The cool-down

The key components of a cool-down are:
1. Low-intensity exercises – gradually lower the pulse rate and the heart rate and reduce the body's temperature, for example, easy movement exercises or light running/jogging.
2. Stretching – includes steady and static stretches, for example, hamstring stretch.

Physical benefits of a cool-down

The cool-down is important for effective training. If light exercise follows training, then the oxygen can more effectively be flushed through the muscle tissue and will oxidise any lactic acid, which needs to be dispersed. Cool-downs also prevent blood pooling in the veins, which can cause dizziness.

The cool-down is crucial in:
- helping the body's transition back to a resting state
- gradually lowering heart rate
- gradually lowering temperature
- circulating blood and oxygen
- gradually reducing breathing (respiratory) rate
- increasing the removal of waste products such as lactic acid
- reducing the risk of muscle soreness (or delayed onset of muscle soreness – DOMS) and stiffness
- reducing the risk of blood pooling
- reducing the risk of damage to joints
- aiding recovery by stretching muscles, i.e. lengthening and strengthening muscles for next workout/use.

▲ Figure 2.2.5 The warm-up and the cool-down are important elements of a fitness training programme

IN THE NEWS

Use of ice vests

The Japanese Tokyo Olympics summer temperature was expected to reach over 33 °C. This meant athletes would have to perform under very hot and humid conditions.

High temperatures were also predicted for the 2022 FIFA World Cup in Qatar (still planned for at the time of writing) with athletes compelled to use cooling strategies during the competition.

An expert at Hiroshima University commented that the combined factors of competition timing and global warming leading to increased temperatures, presented a growing problem for athletes. If their core body temperature gets too high, they are at risk of dehydration as well as a decrease in sporting performance and brain function.

Athletes from the Hiroshima University football team were recruited by the expert to test a prototype 'cooling vest'. It is filled with ice packs and a collar to keep the neck cool and is designed to cool the athletes' upper-body skin and neck, which can lower their temperature and decrease their heart rate.

In the test, the participants played a game of football for 30 minutes followed by 15 minutes of rest. Some of them wore the cooling vest during the rest period and some did not. All the participants then went on to play soccer for a further 30 minutes. The athletes who wore the vest at half-time showed increased performance in the second half and reported that they felt more comfortable. This is important because comfort and relaxation during half-time help to avoid stress during the remainder of a game.

SUMMARY

- The four principles of training are that it should:
  - be specific to the sport
  - work the body harder than normal (overload)
  - progress incrementally
  - be reversible – all training achievements can be undone if training stops or slows down.
- The FITT principle includes frequency, intensity, time and type.
- Continuous training seeks to maintain and improve cardiovascular endurance.
- Fartlek is also known as 'speed play' and is often used to maintain and improve aerobic endurance.
- Interval training is one of the most popular types of training for aerobic endurance but can improve both aerobic and anaerobic fitness.
- Circuit training involves a series of exercises arranged in a particular way called a circuit because the training involves repetition of each activity.
- Weight training involves a number of repetitions and sets, depending on the type of strength that needs to be developed.
- Plyometrics improves the speed with which muscles contract and therefore affects power.
- High-intensity interval training (HIIT) is a cardiorespiratory training technique that alternates brief speed and recovery intervals to increase the overall intensity of a workout.
- The benefits of a warm-up are that it:
  - improves flexibility
  - increases pliability of ligaments and tendons
  - increases the amount of oxygen to the muscles
  - increases the speed of muscle contractions.
- The benefits of a cool-down are that it:
  - flushes oxygen through the muscles more effectively
  - helps to oxide lactic acid
  - prevents blood pooling in the veins.

Section 2 Physical Training

Practice questions

1. Compare fartlek training with circuit training. **(2 marks)**
2. Explain high intensity interval training (HIIT). **(3 marks)**
3. 'Frequency' is one of the components of the FITT principle of training. Training three times a week is an example of 'frequency'.

   Give two other practical examples of 'frequency' in personal exercise programmes and assess two ways in which applying this principle might improve fitness. **(4 marks)**
4. 'Type' is a principle of training.

   Using a practical example, explain what is meant by the term 'type'. **(2 marks)**
5. Describe a suitable cool-down for a gymnast. **(2 marks)**
6. *Before a basketball player participates in a game, they will complete a warm-up to prepare their body and mind for the competitive game.

   Using practical examples, outline the components of a warm-up and explain the different mental preparation techniques that could be used to improve performance of this basketball player. **(6 marks)**
7. *Using practical examples from sport, explain how the principles of training and the setting of goals can help to ensure the success of a personal exercise programme. **(6 marks)**

*These questions include an assessment of the quality of your written communication.

Chapter 2.3
Preventing injury in physical activity and training

Understanding the Specification

You should know and understand how the risk of injury in physical activity and sport can be minimised and be able to apply examples, including:
- personal protective equipment
- correct clothing/footwear
- appropriate level of competition
- lifting and carrying equipment safely
- use of warm-up and cool-down.

You should also know the potential hazards in a range of physical activity and sport settings and be able to apply examples, including:
- sports hall
- fitness centre
- playing field
- artificial outdoor areas
- swimming pool.

Minimising the risk of injury in physical activity and sport

The following are ways of helping to prevent injuries or health problems associated with physical activities and sport.

Personal protective equipment

The risks arising from some hazards can be limited by using **personal protective equipment** (PPE), for instance when people wear protective gloves while handling cleaning equipment or a rugby player wearing a gum shield.

An example of a piece of protective equipment in a physical activity is a squash player wearing protective goggles to minimise the risk of impact with the ball.

Other examples of personal protective equipment include:
- scrumcaps in rugby and safety helmets in canoeing
- gloves as a cricket wicketkeeper or hockey goalkeeper
- shin pads in football and hockey.

Key term

Personal protective equipment PPE (including correct clothing and footwear) is defined by the government's Health and Safety Executive as 'all equipment (including clothing affording protection against the weather) which is intended to be worn or held by a person at work and which protects him (or her) against one or more risks to his health or safety'.

▲ Figure 2.3.1 The risks arising from some hazards can be limited by using protective equipment

Section 2 Physical Training

Activity
Choose three different types of sports and list the PPE commonly used in each of these sports.

❓ Extend your knowledge

Inappropriate or damaged equipment

The equipment that is used in physical activity and sport should be correct for the activity and the age/ability of the people involved. For example, in gymnastics, the vaulting box should be at an appropriate height. For very young tennis players, the rackets may be lighter and smaller than full size. Unsuitable equipment can cause injury. For example, if a vault is too high, there is a greater chance of the gymnast colliding with the box. A tennis player who has too heavy a racket may strain their arm muscles.

Make sure that all equipment is 'fit for purpose', in other words that it is in good working order and is safe to use. Damaged equipment can cause injury. For example, if a basketball backboard is damaged, it may become loose and fall on a competitor, causing serious injury.

▼ Table 2.3.1 A selection of OCR GCSE PE assessed sports and examples of associated PPE

Examples of GCSE assessed sports	Examples of associated PPE
Acrobatic gymnastics	Heel and foot pads
Camogie	Helmet
Cricket	Wicketkeeper gloves
Squash	Eye guard/goggles
Wheelchair rugby	Gloves
Snowboarding	Hip guard
Windsurfing	Wetsuit

Correct clothing and footwear

It is also important to wear the correct clothing and footwear for the sport to be played, for example, football boots with appropriate studs in football, and warm, waterproof clothing for outdoor adventurous activities such as skiing.

Appropriate level of competition

Make sure that you are fit for the level of competition in a physical activity or sport. If you are going to undertake an activity requiring stamina, make sure you have good cardiorespiratory fitness. If in basketball, for example, you are required to stretch suddenly, make sure that you have worked on your flexibility to prevent injury.

Be aware of the main principles of fitness training that have been covered in this book. Any exercise and training programme must take into account the individual. The participant's age, time available, equipment available and skill level must all be taken into consideration before the principles of training are applied.

Each participant must get to a particular skill level and have good technique before performing seriously in physical activity and sport. Exercise and training should include basic skills which when practised enough become almost second nature. Injury is much less likely the higher your personal skill level. Ensure that skills and techniques follow technical models of how the skill ought to be performed to ensure personal health and safety.

Lifting and carrying equipment safely

Back strains and even broken limbs have been caused by incorrect methods of lifting and carrying sports equipment. The correct technique for lifting heavy equipment involves bending the knees rather than the back.

Some equipment needs to be lifted with mechanical assistance. If there are special instructions concerning the method of lifting or moving a particular piece of equipment these should always be followed.

Chapter 2.3 Preventing injury in physical activity and training

Additional hazards can arise during assembly of equipment. For instance, a trampoline should be put up only by people who have been trained to do it properly, otherwise there is a danger of the trampoline's legs springing up and causing injury.

Warm-up and cool-down

Whatever the level of the physical activity or sport – whether it is serious competition or just recreational play – you should be prepared for it by carrying out an effective warm-up. A cool-down is equally important and should take place immediately after exercise. Refer to Chapter 2.2 for further detail on the steps involved.

Always ensure that your training is safe. After warming up sufficiently, your exercise regime should suit your age, ability and physical fitness. You should also ensure that you do not push yourself too hard and that you 'listen' to your body and stop if any exercise hurts or you are getting unduly tired.

> **Extend your knowledge**
>
> ### Correct wheelchair equipment for powerchair football
> Powerchair football is played in specialised electric wheelchairs, called powerchairs. Each powerchair must have four or more wheels, a lap belt and a foot guard. The players use the foot guard to kick and block an oversized soccer ball (33 cm in diameter).
>
> ▲ Figure 2.3.2 Powerchair football players use specialised wheelchairs

> **Extend your knowledge**
>
> ### Exercising safely
> - Identify the individual's training goal.
> - Identify medium- and long-term goals.
> - Identify the fitness components to be improved.
> - Establish the energy systems to be used.
> - Identify the muscle groups that will be used.
> - Evaluate the fitness components involved.
> - Use a training diary.
> - Vary the programme to maintain motivation.
> - Include rest in the programme for recovery.
> - Evaluate and reassess goals.

Section 2 Physical Training

> **STUDY HINT**
> Injuries and their treatment are not directly examined in the Specification, but background knowledge of injuries will help your understanding of how to reduce risks and injuries.

❓ Extend your knowledge

Concussion in rugby

Rugby union has recently announced new rules around concussion including:

- doubling the time for doctors to assess a player for concussion to 10 minutes
- requiring all players, coaches and officials to take and pass a training course to improve the awareness and understanding of concussion
- penalties for non-compliance, including fines and suspensions
- strengthening the pitch-side memory test and altering the balance test
- providing all medical teams at Premiership grounds and Twickenham with access to replays to help their decision-making
- barring any player with confirmed or suspected concussion from re-entering the game
- an independent review of the on-field management of all head injuries during Premiership and England matches.

IN THE NEWS

Sports injuries in children and adolescents

Sport can boost children's fitness, self-esteem, co-ordination and self-discipline, but it can also put them at risk of sports injuries, ranging from minor to serious, and even ones that could lead to medical problems throughout their lives.

Because young athletes' bones, muscles, tendons and ligaments are still growing, they are more susceptible to injury. Growth plates – the areas of developing cartilage where bone growth occurs in growing children – are weaker than the nearby ligaments and tendons. What might be a bruise or sprain for an adult could be a serious growth-plate injury in a child; a trauma that would tear an adult's muscle or ligament is more likely to break a child's bone.

There is also the added risk that some young athletes will try to perform beyond their abilities in a bid to keep up with stronger/more physically mature peers.

Young athletes who take part in contact sports are at particular risk of severe injuries to the neck, spinal cord and growth plates, even when stringent training and safety measures are put in place.

❓ Extend your knowledge

Injuries and cycling in Scotland

In the whole period examined (1995–2018) reported cycling casualties of all types reduced by more than half, but the rate of serious injuries and fatalities increased by 18 per cent between 2004–2018.

- Most (82 per cent) casualties were male.
- Far fewer children were casualties in 2018 compared with 1995.
- In recent years cycling casualties were highest among young to middle-aged adults; in the last five years, 65 per cent of all casualties were in the age range 25–54 years.

Source: www.gcph.co.uk/assets/0000/7810/Cycling_Casualties_in_Scotland.pd

Common types of sports injuries

Head injuries

A likely head injury in sport is to be knocked unconscious and to suffer from concussion. Players with suspected concussion should not continue with the activity until they have been correctly medically assessed, following the governing body guidelines.

Chapter 2.3 Preventing injury in physical activity and training

Post-concussion syndrome (a collection of symptoms that can last for several weeks or months after the concussion) can occur after weeks or months if proper treatment is not given after the injury.

IN THE NEWS

Concussion

A field study commissioned in 2020 by the Football Association and Professional Footballers' Association shows that modern footballers could be at greater risk of neurodegenerative disease from head injuries than their predecessors. The study, which looked at dementia and other neurological diseases among retired players, observed that the risk of developing conditions like these was three and a half times greater than among the general population.

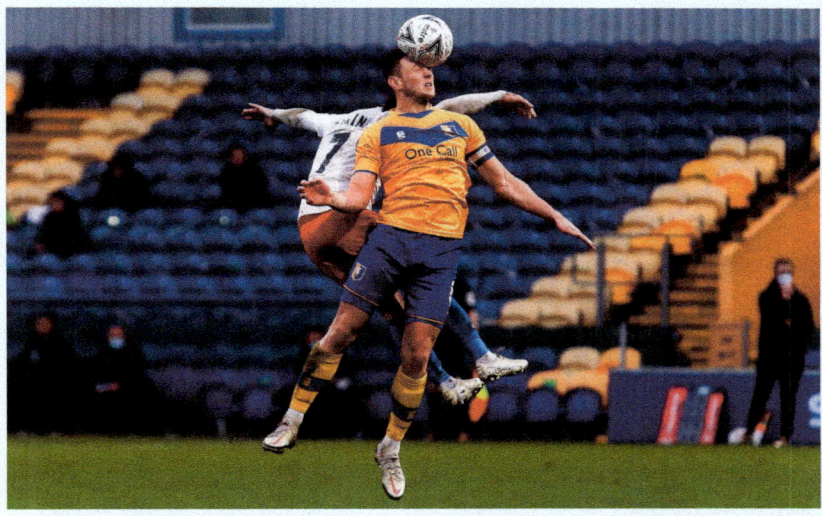

▲ Figure 2.3.3 Studies suggest that football players may be more prone to develop dementia and other neurological diseases later in life

Spinal injury

Any injury to the spine should be treated extremely seriously. It could result in lasting damage to someone's health and their fitness to operate normally, let alone play sport. Damage to the spinal cord may cause very painful conditions. A break in the cord high up in the spine is usually fatal.

If there is a suspected injury to the spine, it is important to get expert help immediately without moving the injured person. Spinal injuries can be caused by incidents such as a collapsed rugby scrum or falling off a horse in equestrian events.

Fractures

Bone fractures can be serious injuries. As well as damaging the bone, they often injure the tissues around the bone such as tendons, ligaments, muscles and skin. A fracture occurs when there is a physical impact or

Section 2 Physical Training

indirect blow to the bone. Anyone involved in contact sports is in danger of sustaining a fractured bone.

To treat the fracture, cover and elevate the injured limb and keep it completely still. The casualty should go to hospital for treatment. The limb will probably be put in a cast to keep it still while the bone heals. The injured person can be back in training after 5–12 weeks.

Dislocations

Dislocation involves movement of a joint from its normal position and is caused by a blow or a fall. When a joint has a lot of pressure put upon it in a certain direction, the bones that usually join in the joint disconnect. The joint capsule often tears because of this movement of bones, along with the ligaments involved. The exerciser or sports person will have limited movement and will experience severe pain.

Sprain

This is a tear to a ligament and is often caused by an overstretch. Ankles, knees and wrists are particularly susceptible to sprains.

Ankle sprains, caused by going over on your ankle, are common among people involved in sport or outdoor activities. Sometimes a 'snap' or 'tear' is felt or heard. Treatment involves rest, ice, compression and elevation (RICE). Do not remove the shoe until ice has reduced the ankle swelling.

Recovery takes between one week and three months, depending on the grade of injury. The usual recovery time is two weeks.

Strain

This is a twist or tear to a muscle or a tendon. Causes include over-use of the joint, force or overstretching.

Blisters

A blister is the body's way of trying to put protection between the skin and what is causing friction, e.g. in a footballer's case, their boot.

The skin is in various layers. Friction and force cause these layers to tear. Fluid called serum flows in between the damaged layers, producing a bubble of liquid. The pain begins when this swelling rubs against another surface.

To treat blisters, the first thing you have to do is cleanse the skin with a sterilising solution. The next step is to put a protective covering over the blister to prevent infections.

The amount of time a blister takes to heal depends upon how big it is, but on average a couple of days is enough.

Risk assessment

To be able to prepare a **risk assessment**, it is important to identify the following:

- The health and safety hazards in a given situation. This includes identifying equipment faults, use of chemicals, other substances hazardous to health and the possibility of spillages.

Key term

Risk assessment This is the technique by which you measure the chances of an accident happening, anticipate what the consequences would be and plan actions to prevent it.

Chapter 2.3 Preventing injury in physical activity and training

> **STUDY HINT**
> Be able to identify a hazard for each area named in the Specification:
> ✔ Sports hall   ✔ Artificial outdoor areas
> ✔ Fitness centre   ✔ Swimming pool
> ✔ Playing field

- The purpose of the assessment. Identify the level of risk. The assessment is designed mostly to minimise injury to participants and workers. It is also designed to ensure that the activity involved can be successful with no injury or accident but hopefully keeping the pleasure and excitement. A safe environment is crucial if physical activity is to be successful.
- The risks involved. Participants, coaches, supervisors, etc. must be aware of their responsibilities in limiting the risks in any sports activity. The risks should be calculated, specialist equipment used and record sheets and other documents kept up to date.
- Procedures for monitoring or checking that risks are kept to a minimum. If there are any changes to the planning of an activity, these should be reviewed to identify their levels of success. There may be other equipment to buy to make the environment safe, or new procedures to be used. All this must be planned within an identified time cycle.

The hazard is often supervised so that the risks are minimised. A supervisory function is performed by, for example, a lifeguard at a swimming pool, spotters around a trampoline (those that stand around the trampoline to stop the performer jumping off) or a coach supporting a gymnast on the beam.

Identifying potential hazards in a range of physical activity and sport settings

The area in which the activity takes place must be looked at carefully to recognise possible **hazards**. The facilities and equipment that are used in physical activities often carry warnings of possible injuries and these must be noted.

There may be obvious **risks** associated with the activity, the equipment or the facilities – for example, on an all-weather surface, if a player falls or slides, they may experience friction burns.

It is important to take care with anyone who may not be fully aware of risks, for instance children or those with learning difficulties, or someone new to a job in a leisure centre or a beginner in a sports activity. Once those who are at particular risk have been identified, an assessment of how they might be harmed needs to be made and safety procedures put into place to protect them.

There must be an assessment of how dangerous a particular hazard is and then whether the risks associated with that hazard are high, moderate or low. If the hazard is particularly dangerous and the risks are high, more care clearly needs to be taken.

Key terms
Hazard Something that has the potential to cause harm.
Risk The chance that someone will be harmed by the hazard.

? Extend your knowledge

The main causes of accidents are:
- objects falling – e.g. a container falling off a shelf in a leisure centre
- trips and falls – e.g. a path leading up to a sports facility may be uneven
- electric shock – e.g. from a hi-fi used to provide music for an aerobics session
- crowds – e.g. supporters at a football match tripping over each other
- poisoning – e.g. by toxic chemicals used in a swimming pool
- being hit by something – e.g. a javelin
- fire – e.g. in the changing rooms of a sports centre
- explosion – e.g. in the store area of a leisure centre
- asphyxiation – e.g. by chemicals used for cleaning.

Section 2 Physical Training

> **STUDY HINT**
> Don't get hazard and injury mixed up. If you are asked to identify a hazard, do not give the injury that might be caused by the hazard. For instance, a hazard might be a broken bottle on a playing field – the hazard is not the cut that might be caused by the broken glass.
> In many cases, it may be possible to remove the hazard altogether, for instance an uneven path is declared out of bounds or a broken indoor football goal is removed from a sports hall.
> In some cases the hazard has to be made safer to reduce the risks – for example, glass in a door that is used frequently can be replaced with non-breakable plastic, or a trampoline can be surrounded by additional safety mats.

Examples of hazards in a sports hall:
- worn exercise/gym equipment
- hard walls
- doors without safety glass
- cracked windows
- poor lighting
- slippery floor
- other participants.

Examples of hazards in a fitness centre:
- equipment (broken or badly positioned)
- hard flooring
- open windows
- free weights (e.g. trip hazard; use with incorrect technique)
- other participants.

Examples of hazards on a playing field:
- litter, including broken bottles and dog excrement
- goal posts and other semi-permanent equipment (obstacles)
- movable equipment (e.g. trip hazard; incorrectly moved)
- poorly maintained fencing (e.g. weak, sharp and/or rusty)
- pitch surface (e.g. uneven, hard)
- other participants.

Examples of hazards on artificial outdoor areas:
- slippery surface of pitch
- litter, including broken bottles and dog excrement
- goal posts and other semi-permanent equipment (obstacles)
- movable equipment (e.g. trip hazard; incorrectly positioned)
- poorly maintained fencing (e.g. weak, sharp and/or rusty)
- other participants.

Examples of hazards in and around a swimming pool:
- water
- chemicals in the water
- hard and slippery surface of surrounding area
- equipment (e.g. trip hazard)
- other participants.

Chapter 2.3 Preventing injury in physical activity and training

SUMMARY

- Risks of injury in sport can be minimised by using personal protective equipment, correct clothing/footwear, appropriate level of competition, lifting and carrying equipment safely and through the use of a warm-up and a cool-down.
- Make sure you are fit for physical activity and sport. If you are intending to be involved in an activity requiring stamina, make sure you have good cardiorespiratory fitness.
- Each participant must get to a particular skill level and have good technique before performing seriously in physical activity and sport.
- The correct technique for lifting heavy equipment involves bending the knees rather than the back.
- Hazard is something that has the potential to cause harm.
- Risk is the chance that someone will be harmed by the hazard.
- Common hazards in sport include playing surface, equipment, litter, water (swimming) and other participants.

✔ Check your understanding

1. How can personal protective equipment minimise the risk of injuries?
2. Why is it important to wear the correct clothes and footwear for physical activities?
3. What is meant by ensuring the appropriate level of competition, especially for young people?
4. How can the safe lifting and carrying of sports equipment minimise the risks of injury?
5. How can a warm-up and a cool-down minimise the risks of injury in sport?
6. What is meant by a hazard in physical activities?
7. What hazards are associated with the gymnasium/sports hall/fitness centre?
8. What hazards are associated with a playing field and an artificial outdoor area?
9. What hazards are associated with a swimming pool?
10. How would you reduce the risk of hazards in each of these areas?

Practice questions

1. Using a practical example, explain one way correct clothing can minimise the risk of injury in sport. **(1 mark)**
2. Give two different examples of personal protective equipment that will help prevent injury. **(2 marks)**
3. Give an example from one of your assessed sports that shows how the appropriate level of competition can prevent injury. **(1 mark)**
4. *Explain, using practical examples, how a coach might reduce the risk of injury to a participant when delivering a training session on an artificial outdoor area.

    How could the health and well-being of a sports performer influence their risk of injury? **(6 marks)**
5. Identify two potential hazards that might be found in a fitness centre. **(2 marks)**
6. Using sports examples, describe the potential hazards associated with a sports hall. **(4 marks)**

*This question includes an assessment of the quality of your written communication.

Section 3
Socio-cultural Influences

3.1 Engagement patterns of different social groups in physical activities and sports

3.2 Commercialisation of physical activity and sport

3.3 Ethical and socio-cultural issues in physical activity and sport

Chapter 3.1
Engagement patterns of different social groups in physical activities and sports

Understanding the Specification

You should be familiar with current trends in different social groups' participation in physical activity and sport.
You should understand how different socio-cultural factors can affect participation and understand strategies that can be used to improve participation through promotion, provision and access.
You should be able to apply examples from physical activity/sport to these participation issues.

Key terms

Sport This involves organised competition between individuals or teams that includes physical activity.

Sport England This organisation tries to help communities develop sporting habits for life. It funds other organisations and projects to get people more involved in sport and to help those who wish to pursue sport to the highest level.

Moderate activity In September 2019, the Chief Medical Officer updated the guidelines on physical activity. Instead of the measure of children and young people doing 60+ minutes of moderate activity every day, this has now changed to 60+ minutes a day across the week. This effectively means they need to do 420 moderate minutes or more a week to meet the guidelines.

STUDY HINT
Get to know the current trends in participation using different sources, such as Sport England:
- ✓ trends related to different social groups
- ✓ trends in a range of different physical activities and sports.

Current trends in participation in physical activity and sport in the UK

For the health and fitness of all age groups in the UK, it is important to be aware of and to understand the current position regarding participation in physical activities. This information about levels of engagement will then enable the UK government and sports organisations to target particular groups to increase levels of exercise and sports activities. A population that regularly exercises and gets involved in **sport** is more likely to be healthier and happier. The data referred to in this section is derived largely from publications of **Sport England** research: *Active Lives Children and Young People Survey,* published in 2019 and the *Active Lives Adult Survey,* published in 2020.

Note that this information is taken from Sport England surveys during pre-pandemic England.

Participation for children and young people aged 5–16 (2019)

- 46.8 per cent of children and young people (3.3 million) are meeting the Chief Medical Officer guidelines of taking part in sport and physical activity for an average of 60 minutes or more every day.
- 29.0 per cent (2.1 million) do less than an average of 30 minutes a day.
- 24.2 per cent are 'fairly active' (30–59 minutes per day).

Sport England target for young people (2019)

The target is for young people to do 60+ minutes of **moderate activity** a day across the week.

Participation for children and young people by gender (2019)

Boys (51 per cent or 1.8 million) are more likely to be active than girls (43 per cent or 1.5 million), with a gap of 319 200 between them.

Participation for children and young people by socio-economic status (2019)

Those from low socio-economic (affluence) families are the least likely to be active (42 per cent).

Participation for children and young people by disability and long-term health conditions (2019)

Children and young people with a disability or long-term health condition are more likely to be less active than those without.

Participation for children and young people by ethnicity (2019)

- Asian (35 per cent) and black (34 per cent) children and young people are the most likely to be less active.
- For example: white British are 27 per cent less likely to be active, whereas Asian are 35 per cent less likely to be active.

Participation for children and young people by types of activity (2019)

- Active play and informal activity are common for young people in Years 7–11 (ages 11–16), with nearly half taking part in one typical week.
- Swimming activities do not feature in the top ten for young people in Years 7–11 (ages 11–16), but 14 per cent take part.
- Gym or fitness moves into the top ten for this age group, with a quarter taking part.
- Team sports is the most common activity amongst young people in Years 7–11
- A wide range of activities, from team sports to active play and walking, have seen an increase in the proportion of young people taking part (from 2015–2019).

Summary of participation levels by activity (2019):
- team sports – 63 per cent
- running and athletics – 32 per cent
- gym or fitness activities – 25 per cent
- dance – 22 per cent
- cycling – 19 per cent
- racket sports – 17 per cent.

Extend your knowledge

Further data is available for **participation rates** in physical activities from other sources such as:
- National Governing Bodies – www.uksport.gov.uk/sports
- Government's Department of Culture Media and Sport – www.gov.uk/government/organisations/department-for-digital-culture-media-sport

Key terms

Participation rates This refers to the number of people within a group who are involved in sport compared with those who are not. For example, in a school the participation rates of girls in extra-curricular sport could be 30 per cent. In other words, three out of every ten girls in the school are members of a sports team or club.

Recreation Activities that you enjoy that are not work-related.

Activity

Draw a graph showing the participation levels for each type of activity shown in the Summary of participation levels by activity (2019).

Think of reasons why some activities are more popular than others.

Section 3 Socio-cultural Influences

> **? Extend your knowledge**
>
> There is a positive association between levels of engagement in sport and physical activity and levels of mental well-being. Mental well-being scores are higher for those who are active than for those who are fairly active, which in turn are higher than for those who are less active.
>
> Source: **Sport England 2019**

IN THE NEWS

Can sport make us feel happy?

Research by the NHS shows that the five most important ways to feel happy spring from:
- positive emotions
- mental engagement
- strong relationships
- meaning in life
- goal accomplishment.

It probably seems like a tough goal, but many sporting activities can help us to achieve all five at once. Evidence also suggests that if we can do this, we are more likely to sleep better and to thrive at school or work.

Participation for Adults (2019)

Overall, data from Sport England shows that:
- 63.2 per cent (28.6 million) did an average of 150 minutes or more of active exercise per week
- 12.2 per cent (5.5 million) were fairly active but did not reach an average of 150 minutes a week
- 24.6 per cent of adults (11.1 million) did less than an average of 30 minutes a week.

Sport England target for adults

The target from Sport England (2019) is for adults to be physically active for at least 150 minutes a week. More detailed targets show the aspiration of half a million more people becoming more active, with a focus on women and those in lower socio-economic groups (2019).

Participation for adults by gender (2019)

- Men (65 per cent or 14.4 million) are more likely to be active than women (61 per cent or 14.2 million).
- There has been a growth in activity levels for both men and women since 2016 until 2019.
- More women are active (+0.7 per cent, up over 210 000).
- Male participation has remained largely unchanged since 2016.
- In 2020, the gender gap has reduced to 210 900 (3.9 per cent) – down 145 200 (0.7 per cent) since 2016.

Participation for adults by socio-economic status (2019)

- Those in routine/semi-routine jobs and those who are long-term unemployed or who have never worked are the least likely to be active (54 per cent) and most likely to be inactive (33 per cent).
- Activity levels fall from managerial, administrative and professional occupations to routine/semi-routine jobs and those who are long-term unemployed or who have never worked.

Chapter 3.1 Engagement patterns of different social groups in physical activities and sports

- The gap between the higher socio-economic status groups to the lower remains roughly the same, with 18 per cent fewer people from lower social groups being active compared to higher social groups.

Participation for adults by age (2019)

- Activity levels of adults generally decrease with age, with the sharpest decrease coming at age 75+ (to 40 per cent).
- In 2019, there has been a strong growth in activity levels amongst the 55–74 and 75+ age groups.
- The 75+ age group has seen an increase of 250 100 (5.1 per cent) in those who are active, compared to 2018.
- Activity levels are unchanged for the 35–54 age group.
- The 16–34 age group has seen a decline in activity levels in 2019, with those who are active falling by 1.7 per cent, or over 260 000 people, compared to 2018.

Participation for adults by disability and long-term health conditions (2019)

- Activity is less common for adults with a **limiting disability and long-term health condition** (47 per cent) than those without (68 per cent).
- Activity levels decrease sharply the more impairments an individual has – and just 39 per cent of those with three or more impairments are active.
- Amongst adults with a disability or long-term health condition, there has been a steady increase in activity levels amongst those with one or two impairments between 2018 and 2020.

Participation for adults by ethnicity (2019)

- Figures for 'active' in 2020, based on ethnicity:
    - mixed – 68 per cent
    - white other – 65 per cent
    - white British – 65 per cent
    - Chinese – 61 per cent
    - other ethnic group – 61 per cent
    - black – 58 per cent
    - Asian (excluding Chinese) – 54 per cent.
- There are differences observed in activity levels of adults based on ethnicity.
- Activity levels for white British adults are showing a steady increase, but for most ethnic backgrounds there is an underlying flat trend.
- Asian (excluding Chinese) adults have an underlying flat trend despite a drop compared to 12 months ago (–2.5 per cent)
- Adults from mixed ethnic backgrounds have seen a larger drop compared to 12 months ago (–4.8 per cent) which indicates a potential reduction in the proportion who are active.

Key term

Limiting disability and long-term health conditions Defined as an individual reporting they have a physical or mental health condition or illness that has lasted or is expected to last 12 months or more, and that this has a substantial effect on their ability to do normal daily activities. (Sport England 2020)

? Extend your knowledge

Other factors combine with ethnic background to influence levels of activity.
When ethnicity and gender are taken into account, black and Asian (excluding Chinese) women are the least active.

Participation for adults by types of activity (2019)

Sport England's research looks at the participation in activities that have been played at least twice over 28 days.

Section 3 Socio-cultural Influences

- There are strong upward trends in walking and adventure sports (from 2016–2019).
- Fitness activities have dropped by 619 100 (−1.5 per cent) (2018–2019).
- Running, athletics or multi-sports have dropped by 264 400 (−0.7 per cent) (2018–2019).
- Swimming activities have dropped by 518 800 (−1.2 per cent) (2018–2019).
- Racket sports have seen a drop (2018–2019).

Activity

Table 3.1.1 shows the number of people aged 16 and over playing at least 30 minutes of sport at moderate intensity at least once a week. Analyse this data.

1. Rank order the most popular sports in Year 1.
2. State which sport's participation rates fell the most.
3. State which sport's participation rates rose the most.

▼ Table 3.1.1 Data from government UK source

	Year 1	Year 2	% change
Swimming	2.89 m	2.82 m	+2.39%
Athletics	1.96 m	1.99 m	−1.82%
Football	1.94 m	2.2 m	−11.76%
Cycling	1.87 m	1.93 m	−3.54%
Golf	772 800	908 000	−14.89%
Tennis	424 300	420 300	+0.95%
Squash	257 700	281 100	−8.32%
Cricket	189 400	211 300	−10.36%
Rugby union	166 400	197 500	−15.75%

IN THE NEWS

Participation in physical activities during the pandemic (2020)

During the COVID-19 pandemic, each week for the initial eight weeks of lockdown, Sport England commissioned a survey of the English public to assess their activity levels and attitudes towards physical activity.

- Different types of activity became popular, for example, online 'zoom' fitness classes.
- Older people, lower-income people and those who had to self-isolate, did less activity.
- One quarter of people exercising in April 2020, reported that Joe Wicks was the most influential figure for exercise.
- There was a growth in cycling and walking from March to May 2020.

Chapter 3.1 Engagement patterns of different social groups in physical activities and sports

Summary of the numbers participating by physical activity in England (2019)

- Walking for leisure – 20.3 million
- Fitness activities – 12.9 million
- Running and athletics – 6.6 million
- Cycling – 6 million
- Swimming – 4.2 million
- Team sports – 3 million
- Racket sports – 2 million

IN THE NEWS

Sportswomen 'rich list'

In the period between 1 June 2019 and 1 June 2020, nine of the top 10 highest earning sportswomen were tennis players, with Naomi Osaka at the top. She replaced Serena Williams as the world's highest-earning female athlete.

Osaka and Williams were the only two women to appear in the top 100 highest earning sportspeople: Osaka in 29th place and Williams in 33rd place.

Osaka earned $37.4 million – and $34 million of that came from endorsements. (Only Roger Federer had earned more from endorsements in the same period.)

There was only one non-tennis player in the top 10 highest earning sportswomen and that was US soccer player Alex Morgan. She earned $4.6 million – of that amount, the money she received for endorsements was 10 times that of her actual salary.

Megan Rapinoe, Alex Morgan's team-mate, earned $4.2 million. Her earnings went up after a boost to her professional profile, when she was offered many sponsorship deals and opportunities to earn speaking fees.

As the period analysed ended in 1 June 2020, the COVID-19 pandemic would only have had a marginal effect. However, it was predicted that the following year's figures would reflect the effects of the pandemic to a greater extent.

> **Extend your knowledge**
>
> Team GB's top Olympians are four times more likely to have attended private school than the UK population as a whole. Top performers in rowing and hockey in particular are very likely to have been schooled privately. Half of Team GB's winning women's hockey team attended fee-paying schools, as did more than 50 per cent of the medal-winning rowers.

The main factors affecting participation in physical activity and sport

There are many influences on whether people participate in physical activity and sport. There are, of course, people who show no interest in sports whatsoever, but even they may be interested in keeping healthy and may well do some exercise or consider carefully what they eat.

Section 3 Socio-cultural Influences

> **STUDY HINT**
> In addition to age, disability, ethnicity and gender, the following are key socio-cultural factors that affect participation in sport, which you'll need to learn:
> - religion/culture
> - family
> - education
> - time/work commitments
> - cost/disposable income
> - opportunity/access
> - discrimination
> - environment/climate
> - media coverage
> - role models.
>
> The following are some of the main reasons why people often participate in physical activity:
> - to manage stress
> - to feel good
> - for a sense of well-being
> - to live longer
> - to improve/maintain image
> - for enjoyment
> - to meet people and make friends
> - as a hobby – to learn new skills
> - to please or to copy parents/role models
> - to make money or as a job/vocation.

Age

The average life expectancy has increased and so there are more and more older people who could take advantage of sports opportunities. There are more veterans' teams in a variety of sports and there is a growing awareness that activity in old age can enrich the quality of life experiences. Sport, however, is often perceived as a 'young person's activity' and older age groups may lack confidence in participating.

IN THE NEWS

Age is a factor in participation

▲ Figure 3.1.1 As people reach old age, participation in sport decreases for some

The Sport England research (2019) reveals that as people get older, they are not only more likely to be inactive, they are also more likely to do no physical activity (zero minutes per week).

Around half of those aged 55–64 and 65–74 who are inactive, do no physical activity. This trend of zero physical activity rises even further for those aged 75–84 and those aged 85+.

In addition, we know that over half (51 per cent) of people aged 55 and over who have done no physical activity in the last 28 days have also done nothing throughout the year. This pattern of consistent inactivity is amplified for those aged 75 and over. For example, 70 per cent of those aged 85 and over do no physical activity at all throughout the year.

This demonstrates that many older adults do not have activity as part of their lifestyles at all, and this becomes more common amongst the oldest in our population.

Chapter 3.1 Engagement patterns of different social groups in physical activities and sports

> **? Extend your knowledge**
>
> **Health problems**
>
> There are genuine health reasons for some people not to participate in sport, although many medical practitioners will encourage an active lifestyle. Most rehabilitation regimes include physical exercise and what better way to exercise than sport?
>
> There is an increase in obesity in the Western world due to our diets and lack of exercise. Embarrassment is a powerful emotion that prevents many people taking the step towards sport. There needs to be encouragement and the right environment for such people to be involved in sport. Joining clubs such as 'Weight Watchers' can encourage some to take exercise, which may lead to participation in a sport. Others would disagree and would find joining such an organisation demeaning and only reinforces individuals' lack of self-worth. This lack of self-esteem is an important factor and must be tackled for an individual to gain the confidence necessary to join others and participate in sport.
>
> ▲ Figure 3.1.2 There is an increase in obesity in the Western world due to our diets and lack of exercise

Much evidence points towards a real fall in the levels of participation by 16–19 year olds.

One particular study (Moran (2014) Sport and Exercise Psychology) sampled youth sport participants and found that while over a quarter of children were participating in sport at 10 years of age, this dropped significantly to just over 3 per cent at age 18. Females indicated that negative physical and emotional experiences in sport led to their decision to discontinue participation. Males suggested that the competitive nature of participation led to them giving up (especially if they lost in competition).

Gender

There are far more men than women who get involved in sport either to participate or to spectate. Some people still believe that being good at or interested in sport is somehow 'unfeminine', thus reinforcing male dominance in sport and sport coverage. Certain activities are traditionally linked to either males or females and this can lead to discrimination. For example, the funding for women's football is significantly lower than the funding for men's football in the UK.

A wide-ranging report was published in 2018 by Fifpro, the World Players' Union, which represents 60 000 football players globally.

The report surveyed 3500 Fifpro members and showed that only 1 per cent of players in the FA Women's Super League are mothers, suggesting that clubs do not do enough to support those who have or who would like to have children.

The report also finds that:
- Ninety per cent of professional female players worldwide are considering ending their football careers early.
- Only 9.4 per cent of female players globally are aged 29 and over, compared to 22.4 per cent of male players.
- Twenty-six per cent of Super League players said their clubs do not cover their football expenses.
- Only 1 per cent of Super League players are mothers – while the PFA was unable to supply any figure, it is believed the proportion of male players who have children is multiple times that.

The report continues to show the massive gender equality pay gap, with 88 per cent of players in the Women's Super League, the top tier in England, earning under £18,000 a year, as well as 58 per cent of players considering quitting because of the low level of income.

Work is being done to improve funding in the women's game, after England's women's team achieved their best ever finish at the World Cup in 2015, earning a gold medal, and their semi-final position at the 2019 World Cup. Since then, the number of girls participating in the game has risen – 147 000 female players competed in affiliated league and cup competitions in 2019 (source FA) – a figure which has risen from just 10 400 in 1993, when records began.

IN THE NEWS

Trans women and sport

In the autumn of 2020, World Rugby updated its guidelines to exclude trans women from playing women's rugby on the grounds of safety. It was suggested that there may be a 20–30% greater risk of injury to a woman who was tackled by another player who has gone through male puberty.

This was criticised by the LGBTQ community, who felt there was not enough scientific evidence to back up the decision. One spokesperson called upon all rugby clubs, at whatever level of the game, to speak out against any ruling that might exclude and impact upon people who are already vulnerable.

Chapter 3.1 Engagement patterns of different social groups in physical activities and sports

Nevertheless, more women are now involved in physical exercise and there is far more interest in health and fitness matters. The participation rates for women in sports such as football and rugby continue to grow, there is an increase in the number of female sports presenters, which may encourage more women to take an interest in sport, and there are fewer instances of open discrimination against women participating in clubs such as golf clubs.

In spite of this progress, however, even now women's sport in the media is often covered because of what they look like rather than their achievements. For example, in newspapers, photographs of women tennis players with comments about their clothing is often at the detriment to discussion of their merits as players. Career earnings and media and television coverage for women severely lag behind.

▲ Figure 3.1.3 The number of female sports presenters is increasing

❓ Extend your knowledge

Women medallists at Rio 2016

At the Rio Olympics in 2016, watched by a home audience of 9.7 million people, Team GB won 67 medals and finished second on the medal table (with the USA at the top). Team GB had won 65 medals at the London Olympics in 2012 and this was the first time an Olympic team had won more medals immediately after they had hosted the games.
To cap this success, Team GB's female athletes won more medals than ever before:

- Laura Kenny won four Olympic titles (the first British female Olympian to do so).
- Dame Katherine Grainger won one gold and four silver medals, becoming Team GB's most decorated female Olympian.
- Amy Tinkler was Team GB's youngest athlete and medallist at a mere 16 years of age.
- The women's hockey team won gold after they defeated The Netherlands' team (the defending champions) on penalties.

▲ Figure 3.1.4 Women are regularly involved at the highest level in many sports previously dominated by men

Section 3 Socio-cultural Influences

> **STUDY HINT**
> Be prepared for examination questions to link data on participation rates with factors such as gender. For example, men (65 per cent or 14.4 million) are more likely to be active than women (61 per cent or 14.2 million) (Sport England 2019).

> **? Extend your knowledge**
> In 2019, UK football introduced the **Rooney Rule**, which means English Football League clubs must interview at least one black, Asian or minority ethnic candidate when searching for a new first-team manager.
> However, the rule does not include the Premier League, who say they are pushing other initiatives.

Key term

Rooney Rule This dictates that sporting authorities must interview a black, Asian and minority ethnic (BAME) applicant when recruiting for senior coaching positions. There is no quota or preference given to minorities in the hiring of candidates. The rule is not restricted to sport and has been adopted across a number of other industries. The rule is named after Dan Rooney, former owner of the Pittsburgh Steelers in the USA and former chairman of the NFL's diversity committee.

Ethnicity, religion and culture

Some ethnic groups and religions may support physical activity and sport, or may have high regard for some activities rather than others, and these views may influence participation. Some cultures or religious beliefs may act as barriers for those who wish to participate.

IN THE NEWS

Lack of BAME coaches in English football

In 2020, the top 92 clubs in the English professional leagues had only six black or non-white head football coaches. This followed the FA's plan, announced in 2018, to increase the number of people from a BAME background in leadership and coaching roles.

More than a quarter of the 500 players in the 20 premier league squads are black or mixed race. However, very few of these players go into football management when they retire.

In a bid to address this by the end of 2021, the FA aims for 20 per cent of the England team's coaching staff to come from a BAME background.

Kick It Out

Kick It Out is an independent charity organisation that is concerned with equality and inclusion in English football.

The Kick It Out campaign works with football organisations, education establishments and communities to combat discrimination for everyone throughout the game, including players, spectators and all those who work in the football industry.

The campaign has been associated with anti-racism, but their strategy is to support all those who are under-represented in football.

Kick It Out also campaigns against on-line abuse and provides rehabilitative education for football fans who have been found guilty of discriminatory conduct. Social media companies have faced a lot of criticism for failing to take enough responsibility for offensive comments posted on their sites. Kick It Out has included a drive to 'turn bystanders into activists', for example, via their Take A Stand campaign against on-line abuse.

Black Lives Matter

'Black Lives Matter' is an organisation campaigning against racism, not just in sport but in all walks of life throughout the world.

However, for many years, sportspeople have been using their platform to protest against racial injustice and police brutality. For example:

- 1968 Mexico Olympics – Tommie Smith and John Carlos made the Black Power salute from the winners' podium in a protest about racial inequality.
- August 2016 – Colin Kaepernick of the San Francisco 49ers US football team knelt instead of standing during the pre-game anthems as a protest against racial injustice and police brutality.

However, while Kaepernick's actions hit the world's headlines, they also led to him being criticised by the US President, Donald Trump, and left him without a team to play for.
- August 2020 – two US basketball teams protested against the shooting of Jacob Blake, a black man who was shot in the back seven times by US police. The players wore T-shirts with holes in them, representing how many times he was shot.

In fact, the shooting of Jacob Blake in May 2020 brought sport in the USA to a halt, with protests in support of the Black Lives Matter movement taking centre stage. The US National Football League has since apologised for not listening to players in the past and has encouraged all sportspeople to speak out and protest peacefully. In a role reversal, the players who now attract media attention are the ones who don't 'take the knee'.

Discrimination of any kind has no place in sport or any aspect of society, yet regrettably it may well be a factor that stops those from minority ethnic backgrounds from participating in sport. Some people from minority ethnic backgrounds may feel that they 'don't belong' in certain sports or sports clubs because of the actual or perceived prejudice that might be exhibited by other participants, officials or administrators.

Family

It is much more likely for you to be involved in sport if your parents or guardians participate themselves or promote the benefits of participation. Those whose families do not participate or who show little interest in sport are much less likely to be involved themselves.

Family support is often crucial for young people to be involved in higher levels of competition, with parents and guardians often having to provide transport and funding for their children for sporting activities.

Parents, guardians and other significant members of the family can also make participation difficult through their own high or unrealistic expectations. Some family members put undue pressure on young people, who then become demotivated and disillusioned with sport and therefore give up or are unhappy when they compete.

IN THE NEWS
Parents' sideline behaviour

In 2016, the Director of Grass Roots Football reported that the organisation received around 900 reports every weekend of parents resorting to verbal and/or physical abuse of officials during children's football games. Feelings clearly ran high on the touchline in Surrey one weekend when parents physically assaulted officials. Grass Roots claim that the complaints about incidents are usually very similar, sparked by parents who go over the top, leading to a shove or slanging match.

Section 3 Socio-cultural Influences

Disability

More people with disabilities are taking part in physical activities and sport. There has been a rise from 2015 to 2019 of those with disabilities being involved in physical activities but not by a great deal, with those who have three or more impairments seeing the greatest rise of 2.5% between 2016 and 2019. Physical activity is less common for disabled people or those with a long-term health condition (47%) than those without (68%). (Sport England 2019)

▲ Figure 3.1.5 In recent years, there has been a slight increase in participation in sport of people with disabilities

IN THE NEWS

Do the Paralympics increase participation of people with disabilities?

The Paralympics of 2012 in London and 2016 in Rio, and hopefully for the future 2021 Games in Tokyo, can inspire people who watch, and encourage them to participate. Unfortunately, this is not always the case.

One of the main aims of the London 2012 Paralympics was to increase the participation in sport of people with disabilities. Initially there was a significant rise in participation after 2012 in the UK (19.1 per cent in 2013) but it fell back to pre-Games participation levels in 2013.

Many sports organisations were not prepared for the level of interest from people with disabilities following the Paralympics of 2012 and 2016 and could not respond accordingly. For some people with disabilities, the Paralympians did not seem relevant because they may have been perceived as the elite few who could not realistically be copied. People's reduced incomes (caused by austerity) also created a barrier to participation.

▲ Figure 3.1.6 A wheelchair athlete from the 2016 Rio Paralympics

Chapter 3.1 Engagement patterns of different social groups in physical activities and sports

> **? Extend your knowledge**
>
> **Activity Alliance**
>
> From April 2018, the Activity Alliance (previously known as the English Federation of Disability Sport) has encouraged members, partners and people with disabilities to make active lives possible for those with a wide range of disabilities. They seek to challenge perceptions and change the reality of disability, inclusion and sport. They help to enable organisations to support individual people with a disability to be active and stay active for life.
>
> The Activity Alliance has a strategy for 2020–2025 to achieve fairness by seeking to close the gap between the level of inactivity of those with disabilities and that of those without disabilities. They have stated that they will do this by:
> 1. embedding inclusive practice into organisations
> 2. changing attitudes towards disabled people in sport and activity.

Those with a disability who wish to be involved in sport and physical activities face problems in getting access to facilities and may well feel discriminated against through this lack of suitable facilities and equipment. Some people with disabilities lack the confidence to get involved and also cannot find suitable activities that accommodate their disability and this results in a low rate of participation.

There are many reasons that people get involved in sport:

- Benefits to our health and fitness – sport can make us fitter and therefore healthier.
- Benefits to our well-being. Many people report that they feel better after participating in sport. It is accepted that certain hormones are released during exercise and that these can help us to feel more optimistic about life and better about ourselves.
- Benefits to manage stress. People often use sport as an escape from their working life. It has been recognised that by playing sport we can release some of our pent-up frustrations and aggressions – the squash ball can be hit hard to get rid of anger caused by frustrations at work or at school.
- Benefits to learning new skills – again giving a sense of accomplishment and also being able to compete eventually at a higher level and increasing our self-satisfaction when we overcome challenges and barriers.
- There is of course the huge benefit of meeting and participating with other people. New friends can be made through sport, which again is important for our sense of well-being.

Section 3 Socio-cultural Influences

▲ Figure 3.1.7 Sport can make us fitter and therefore healthier

IN THE NEWS

Media coverage can stimulate interest

Michael Phelps's first gold medal of the 2016 Rio Olympics was accompanied by widespread media interest in the large purple circles visible across his back and shoulders when he competed in the men's 4 × 100 m freestyle relay.

Social media also joined in, with many guessing that the origin of these circles ranged from crop circles to tattoos. But it was confirmed by Phelps that these marks were caused by a suction-based massage treatment popular with the US Olympic team.

The ancient form of the therapy is believed to originate in Egypt or China. In the modern version of cupping, the air inside the cup is heated and then placed on the skin, creating suction in that cupped area. It is supposed to allow overworked muscles to heal more quickly, although there is some doubt about whether this treatment is effective.

▲ Figure 3.1.8 The jury is out on whether the practice of cupping can speed up the process of healing tired muscles

Chapter 3.1 Engagement patterns of different social groups in physical activities and sports

Media coverage

The media and commercialisation will be dealt with in chapter 3.2. The media can play an important role in shaping attitudes to sports participation.

The type of sports that get the most media coverage is limited, with football getting the most. Male sport dominates media coverage, although there is an increase in women's football coverage, following the 2019 World Cup, when the England women's team reached the semi-finals. The Great Britain women's Olympic football team (Team GB) reached the quarter-finals on their debut at the London 2012 Olympic Games. This success and subsequent media coverage helped a growth in participation across all levels of the women's game. An FA report after the 2019 World Cup revealed that more than 2.63 million women aged 16 and over in England were playing football.

The media can stimulate participation in sport. You only have to see the greater activity on municipal tennis courts during the Wimbledon fortnight to appreciate that watching sport can encourage participation.

Our interest in playing a sport is particularly increased when the media highlights the success of UK sportspeople. There was a surge of interest in cycling, for instance, after success in the 2012 London Olympics when six world track records were achieved.

▲ Figure 3.1.9 Wimbledon fortnight can stimulate participation in tennis

Section 3 Socio-cultural Influences

> **STUDY HINT**
> To prepare for the examination, it is helpful if you can learn a summary of how the media can affect participation in sport positively and negatively:
>
> Positive:
> - promotes or encourages sport and exercise, and increases interest through sports coverage
> - promotes healthy living
> - can motivate through role models
> - promotional campaigns or public service broadcasting or through advertising
> - provides a wide variety of sports, including minority and novel sports
> - will create funds and sponsorship that can be used to encourage activity
> - gives information about healthy lifestyles and fitness, e.g. via the internet or new training methods.
>
> Negative:
> - may encourage or reinforce unhealthy or inactive lifestyle
> - may show negative role models
> - too much passive watching and listening to media discourages activity, causing the 'couch potato' syndrome
> - minority sports (those in which few people participate) are often under-represented
> - women's sports are under-represented or misrepresented
> - disability sport is under-represented or misrepresented
> - older performers are often under-represented
> - can make people feel inadequate by not having the ability or skill or the 'sporty' body image
> - might show the dangers of participation or (high) risk of injury that might put people off participation.

Other possible reasons that people do not get involved in sport

- **Environment and climate:** this often dictates whether the activity can be indoors or outdoors and in some cases may well stop participation in a particular activity. Bringing down core body temperature is vital before, during and after exercise or competing. Ice jackets, wrist and feet cooling in tanks of cold water, and ice towels for the head and neck all help. Tennis player Andy Murray often uses a post training/game ice bath. For 8 minutes, he sits in iced water kept at 8–10°C (46–50°F). Heptathlete Jessica Ennis-Hill used to stand in a wheelie bin of iced water to help her muscle recovery. Many sports people use ice baths and ice jackets as part of their recovery, but evidence is contradictory about how useful this type of therapy really is. Some feel that the inhibition of inflammation can in fact slow down the repair of muscles. The English Institute of Sport researches other environmental factors such as pollution and the cold of winter games.
- **Time:** work commitments can get in the way of finding enough time for sport.
- **Resources:** you may or may not have appropriate facilities or sports clubs near to you. This can dictate whether you participate in sport or not. Some local authorities lay on a transport service for those who wish to visit a sports facility, for example, the elderly may catch a specially run bus to a local leisure centre.

- **Role models**: like parents, other significant individuals can influence whether you participate in sport. If your peers are very sporty and they see sport as a worthwhile activity, then as a member of that peer group you too are more likely to participate. If those within your peer group do not take part in sport or have an anti-sport/fitness culture, then you are less likely to participate.

▲ Figure 3.1.10 If your area of the country has regular snow then snow-based activities are more likely

Strategies to improve participation

The three important factors that can deliver successful strategies for improving participation are:
- promotion or convincing people they should take up sport
- provision of facilities, equipment, coaching, etc.
- access, or giving people opportunity to participate by making it easier for them to engage in sport.

The promotion, provision and access for sport are delivered by a number of agencies, such as UK Sport and Sport England, as well as government strategies to promote participation in sport.

Public, private and voluntary agencies

Public, private and voluntary agencies all promote sport in the UK.

We all pay through our taxes to the government, which in turn funds public organisations. Private sector organisations include commercial businesses trying to make a profit and non-profit-making voluntary organisations such as the Youth Hostels Association or amateur sports clubs.
- Public facilities include local leisure centres, run by the local authority and funded via the taxpayer.
- Private facilities include local private health and fitness clubs.
- The voluntary sector facilities include local athletic clubs where you could train to keep fit. The Youth Hostels Association is another example of a voluntary organisation, which would give you information and concessionary rates to stay at youth hostels so that you can walk or ramble to keep fit.

Section 3 Socio-cultural Influences

▲ Figure 3.1.11 Sport is provided through public, private and voluntary agencies

The public sector includes local authorities (councils), which promote sport according to what they perceive to be the interests of the local population – for example, basketball to improve levels of participation and excellence and to improve basketball court facilities.

The private sector provides sport, again according to local needs and often strives to get as many people involved as possible, to raise attendance levels and, importantly, because they are money-making organisations, to improve their profits. An example of a private club would be a David Lloyd Leisure club, which provides the equipment, instruction in fitness activities and also, increasingly, personal training.

The voluntary sector aims to help provide support for local needs. It promotes specific sports, for example, the local hockey club, which strives to get as many people to play hockey as possible and to attract men and women from all walks of life to the game. Such a club would run teams in local leagues and hold training sessions for its members.

Department for Culture, Media & Sport (DCMS)

This is a government department that has responsibility for government policy related to sport. The department has a minister associated with it who is responsible for sport, as well as culture and the building of a digital economy, and some aspects of the media throughout the whole UK, such as broadcasting and internet.

UK Sport

The role of UK Sport, an agency under government direction, is to provide support for elite sportspeople who have a high level of performance or have the potential to reach the top. The organisation not only distributes government funds, including lottery money, but also supports world-class performers and promotes ethical standards of behaviour, including the fight against the use of performance-enhancing drugs through its anti-doping programme.

UK Sport oversees the work of sports councils in England, Scotland, Wales and Northern Ireland. These are:

- Sport England
- **sport**scotland
- Sports Council for Northern Ireland
- Sports Council for Wales.

UK Sports Institute (UKSI)

The aim of this organisation is to provide the very best sportspeople with appropriate facilities and support. It offers sports science advice, coaching expertise and top training facilities. The UKSI comprises a number of centres located around the UK. Each individual sports council of England, Scotland, Wales and Northern Ireland has responsibility for the development of the UKSI in its area.

Youth Sports Trust (YST)

The YST is a sports agency responsible for the development of sport for young people. It has created a sporting pathway for all children through a series of

> **? Extend your knowledge**
>
> UK Sport feels that its purpose is to lead the UK to sporting excellence by supporting winning athletes, world-class events and ethically fair and drug-free sport. UK Sport receives government funding in order to fulfil its role as the UK's national anti-doping agency, as well as funding a number of support programmes.

linked schemes called the TOP programmes, aimed at encouraging young people from 18 months to 18 years to follow a healthy and active lifestyle.

Governing bodies

The majority of sports that we know today were developed and organised in the late 19th century. The participants needed to agree rules and regulations for their sports and so they met and formed committees called governing bodies – for example, the Football Association (FA), the Lawn Tennis Association (LTA), the Amateur Swimming Association (ASA), the Rugby Football Union (RFU), etc. There are more than 265 governing bodies in the UK. The teams and clubs pay a subscription to the governing body. They in turn administer the sport nationally and organise competitions and the national team. There are still many amateur positions within each governing body, but increasingly more salaried members of staff are involved.

The national governing bodies are also members of international governing bodies, for example, Union des Associations Européennes de Football (UEFA) and Fédération Internationale de Football Association (FIFA). These international bodies control and organise international competitions.

Methods of encouraging people into physical activity:
- ensuring that images and photos used illustrate the range of participants currently involved in the physical activity
- featuring in governing body publications, stories or articles that address the issue of equity within physical activity, from both positive and negative standpoints
- senior figures in the sport and physical activity making a public statement about their intention to tackle inequality issues
- allocating financial resources for physical activity.

Methods of encouraging disabled people into physical activity:
- promoting the inclusion of disabled people in the mainstream programmes of national governing bodies of sport, local authorities and other providers
- increasing funding
- raising the profile of physical activity and sport for people with disabilities.

IN THE NEWS

Effects of COVID-19 on women's participation in fitness activities

In 2020, Sport England representatives told MPs that the COVID-19 pandemic had led to 'a return to gender stereotypes' in some households. Women's caring and childcare responsibilities were being 're-amplified' and this was having an effect on their fitness and well-being.

Regular fitness classes in leisure centres are normally attended by about 80 per cent women, and so the closure and restrictions of these classes due to the pandemic also had a disproportionally negative affect on women's participation.

For women in physical activity

Women in Sport is a charity organisation in the UK that researches sport from the perspective of women and girls only. One of their recent reports (2018) revealed that 40 per cent of women experience gender discrimination in the sport industry. In the report, 38 per cent of the women involved stated that they have experienced gender discrimination in the workplace, in comparison to a fifth of the men. Other evidence showed that 40 per cent of the women felt that their gender can have a negative impact on the way in which they are valued by others at work, while 30 per cent have experienced inappropriate behaviour from someone of the opposite sex in comparison to a tenth of the men.

When asked whether men and women in their workplace are treated equally and fairly, 72 per cent of the men believed that they were. However, when asked the same question, only 46 per cent of women agreed.

According to the report, less than half of the National Governing Bodies of sport have succeeded in achieving the minimum requirement of 30 per cent of women on their board.

Gender equity (equality)

To ensure that males and females are treated equally in sport, there are some principles that might lead to an increase in women's involvement and participation, including:
- an increase in awareness of the issues surrounding women's and girls' involvement in physical activity
- giving support to women and girls to become involved in physical activity at all levels and in all capacities
- encouraging organisations to improve access to physical activity opportunities for women and girls
- challenging instances of inequality found in physical activity and sport and seeking to bring about change
- raising the visibility of all British sportswomen.

Other strategies for gender equity
- To provide gender awareness training for governing body coaches, leaders and organisers.
- To establish a programme of courses that will recruit women into the management of physical activity and sport.
- To raise the profile of women in officiating.

Active Communities

Active Communities is a 'framework' comprising services, products and sources of funding provided by Sport England, often in partnership with other organisations and agencies, to assist individuals and organisations to create their own Active Communities. The framework is organised under five core headings, which reflect the most important issues leading to the development of an Active Community:
- promoting social justice
- increasing participation in sport
- developing community sports leaders

Chapter 3.1 Engagement patterns of different social groups in physical activities and sports

- developing community sports programmes and facilities
- planning for sport and recreation.

Government healthy living initiative

The government was prompted to act following a recognition of the barriers against healthy eating:

- limited parental awareness of weight status and associated health risks
- parental beliefs that a healthy lifestyle is too challenging
- pressures on parents that undermine healthy food choices
- a perception that there are limited opportunities for active lifestyles.

The government's healthy living programme aims to tackle these barriers through a range of initiatives aimed at families with young children. Young families are aware of the '5 A Day' message but are not necessarily eating 5 A Day.

Top Tips for Top Mums

This is an extension of the highly successful 5 A Day campaign and encourages parents across the country to share tips and ideas on how they get their children to eat more fruit and vegetables. Top Tips for Top Mums targets young families from low-income backgrounds with children aged between 2 and 11. Recent research by the Food Standards Agency showed that only 46 per cent of people on lower incomes eat 5 A Day compared with 72 per cent of those on higher incomes.

5 A Day

Eating 5 A Day sets children up for a healthy lifestyle. Fruit and vegetables of different colours provide a wide range of vitamins, minerals, fibre and healthy antioxidants, which can help to protect the body throughout life.

Research has shown that eating five or more a day can help a person to maintain a healthier diet. People who eat lots of fruit and vegetables can have a lower risk of heart disease, high blood pressure, strokes and some cancers. To get the best benefit from the nutrients packed into fruit and vegetables, everyone should aim for a variety of types and colours every day.

Change4Life

Change4Life is a movement, supported by the Department of Health, which aims to improve children's diets and levels of activity, thus reducing the threat to their future health and happiness. The goal is to help every family in England eat well, move more and live longer. For more information, look up: Change 4 Life at www.nhs.uk/change4life

Five choices to help you stay healthy

1. You should not smoke. Stopping smoking is often the single most effective thing that you can do to reduce your risk of future illness. The risk to health falls rapidly as soon as you stop smoking (but it takes a few years before the increased risk reduces completely).

> **Extend your knowledge**
>
> There have been many government initiatives to promote healthy lifestyles. It is important to keep in touch with the latest developments and information can be found from the following sources:
>
> - Local Government Association www.local.gov.uk/
> - Active Places www.activeplacespower.com/
> - UK Sport www.uksport.gov.uk/
> - Sport England www.sportengland.org/
> - Department for Culture, Media and Sport www.gov.uk/government/organisations/department-for-digital-culture-media-sport
>
> Other useful links:
>
> - www.heartforum.org.uk
> - www.skillsactive.com
> - www.gov.wales/
> - www.gov.scot/
> - www.patient.info/
> - www.bhf.org.uk/active

2. Do some regular physical activity. Anything that gets you mildly out of breath and a little sweaty is fine – for example, jogging, heavy gardening, swimming, cycling, etc. A brisk walk each day is what many people do – and that is fine. However, it is thought that the more vigorous the activity, the better. To gain most benefit, you should do at least 30 minutes of physical activity on most days. Two shorter bursts is thought to be just as good, for example, two 15-minute bouts of activity at different times in a day.

3. Eat a healthy diet. Briefly, a healthy diet means:
   - At least five portions, and ideally 7–9 portions, of *a range of* fruit and vegetables per day.
   - The bulk of most meals should be starch-based foods (such as cereals, wholegrain bread, potatoes, rice, pasta), plus fruit and vegetables.
   - Not much fatty food such as fatty meats, cheeses, full-cream milk, fried food, butter, etc. Use low fat, mono- or poly-unsaturated spreads.
   - Include 2–3 portions of fish per week, at least one of which should be 'oily' (such as herring, mackerel, sardines, kippers, pilchards, salmon or *fresh* tuna).
   - If you eat meat it is best to eat lean meat, or poultry such as chicken.
   - If you do fry, choose a vegetable oil such as sunflower, rapeseed or olive oil.
   - Try not to add salt to food, and limit foods that are salty.

4. Try to lose weight if you are overweight or obese.
   - You don't need to get to a perfect weight.
   - If you are overweight, you can gain great health benefits by losing 5–10 per cent of your weight.

5. Don't drink too much alcohol.
   - A small amount of alcohol is usually fine (for over 18 years only), but too much can be harmful. Guidelines from the Chief Medical Officer state that, for both men and women, it is safest not to drink more than 14 units a week on a regular basis. It is also stated that it is best to spread out alcohol consumption evenly over three or more days.
   - One unit is about half a pint of normal-strength beer, or two thirds of a small glass of wine, or one small pub measure of spirits.

IN THE NEWS

Boosting physical activity in schools during the COVID-19 pandemic 2020

The Department for Education launched online resources to encourage children to get active to mark National Fitness Day 2020, following the return for most children to schools during the pandemic of 2020.

Schools could access videos on YouTube to encourage pupils to get active for 30 minutes in a COVID-secure environment. The content included:
- videos from schools across the country sharing tips on how to get active during lessons, break times and travel times
- Sport England's Daily Activators doing the 'Daily Mile'
- inclusive activities for pupils with Special Educational Needs and Disabilities (SEND)
- encouragement for more girls to get involved in physical activity.

Chapter 3.1 Engagement patterns of different social groups in physical activities and sports

> **SUMMARY**
> - 46.8 per cent of children and young people (3.3 million) are meeting the Chief Medical Officer guidelines of taking part in sport and physical activity for an average of 60 minutes or more every day.
> - Sport England Target for young people (2019) – for young people to do 60+ minutes of moderate activity a day across the week.
> - Boys (51 per cent or 1.8 million) are more likely to be active than girls (43 per cent or 1.5 million).
> - Those from low socio-economic (affluence) families are the least likely to be active (42 per cent).
> - Children and young people with a disability or long-term health condition are more likely to be less active than those without.
> - Asian (35 per cent) and black (34 per cent) children and young people are the most likely to be less active.
> - Team sports is the most common activity amongst young people in Years 7–11.
> - A wide range of activities, from team sports to active play and walking, have seen an increase in the proportion of young people taking part (from 2015–2019).
> - 24.6 per cent of adults (11.1 million) did less than an average of 30 minutes a week.
> - The target from Sport England (2019) is for adults to be physically active for at least 150 minutes a week.
> - Men (65 per cent or 14.4 million) are more likely to be active than women (61 per cent or 14.2 million).
> - Those in routine/semi-routine jobs and those who are long-term unemployed or have never worked are the least likely to be active (54 per cent) and most likely to be inactive (33 per cent).
> - Activity levels of adults generally decrease with age, with the sharpest decrease coming at age 75+ (to 40 per cent).
> - Activity is less common for adults with a disability or those with a long-term health condition (47 per cent) than those without (68 per cent).
> - Activity levels for white British adults are showing a steady increase, but for most ethnic backgrounds there is an underlying flat trend.
> - There are strong upward trends in walking and adventure sports (from 2016–2019).
>
> *Sources: Active Lives Children and Young People Survey, published in 2019 and the Active Lives Adult Survey, published in 2020.*

Section 3 Socio-cultural Influences

Practice questions

1. *Assess the current trends in participation in physical activities for young people. **(6 marks)**

2. *Research in the UK has shown that physical activity levels reported for those with a disability are generally low.

   Discuss the possible reasons for low participation levels for those with a disability and the long-term physical effects that such low levels of activity could have. **(6 marks)**

3. Using practical examples, describe the strategies to increase the participation of adults in physical activities. **(4 marks)**

4. Give two ways in which the family might affect participation in sport. **(2 marks)**

5. Which one of the following is the best strategy to improve participation? **(1 mark)**
   a. The UK government funding GB athletes
   b. A mineral water company funding the Premier League
   c. A local authority supplying outdoor table tennis tables
   d. A fitness club increasing the number of personal trainers

6. Describe three ways the media may promote sport to the general public. **(3 marks)**

*This question includes an assessment of the quality of your written communication.

Chapter 3.2
Commercialisation of physical activity and sport

Understanding the Specification

You should understand the influence of the media on the commercialisation of physical activity and sport. You should know different types of media:

- social
- internet
- TV/visual
- newspapers/magazines.

You should know the meaning of commercialisation, including sport, sponsorship and the media (the golden triangle), and recognise the positive and negative effects of the media on commercialisation and be able to apply practical examples to these issues. Finally, you should understand the influence of sponsorship on the commercialisation of physical activity and sport, including the positive and negative effects of sponsorship on commercialisation and be able to apply practical examples to the issue of sponsorship.

The influence of the media

This chapter looks at the **commercialisation** of physical activity and sport. Television companies spend an enormous amount of money on the broadcasting rights to sports-related events. To view certain events such as boxing, the subscriber often needs to make an extra payment (pay-per-view). Sky, for example, holds the rights to many Premier League football games, which can be viewed only if you subscribe to a Sky package. Digital TV has also influenced sport – and not always to everyone's benefit.

There has never before been so much coverage of sport on TV, but because of satellite TV dominating this coverage, only those who can afford to subscribe have access to many sports events. The terrestrial channels such as BBC and ITV have lost many of the major sports events. An example of this is when BBC News is unable to show a clip of a boxing match because the rights to that match are owned by another company.

Social media has become an increasingly important influence on the commercialisation of sport. The live streaming of sporting events has become very popular, along with sports clubs and associations' pages using social media platforms such as Facebook and Twitter. Social media has also been a route for sports fans and sports stars to communicate with each other, which can be of mutual benefit both personally and commercially.

Key term

Commercialisation This refers to the influence of commerce, trade or business on an industry (e.g. sport) to make a profit.

The 'golden triangle' – sport, sponsorship and the media

This is the term used to show the interdependence and influences of the three factors of sport, sponsorship and the media. All these factors influence one another.

Section 3 Socio-cultural Influences

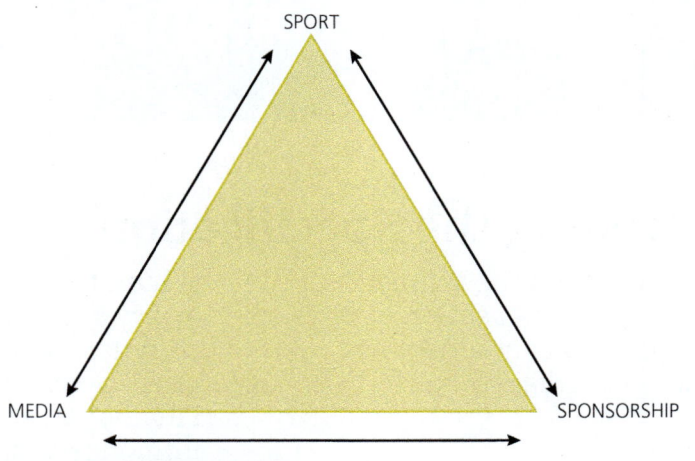

```
              SPORT
               /\
              /  \
             /    \
            /      \
           /        \
          /          \
       MEDIA ———————— SPONSORSHIP
```

▲ Figure 3.2.1 The 'golden triangle'

Types of media are as follows:
- **television**: BBC, ITV, Channel 4, Channel 5, satellite, cable, digital, factual/fiction/advertising
- **press**: broadsheets, tabloids, local, weekly, magazines, periodicals
- **radio**: national, local, commercial
- **internet**: including social media
- **cinema**: documentaries, movies (USA/UK/Bollywood, etc.).

Event programming has been revised because of the needs of the TV companies. Football fans, for instance, are finding that their team may play on a Friday at 6 p.m., which has not traditionally been a time slot for the game. Olympic Games events are often scheduled at irregular times because of the demands of TV companies that are beaming the events around the world across different time zones.

The rules of sport have also been influenced by the media. For instance, in cricket the third umpire, in the form of a video replay analysis, has come into force, largely due to the influence of TV. There has been a similar development in rugby union and rugby league. The armchair spectator can now see the event at every angle and the officials' decisions are laid bare for scrutiny, hence the need for new technology to aid the decision makers on and off the field of play.

The extent of media involvement has also influenced the amount of sponsorship and advertising revenue available to participants, clubs and other sports organisations. This has brought much welcomed money into sport, but some may argue that this has been to only a small number of participants in a small number of sports and may well have led to the decrease in participation in minority sports and other physical activities.

The influence of sponsorship

The influence of sponsorship on the development of physical activity and sport has been enormous over the last 20 years. The exercise and sport market is now big business, with large amounts of money being spent by commercial companies on sports' participants and events. For example, a company such as Adidas might sponsor a top-class tennis player to wear a particular style of training shoe. At the other end of the scale, a local hockey club might attract a small amount of money to go towards the first team kit.

> **STUDY HINT**
> Summarise the positive and negative effects of the media in preparation for the examination:
> Positive:
> ✔ to provide a 'shop window' (helps to 'sell' or promote) for businesses and their products as well as the sports
> ✔ to provide more funds to sports and participants via advertising and sponsorship
> ✔ to make it exciting, entertaining and interesting and therefore more attractive to people to participate and support
> ✔ influences rules and times of play to make the sport more accessible, which in turn helps to sell goods.
> Negative:
> ✔ can over-sensationalise the negative aspects of sport, e.g. poor behaviour
> ✔ can assert too much control over sport
> ✔ too few sports benefit
> ✔ under-representation of minority groups including those with disabilities.

Chapter 3.2 Commercialisation of physical activity and sport

There has also been a significant increase in sponsorship due to sports clothing being fashionable. Training shoes have seen a huge increase in sales, for instance. Many people who wear trainers would never dream of participating in sport! Nevertheless, commercial companies recognise that top sports stars can be fashion role models for the young and therefore use them in advertising campaigns.

Sports sponsorship is increasingly difficult to find for the 'middle-ranking sports', such as hockey – those sports that are neither hugely popular nor minority sports.

IN THE NEWS

A report presented to national governing bodies blames the current climate on sports' inability to attract sufficient media coverage. Sports sponsorship can be a vital ingredient in the financing of governing bodies' activities. Many sports, however, are unable to attract sponsors because they cannot get television coverage.

Companies will sponsor all different aspects of a sports team, event or individual, including:

- stadiums and grounds – new stands or grounds will often be named after the sponsor who has put money towards the development
- clothing – teams usually get a shirt sponsor and often individual players will get deals for footwear
- equipment – companies, usually one of those that manufacture the equipment, will often sponsor a player's equipment
- accommodation and transport – companies often offer free transport and accommodation to big teams so people see them using their company
- competitions – companies may sponsor an actual competition or league so then their name and logo appear on all of the products and information regarding the competition. Sometimes it is even named after the company (e.g. the Vitality Netball Superleague).

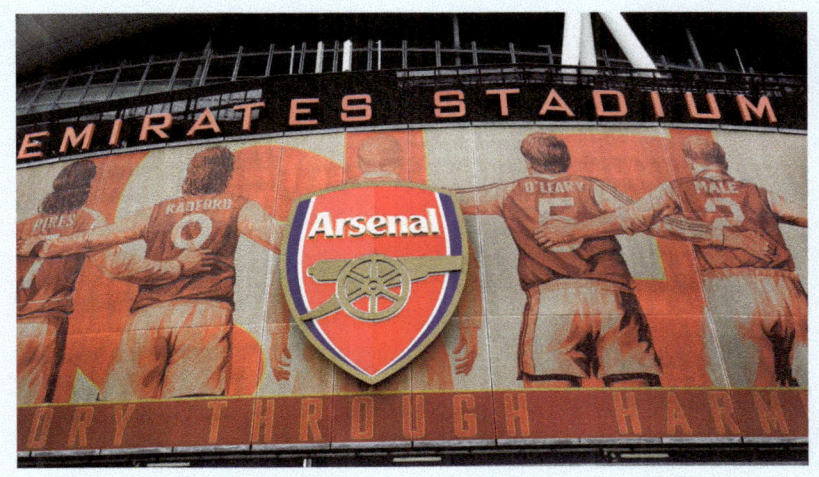

▲ Figure 3.2.2 The Emirates Stadium, named after the international airline and team sponsor, is the home of Arsenal Football Club

119

Sponsorship in sport is good for many reasons:
- It provides money for athletes to train and compete full time.
- It often pays for competitions.
- It promotes the development of new athletes – sponsors offer scholarships, and some universities and colleges offer places to students who excel at a sport for either lower entry grades or reduced tuition fees so that the institution develops a good sporting reputation.
- It is good for the sponsors themselves:
  - They get free advertising – if you see the best players using a product, you might want to use it too.
  - They get an attractive image – most sponsors want to be associated with winners.
  - They benefit through tax concessions and through providing hospitality for clients and business partners – sponsorship money is not usually taxed. Company associates and athletes are also given free tickets in good viewing positions, often with food and drinks included, which they can use to impress possible clients and employees.

Sponsors often give money to charity events. This may be because they believe in a worthy cause. It may also be to help their image.

Sponsorship can also be negative:
- Companies do not want to sponsor teams and athletes who are not successful and so some struggle to get financial help this way.
- A narrow range of sports attracts most sponsors and therefore many sports miss out on useful funding.
- Sponsorship deals are fragile. For example, an injury, loss of form or some bad publicity can mean the contract is terminated and the sponsorship lost.
- Advertising some products in sport can be seen as immoral or unethical, for example, gambling organisations sponsoring football teams.

STUDY HINT
The main points regarding sponsorship to learn for the examination are as follows:
1. Sponsors continue to seek image enhancement and brand awareness through sponsorship and see this to be largely dependent on broadcast and other media coverage.
2. Sponsors are looking to sell their products, develop promotional opportunities and demonstrate that they are good corporate citizens.
3. Sponsors continue to be attracted to the 'top ten' sports and/or to community-based activity; 'middle-ranking' sports such as hockey are rarely considered.
4. Women's sport has the potential to attract more sponsors but to date most of that potential is unfulfilled.
5. Many sports are becoming more commercially aware, but some demonstrate naivety over valuing their rights and approaching sponsors.

Extend your knowledge

Sports organisations have a number of other sources of funding, including grants, subsidies, membership fees and lottery funding:

- **Grants**. These are usually made available to public and voluntary sectors (more about these in a forthcoming chapter). There is an increase in private sector projects being funded as long as the project benefits the local population. Funding is received from the government – local and national. Buildings and equipment are typically funded by such bodies. Many grants involve the sports organisation putting forward a percentage of the funds themselves, for example, 50 per cent government funds, 50 per cent of the costs funded by themselves.
- **Subsidies**. If the local authorities or councils tried to cover all the costs of sport, then few people would be able to participate, for example, in swimming. Therefore there is a system of subsidies whereby members of the public pay a certain cost and the local authority pays the rest. Tax payers fund these subsidies via local government.
- **Membership fees**. All sports organisations with a membership – usually the voluntary sector – can take a significant proportion of their income from membership fees. For example, to join a hockey club, each player pays an annual membership fee and often a 'match fee' for each game they play.
- **The National Lottery**. This is regarded as a grant for sport. World-class performers are also funded through the lottery. UK Sport is lottery funded and this in turn funds high-performance sport in the UK. Sport England, **sport**scotland and Sport Wales are also lottery funds and these fund sport at all levels.

SUMMARY

- Different types of media include television, press (magazines/periodicals), radio, cinema, internet (including social media).
- The media has brought money into sport, but this has gone to only a small number of participants in a small number of sports and may well have led to the decrease in participation in minority sports and other physical activities.
- The 'golden triangle' is the term used to show the interdependence and influences of the three factors of sport, sponsorship and the media.
- The extent of media involvement has also influenced the amount of sponsorship and advertising revenue available to participants, clubs and other sports organisations.
- The exercise and sport market is now big business, with commercial companies spending large amounts of money on sports' participants and events.

Section 3 Socio-cultural Influences

Practice questions

1. Identify four different types of media that might influence the commercialisation of sport. **(4 marks)**
2. Outline two ways in which the media promotes sport. **(2 marks)**
3. Define the term 'sponsorship'. Give two different examples of sponsorship in two of your assessed sports. **(4 marks)**
4. Explain the influence of social media on the commercialisation of sport. **(4 marks)**
5. *Using practical examples from sport, discuss the positive and negative influences of sponsorship on the commercialisation of sport in the UK. **(6 marks)**

*This question includes an assessment of the quality of your written communication.

Chapter 3.3
Ethical and socio-cultural issues in physical activity and sport

Understanding the Specification

You should know the definitions of:
- sportsmanship
- gamesmanship
- deviance

and be able to apply practical examples to these concepts.

You should know the reasons why sports performers use drugs and the types of drugs and their effect on performance, with practical examples of these drugs in sport. You should also know the reasons for player violence and give practical examples of violence in sport.

Ethics and sport

Being ethical in sport is to play by the rules and to show high moral standards in your behaviour. Sport is supposed to be a fair activity, with everyone having an equal opportunity to apply their abilities in whatever activity they are performing. Three aspects that affect ethics in sport are sportsmanship, gamesmanship and deviance.

Sportsmanship

Sportsmanship involves fairness and generosity. Those who show good sportsmanship stick to the rules and regulations but also show that they can lose gracefully and with good humour.

If you compete in a physical activity, it is often good to shake your opponent's hand before and after the event. If you accidentally hurt or injure an opponent, you would show good sportsmanship by seeing that person's well-being as your priority rather than winning the game.

Generally, in exercise, there are good manners in using facilities and equipment. For example, if you are working out in a gymnasium, you return the free weights to the containing rack after you have used them. If you use exercise equipment, then it is good manners or **etiquette** to towel down the machine you have used to remove your sweat.

Key terms

Sportsmanship This involves behaviour that shows fair play, respect for opponents and gracious behaviour, whether winning or losing.

Etiquette This is about the customs we observe surrounding the rules and regulations of the physical activity and also about what is socially acceptable in a particular culture. It involves a convention or an accepted way of behaving in a particular situation.

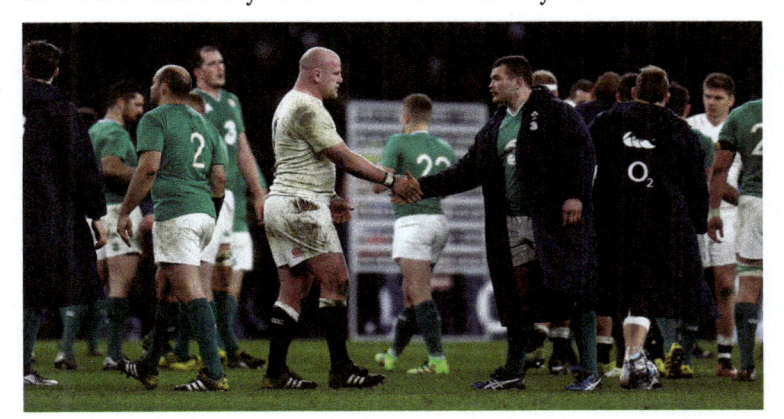

▲ Figure 3.3.1 Good sportsmanship makes for a pleasant and respectful environment

Section 3 Socio-cultural Influences

> **? Extend your knowledge**
>
> **Sportsmanship associated with cricket**
>
> Cricket has always been seen as the 'gentleman's game and that means there are certain traditions of the game that should be respected. Here are some examples of good etiquette:
>
> - **Walk when you're out.** Sadly this is a tradition that has gone out of the game at the highest level. But there will be times when you know you have got an edge through to the wicketkeeper that the umpire has missed. Whether you own up and walk is your decision, but it is regarded as good etiquette to walk.
> - **Umpire's decision is final.** Once a decision has been made, there is no turning back. So that means no arguing with the umpire.
> - **Applaud the new batsman.** No matter whether you are playing for your school or your country, it is good etiquette to clap the new batsman making their way to the wicket.

> **Activity**
>
> Choose one of your assessed activities and then write a set of sportsmanship guidelines for that activity. Do not write about the actual rules but state what is acceptable and what is not as far as behaviour is concerned.

Other examples of good sportsmanship:

- Shake hands with your opponent.
- Thank anyone who has been participating with you or against you.
- Show concern for others, especially when they are injured or under stress.
- Never swear or be abusive.
- Do not stretch the rules to take advantage of someone else.
- Take defeat well and show good humour.
- Do not question officials – accept their decisions.
- Say 'well done' to opponents when they do well.
- Take other people into consideration when participating in exercise – for example, swimming and avoiding colliding with others.
- Do not over-celebrate when you do well – take other people's feelings into account and avoid arrogance in victory.
- Do not deride the efforts of others – be respectful of others, whatever their ability.

Gamesmanship

In many sports competitors are seen to 'bend the rules' or to put aside sportsmanship and use **gamesmanship** to seek an unfair advantage.

There are those who may cheat within the sports competition but in a subtle way that is difficult to control by the rules. The forward in football who dives in the penalty area to seek a penalty, the hockey player who impedes another's stick in a tackle, an athlete who pushes another in a middle-distance race – these are all examples of gamesmanship that most people perceive to be undesirable elements in the sport. Often coaches are guilty of encouraging such behaviour and thus reinforcing the view that gamesmanship is a clever way of undermining your opponent and gaining an advantage in competition.

Key term

Gamesmanship The use of unethical, although often not illegal, methods to win or gain a serious advantage in a game or sport.

IN THE NEWS

Gamesmanship in tennis

The following are typical examples of gamesmanship at competitive professional level tennis, as reported by tennis players and their coaches:

- 'creative' line calling (especially if a big point is at stake) – in other words, stating the ball was out when it was in
- accusing the opponent of 'hooking' even when they hit the ball cleanly
- squeaking their tennis shoes or tapping their racket in an annoying way, just as the opponent begins their service
- making loud noises like grunts or cries long after they have struck the ball
- changing the game score
- stalling at the back fence and making lengthy visits to the toilet to control the match speed
- accusing the innocent opponent of changing the score
- creative let-cord management (especially when a ball from another match rolls close by)
- belittling the opponent under their breath/muttering rude things about them.

Deviance

There is a view that sport may well contribute to **deviance** in our society. Spectators at a sports event may be stirred to commit criminal acts by the sports spectacle. Some have the view that contact sports such as boxing or some martial arts may encourage violence and anti-social behaviour.

There are competitors in sport who use performance-enhancing drugs, which is of course against the rules. The pressure of trying to win and to have that all-important edge over your opponent drives some sportspeople to take drugs to help their performance or to enable them to train more effectively. Competitors' behaviour within a sports event can also be seen as deviant.

Key term

Deviance This involves human behaviour that is against your society's norms and values. Behaviour of this kind is often against the law.

▲ Figure 3.3.2 Some people believe contact sports encourage anti-social behaviour

Section 3 Socio-cultural Influences

> # IN THE NEWS
> ## Example of deviance in cricket
> During the 2020 season, Mitchell Claydon, a Sussex 'seamer' cricket bowler, was banned for nine matches after admitting that he had altered the condition of the ball. He had put hand sanitiser on the ball to try to alter its flight when bowling.
>
> He was charged with a breach of ECB Directives 3.3 and 3.7, which state:
> - 3.3 No Participant may conduct themselves in a manner or do any act or omission at any time which is improper or which may be prejudicial to the interests of cricket or which may bring the ECB, the game of cricket or any cricketer or group of cricketers into disrepute.
> - 3.7 Contravention of the Bob Willis Trophy Playing Conditions 5 or 41.2 … shall be regarded as (i) unfair and improper conduct; and (ii) conduct prejudicial to the interests of cricket and likely to bring the game into disrepute.

Other examples of deviance include:
- hooliganism in football
- violence in sports (e.g. a fight between players in a rugby match)
- taking performance-enhancing drugs
- cheating in sports such as golf.

Drugs in sport

Sportspeople often take drugs to enhance their performance. Many feel that 'others are taking them, so why shouldn't I?' Others are influenced by peers or over-competitive coaches who seek winning by any means.

The use of drugs, whether they be recreational – for example, cannabis – or performance-enhancing – for example, anabolic steroids – is widespread and can seriously affect your health and well-being. Drug taking involves the use of chemicals that alter the way we feel and see things and is one of the oldest activities of the human race.

Even when there are serious consequences to their use – of tobacco, alcohol, cannabis, heroin or performing-enhancing drugs in sport – those consequences will not always make a person want to stop using their drug of choice. If and when they do decide to give up, they may find it is harder than they thought. There is often more to an addiction than the physical withdrawal symptoms. Addiction includes anxiety, depression and lowering of self-esteem. The pattern of these symptoms will depend not only on the drug used but also on the psychological make-up of the person and the circumstances in which they are attempting to remain drug-free.

Chapter 3.3 Ethical and socio-cultural issues in physical activity and sport

UK Sport has been directed by the government to deliver its policy objectives as the national anti-doping organisation, to represent the government in international meetings and to co-ordinate the national anti-doping programme of testing and education and information for sport throughout the UK.

Prohibited substances in sport

Prohibited substances may vary from sport to sport. It is the athlete's responsibility to know their sport's anti-doping regulations. In cases of uncertainty, it is important to check with the appropriate governing body or UK Sport and be sure to read carefully the anti-doping rules adopted by the relevant governing body and international sports federations.

Athletes are advised to check all medications and substances with their doctor or governing body medical officer. All substances should be checked carefully when travelling abroad as many products can, and do, contain substances different to those found in the UK.

Substances and methods are prohibited in sport for various reasons, including:

- Performance-enhancing effects, which contravene the ethics of sport and undermine the principles of fair participation.
- Health and safety of the athlete – some drug misuse may cause serious side-effects, which can compromise an athlete's health. Using substances to mask pain/injury could make an injury worse or cause permanent damage. Some drug misuse may be harmful to other athletes participating in the sport.
- Illegality – it is forbidden by law to possess or supply some substances.

Most sporting federations have anti-doping regulations to ensure all athletes compete by the same principle of being drug-free. The regulations aim to achieve drug-free sport through clearly stated policies, testing and sanctions. They are also intended to raise the awareness of drug misuse and to deter athletes from misusing prohibited drugs and methods.

Examples of performance-enhancing drugs include:

- **Anabolic steroids**: these enable sportspeople to train harder and longer and often lead to them increasing their strength and aggression.
- **Beta blockers**: these help to control the heart rate and keep the athlete calm.
- **Stimulants**: for example, amphetamines – these work as a brain stimulant, which increases alertness.

Extend your knowledge

Addicted to performance-enhancing drugs

The use of steroids is common as they enable faster muscle growth. They often mimic the effects of testosterone and make the body grow more quickly. Addiction is when there is an overriding need to keep using the substance, requiring higher dosages in order to see its effects taking place. In most cases, this also drives up the side-effects and can cause several health issues. Anabolic steroids are frequently abused because they are believed to increase muscle mass and athletic performance. Most people who take anabolic steroids are men, but not all are athletes. Some use them purely to improve their physical appearance. Often, steroid addiction develops when men are trying to cope with underlying mental health issues, ranging from low self-esteem to **body dysmorphia**.

Key term

Body dysmorphia An obsessive mental health disorder where someone cannot stop thinking about an imagined or slight flaw, or flaws, in their physical appearance. (Muscle dysmorphia is when someone perceives themselves to be thin, physically weak and small, regardless of their actual physical size, and despite often being large and muscular.)

Section 3 Socio-cultural Influences

> **STUDY HINT**
> Be able to describe the positive and negative effects of performance-enhancing drugs:
> - ✔ **Positive**: able to play better/perform better/more strength/more assertive/more energy available/control of emotions/able to train harder and longer.
> - ✔ **Negative**: jeopardising health/skin problems, e.g. acne/become addicted/high blood pressure/too aggressive/less self-esteem/masks injury/decreased speed/disqualification/loss of respect from others/gives a bad reputation to the individual and the sport.

? Extend your knowledge

Anabolic steroids

These are man-made drugs that increase muscle growth if taken with vigorous training. This enables the athlete to recover more quickly and therefore to be able to train even harder.

The main problems with taking such drugs are:
- both the liver and the kidneys can develop tumours
- the liver ceases to act properly, causing major health problems
- high blood pressure, severe acne or spots
- shrinking of the testicles, reduced sperm count and the development of breasts in males
- the growth of facial hair, baldness and deepening of the voice in females.

There is also an increase in aggression and other psychological problems.

? Extend your knowledge

Prohibited classes of substances

- Stimulants
- Narcotic analgesics
- Anabolic agents
- Anabolic androgenic steroids
- Other anabolic agents
- Diuretics
- Peptide hormones, mimetics and analogues
- Substances with anti-oestrogenic activity
- Masking agents

Prohibited methods

- Enhancement of oxygen transfer
- Blood doping
- The administration of products that enhance the uptake, transport and delivery of oxygen
- Pharmacological, chemical and physical manipulation
- Gene doping (to alter our genetic make-up, in order to make us stronger or faster)

Classes of prohibited substances in certain circumstances

- Alcohol
- Cannabinoids
- Local anaesthetics
- Glucocorticosteroids
- Beta blockers

IN THE NEWS

Russian athletes banned for state-sponsored drug cheating in sport

The World Anti-Doping Agency (WADA) banned Russia from competing in all major sporting events, including the Tokyo Olympics and Paralympics and the 2022 football World Cup in Qatar. Russia is also not allowed to host any major events for four years. This came after Russia's Anti-Doping Agency (Rusada) was declared non-compliant because it had manipulated laboratory data handed over to investigators in January 2019. A WADA-commissioned report alleged that corruption was widespread and amounted to state-sponsored doping in Russian track and field athletics.

An earlier report, in 2016, had also stated that Russia had run a state-sponsored doping programme for four years across most of the summer and winter Olympic sports.

Violence in sport

The word violence is used frequently and in sport it is often used with the intent to harm others outside the rules of the game or activity. In sport, it is often difficult to distinguish between what is violent and aggressive behaviour and what is not. A foul in rugby may look aggressive, but it could have been unintentional or an accident. Also, what is seemingly accidental on the surface may well have the intent to harm and therefore is aggression.

Possible reasons for player violence

Player violence unfortunately occurs in a number of sports and can lead to injuries to instigator and victim. There are many possible causes of player violence that you need to consider:

1. **We can't help it – it is an instinctive response.** This is known as the instinct theory. In sport, we may have the instinctive urge to strike out and protect ourselves or to defend our territory. For example, in rugby, a player in an offside position may cause an opponent to be aggressive.

2. **We get frustrated.** Again this is a type of instinct – if we feel frustrated, we may well lash out and be aggressive to get rid of the frustration. Such things as playing poorly, or what we feel are poor decisions on the part of the referee, can cause frustration.

3. **We copy others.** To fit into a group and be accepted and to behave in a way that our role models do, we may become aggressive. If someone you look up to behaves aggressively, you are more likely to imitate or copy their behaviour because you think that must be the right thing to do.

4. **We simply get angry.** This might be the result of frustration, or you may have seen someone else not be punished for aggressive

Section 3 Socio-cultural Influences

behaviour. When we get angry, our heart rate and blood pressure increase, and the hormone adrenaline is released more readily into the blood stream. We therefore get agitated and we want to show that we are angry and are therefore aggressive.

5. **The use of performance-enhancing drugs.** The use of drugs such as anaebolic steroids has been shown to increase aggressive behaviour.

▲ Figure 3.3.3 In sport, we may have the instinctive urge to strike out and protect ourselves or to defend our territory

> ### ❓ Extend your knowledge
>
> ### Strategies to control violence or aggression
> The following strategies could be employed to control violence.
> 1. Calm down by relaxing or by concentrating on your own performance in the game or activity. Focusing attention on the job in hand is sometimes called channelling aggression.
> 2. Avoid situations that might make you angry or aggressive – for example, by walking away from trouble or trying a new position on the field of play.
> 3. Remove yourself completely from the situation – for instance, a basketball coach may substitute an aggressive player to calm down.
> 4. Enjoy praise for not being aggressive. Your coach may well praise the fact that you have been a forceful, effective player, but you have not been aggressive and given away territory.
> 5. Recognise others who are successful (role models) but who do not resort to aggression. Most successful sportspeople are not aggressive but are assertive.
> 6. Punishment or fear of being punished may well control aggression. Often fines are used or a player may be dropped from the team.
> 7. Recognise that you have a position of responsibility. Aggression could let the rest of the team down.
> 8. Anger management. Try to identify what makes you angry and to avoid the triggers to anger. You may learn to deal with your feelings early on rather than waiting for your anger to build up out of control.
> 9. Breathing exercises. Relax in your mind and body with deep, controlled and slow breathing. Your heart rate will decrease the more steadily you breathe, and then you will feel calmer.

SUMMARY

- Ethics in sport include the concepts of sportsmanship, gamesmanship and deviance.
- Sportsmanship involves fairness and generosity.
- In many sports, competitors are seen to 'bend the rules' or to put aside sportsmanship and use 'gamesmanship' to seek an unfair advantage.
- Deviance involves human behaviour that is against your society's norms and values.
- Anabolic steroids enable sportspeople to train harder and longer.
- Beta blockers help to control the heart rate and keep the athlete calm.
- Stimulants work to increase alertness for sportspeople.
- The word violence is used in sport as behaviour with the intent to harm others outside the rules of the game or activity. Violence is often used to get an advantage, to retaliate or because of a player's frustration.

Practice questions

1. Using examples from sport, describe the value of sportsmanship. **(4 marks)**
2. Define gamesmanship and give an example from one of your assessed sports. **(2 marks)**
3. Giving an example, describe what is meant by deviance in sport. **(2 marks)**
4. *Discuss the differences between gamesmanship and sportsmanship in sport. **(6 marks)**
5. Identify one reason why a sports performer might use beta blockers. **(1 mark)**
6. *Explain the impact on drug use in sport both on the performers and on the sport itself. **(6 marks)**
7. Identify two reasons why a player in a team sport of your choice might be violent. **(2 marks)**

*These questions include an assessment of the quality of your written communication.

Part 4
Sports Psychology

4.1 Characteristics of skilful movement and classification of skills
4.2 Goal setting
4.3 Mental preparation
4.4 Types of guidance and feedback

Chapter 4.1
Characteristics of skilful movement and classification of skills

Understanding the Specification

You should have knowledge and understanding of the characteristics of skilful movement when performing physical activities and sports and be able to apply them to practical examples.

- Definition of motor skills.
- Characteristics of skilled performers with a range of practical examples.
  - Efficiency
  - Pre-determined
  - Co-ordinated
  - Fluent
  - Aesthetic

You should also have knowledge and understanding of the identified classification of skills in both the learning and improvement of physical skills and be able to apply them to practical examples.

- The difficulty continuum from simple to complex skills.
- The environmental continuum from open to closed skills.
- Examples of skills for each continuum along with justification of their placement on both continua.

To strive to become good at your sport and to be skilful in everything you do, it is useful to be able to picture and describe what skilful movement actually is. We can then compare what we do with this picture of expertise and identify what we have to work on to improve.

Characteristics of skilled performers

When we use the term skill, we often mean a combination of perceptual (how we see our surroundings), cognitive (thinking skills) and **motor skills**. Skilled performers are not born with most motor skills already programmed in their minds – they have to learn them in a number of different ways.

Skilful movement

Skilful movement can be defined as:

A skilled movement is one in which a predetermined objective is accomplished with maximum efficiency with a minimum outlay of energy.

Are skilful people born with their skills or do they learn their skills? The answer is probably a mixture of both. We are all born with abilities and these dictate the potential to be skilful.

We often comment that an experienced sportsperson is 'skilful', but what do we actually mean by the word 'skill'? We use it to describe a task such as kicking a ball, but often we use it to mean the overall actions of someone who is good at what they do.

Key term

Motor skill An action or task that has a target or goal and that requires voluntary body and/or limb movement to achieve this goal. There are two main ways of using the word 'skill':

a. To see skill as a specific task to be performed.
b. To view skill as describing the quality of a particular action, which might include how consistent the performance is and how prepared the performer is to carry out the task.

Chapter 4.1 Characteristics of skilful movement and classification of skills

When we see top-class sportsmen and sportswomen, we are often struck by the seemingly effortless way in which they perform, and it is not until we try to perform ourselves that we realise just how difficult it really is! We know that these performers are very fit, but they don't seem to exert themselves and we are aware that whatever the skill – whether it is a somersault in gymnastics or a perfectly timed rugby tackle – the end product looks good and is aesthetically pleasing. A skilled performer knows what they are trying to achieve and shows a successful movement. A beginner, or novice, will seem clumsy and slow and will lack control. The novice will also tire quickly and use up more energy than is necessary. Characteristics of skilful movement include the movement being fluent, co-ordinated and controlled. The performer seems effortless and looks good, obviously using good technique.

IN THE NEWS

▲ Figure 4.1.2 Gymnast Simone Biles

New gymnastic skills invented

In order to have a move officially named after a gymnast, they must successfully complete the move in the World Championships or at the Olympics. Simone Biles, the US gymnast, has done just that by creating four original and very difficult gymnastic moves which are now called the 'Biles'. They are some of the most difficult elements ever seen in gymnastics.

Biles already had two incredible moves named after her (on the floor and on the vault) but she performed two more original skills (during her floor and beam routines) in 2019 at the World Championships in Stuttgart, Germany. She is the first woman to complete the triple-twisting, double back manoeuvre during her floor routine, which is now called the 'Biles II' in the gymnastics code of points.

Activity

▲ Figure 4.1.1 Lionel Messi: a skilled performer?

Look at the photograph. We would probably all agree that this performer is skilled. Write a list of words and phrases you feel would describe a skilled performer.

Skilful movement, then, is not one that can be described in one specific way, but is a mixture of features that when combined provides movement patterns that are effective and efficient.

Main characteristics with practical examples
- Efficiency, e.g. no wasted energy when hitting a ball in cricket.
- Pre-determined, e.g. the trampolinist knows their routine well before they start.

- Co-ordinated, e.g. the volleyball player can jump and 'spike' successfully, using arms and legs together for co-ordination.
- Fluent, e.g. the rugby player picks up the ball and passes in one flowing movement.
- Aesthetic, e.g. the basketball player shoots the ball using the correct technique that looks good.

> **? Extend your knowledge**
>
> **Other characteristics associated with skilled performers**
> The following is a list of other characteristics of skilled performers, together with examples:
> - Creative, e.g. a rugby player can disguise a pass.
> - Successful technique, e.g. a netball player shows the correct shooting technique.
> - Controlled, e.g. a tennis player controls a smash that goes in.
> - Speed, e.g. a lacrosse player passes with speed.
> - Consistent, e.g. a squash player serves well every time.
> - Able to learn, e.g. a gymnast is able to learn a new technique of somersault.
> - Confident, e.g. a hockey player shows confidence when shooting at goal.

> **? Extend your knowledge**
>
> **Fundamental motor skills**
> We learn fundamental motor skills at a young age, usually through play, and if they are learned thoroughly, a child can move on to the more sophisticated actions that are required in sport. Fundamental motor skills are skills such as throwing, catching and running. These skills are important because they provide the basis for other skills.
>
> Without acquiring the fundamental motor skills, it is unlikely that a person would be able to excel in a sports activity. These skills provide the platform on which we can build the more advanced skills demanded in our sports. Acquiring fundamental motor skills can help children build their self-esteem and make them more accepted in group 'play' situations.

Key terms

Perception A complex concept that involves interpretation of stimuli. Not all stimuli are perceived and what is perceived depends on experience and attention ability.

Cognitive skills These are skills that involve the intellectual ability of the performer. These skills affect the perceptual process and help us to make sense of what is required in any given situation. They are essential if the performer is to make correct and effective decisions.

If a tennis player often serves aces in a match, we would label that player as skilled. If we watched him over a number of matches and he continued to serve aces, we would be more justified in labelling him as skilled. A squash player whom we might regard as skilled would anticipate where the ball is going to land and would put herself in a position to receive the ball early so that she could hit it early, thus putting her opponent at a disadvantage. The player also has to assess the position of the opponents and the players on the same team and will have to decide where to pass the ball and how hard to pass it. This interpretation of information or stimuli is called **perception** and the skill required is called *perceptual skill*.

For skill acquisition to take place, the person also needs **cognitive skills**. These skills are intellectually based and are linked to working out or solving problems; they underpin verbal reasoning. These skills are often seen as innate, although there is considerable debate among psychologists as to how intelligence is acquired and whether there is only one or many ways that people can show intelligence.

Chapter 4.1 Characteristics of skilful movement and classification of skills

Classification of skills

For the nature of skills to be understood fully and for those that teach and learn skills in sport, it is helpful to classify them. Classification makes it clearer about what is required to learn and perform a particular skill. Skills can be placed on a continuum or scale and for OCR GCSE PE the two continua that you need to be concerned with are:

- environmental continuum
  - Open _____ Closed
- difficulty continuum.
  - Complex _____ Simple

If a skill is affected by the surrounding environment and requires the performer to make perceptual decisions, it is called an open skill. If a skill at the other extreme is not affected at all by the environment, it is called a closed skill.

Skills can be classified according to the types of judgements and decisions that you have to make to perform the skill. If there are many decisions to make, then the skill is known as a complex skill and may have to be learned in stages. If the skill is a straightforward one with hardly any judgements and decisions to make, then it is known as a simple skill and can be taught as a whole and in a fairly repetitive way.

Practical examples:

- complex skills – slip catch in cricket, or a pass by a midfield player in hockey who has to make lots of decisions before she passes
- simple skills – a sprint start in swimming, for example, where there are very few decisions – other than to dive – to be made.

▲ Figure 4.1.3 A slip catch in cricket is an example of a complex skill

Implications for training and coaching

If a coach and the performer are familiar with and understand the nature of the task or skill that has to be learned and performed, then training techniques can be adapted depending on these requirements.

If a closed skill is to be coached, it is going to be more effective if it is practised repetitively so that the skill is 'grooved'. It is also unnecessary to vary the situation because closed skills remain mainly constant.

> **STUDY HINT**
> Learn the main characteristics of skilled movement:
> ✔ Efficiency
> ✔ Predetermined goals
> ✔ Co-ordinated
> ✔ Aesthetically pleasing
> ✔ Fluent

> **Activity**
> Your physical activity, sport or exercise programme will require fundamental motor skills, more advanced motor skills and perceptual skills. From one of your assessed physical activities, identify:
> 1. the fundamental skills involved
> 2. the motor skills involved
> 3. any perceptual skills involved.

If an open skill were learned, then a variety of situations would be effective because the performer would build up a repertoire of strategies due to the ever-changing circumstances.

> **SUMMARY**
> - The main characteristics of skilled movement are efficiency, predetermined goals, co-ordination, fluency and aesthetics.
> - Motor skills involve fundamental movement patterns and perceptual and cognitive skills.
> - If a skill is affected by the surrounding environment and requires the performer to make perceptual decisions, it is called an open skill. If a skill at the other extreme is not affected at all by the environment, it is called a closed skill.
> - Skills can be classified according to the types of judgements and amount of decisions that you have to make to perform the skill. If there are many decisions to make, the skill is known as a complex skill and may have to be learned in stages.
> - If the skill is a straightforward one with hardly any judgements and decisions to make, it is known as a simple skill and can be taught as a whole and in a fairly repetitive way.

Practice questions

1. Identify five main characteristics of skilful movement in sport. **(5 marks)**
2. Using a practical example from your assessed physical activity, describe one characteristic of an open motor skill and one characteristic of a complex skill. **(2 marks)**
3. What is meant by the term 'motor skill'? Give a practical example of 'aesthetic' as a characteristic of a skilful performer. **(2 marks)**
4. Is the following statement true or false? A sprint start in athletics is an example of a complex skill. **(1 mark)**
5. *Choose two different skills from one of your assessed activities and classify them using the difficulty continuum and the environmental continuum. Justify your classifications for each of your chosen skills. **(6 marks)**

*This question includes an assessment of the quality of your written communication.

Chapter 4.2
Goal setting

Understanding the Specification

You should understand and be able to apply examples of the use of goal setting for the following reasons:
- for exercise and training adherence
- to motivate performers
- to improve and optimise performance.

You should also be able to understand the 'SMART principle' (Specific, Measurable, Achievable, Recorded, Timed) of goal setting with practical examples.
You should be able to apply the SMART principle, using practical examples to improve and optimise performance.

Goal setting

There are many reasons why goal setting can be important, including to encourage individuals to stick to a routine and to motivate performers. One common way of doing this is through the SMART principle. SMART stands for:

- Specific
- Measurable
- Achievable
- Recorded
- Timed.

For exercise and training adherence

Goal setting has been shown as an effective method in ensuring that those people who wish to exercise or train to improve fitness, health and performance are more likely to stick to their exercise/training programmes. Too many goals can be irrelevant to the performer or can result in them giving up too quickly. Goals that are simply out of reach, too difficult or too demanding can result in a high dropout rate.

To motivate performers

Goal setting can inspire and drive performers to achieve their best and can be useful in motivating them to follow exercise and training programmes. But in order to motivate, goals must follow the SMART principle and also be exciting and realistic. All performers, whether they are elite athletes striving for world records or are simply exercising to keep fit, are often motivated by short-term goals, leading to long-term goals. If goals or targets are reached each step of the way then performers are more likely to continue and to try their best to reach the next step towards further goals.

To improve and optimise performance

Goals that follow the SMART principle often lead to higher levels of performance, but goals should be incrementally more difficult over a period of time. Improvements can be seen only if each short-term goal is

Section 4 Sports Psychology

realistic but challenging. Goals set might lead to a decline in performance if they are set beyond the reach of the performer and this can also lead to demotivation and may result in the performer giving up altogether.

For goals to result in exercise adherence, motivated performers and improved performance, they need to be appropriate to performer's needs. By setting appropriate goals, you can:

- take up an activity or activities
- achieve more when you participate in physical activities
- improve your performance
- improve the quality and quantity of your training
- increase your motivation to succeed
- increase your pride and satisfaction after goal completion.

Goal setting is a very powerful process that can lead to rewards, personal satisfaction and increased motivation levels. By knowing what you want to achieve, you then know what you need to concentrate on and improve and what distractions to ignore.

When you set goals for training in sport, you should try to:

- pace yourself – do not try to do too much too soon
- give yourself rewards
- keep goals realistic
- keep a record of your goals
- not feel bad if things do not go well – plan your next step for future success.

Achieving goals

When you have achieved a goal, enjoy the satisfaction of having done it – pat yourself on the back. Plan to achieve even greater or higher goals.

If you have failed to reach a goal, make sure that you have learned lessons from it to keep motivated and focused.

▲ Figure 4.2.1 Achieving a goal can lead to high levels of satisfaction

Reasons for not attaining goals in physical activities

- You did not try hard enough.
- Poor technique which needs to be adjusted.
- The goal you set was unrealistic at this time.

Use this information to adjust your goals or to set different goals to learn new skills or build to improve fitness. Turn everything into a positive learning experience. Failing to meet a goal is a step forward towards success.

When you have achieved a goal:

- if easily achieved, make your next goals harder
- if the goal took too long to achieve, make the next goals a little easier
- if you learned something that would lead you to change future goals, then change them.

Effective goal setting

For goal setting to be effective, there must be short-term goals leading to longer-term goals. For example, to win the league cup, the netball team may have to concentrate on winning more games away from home. This may require short-term goals of improving the team's defending strategies. For those who simply wish to exercise more, the first step is to walk to school rather than any long-distance running.

Motivation can be increased by splitting long-term goals into medium-term and short-term goals, which are more specific and manageable over a short period of time.

People who exercise and sports performers need to know how they are progressing. Most sportspeople are highly motivated and feedback is essential for them to maintain their enthusiasm and commitment. For those who are exercising to keep fit, positive feedback is also crucial if they are going to keep exercising. Too many people join gyms in this country but stop going after the first few times.

> **Extend your knowledge**
>
> ### Evaluation of goal setting
> Goal evaluation must take place if progress is to be made and performance improved or participation increased. Goals must therefore be clearly defined. This is easier with physical activities and sports that involve objective measurements, e.g. timings. Evaluation can take place only if goals are measurable. The measurement of goals will then evaluate success, which in itself is a motivating factor and will also give useful information about the setting of further goals.

STUDY HINT

SMART goal setting

Be able to identify each element and then apply each one, using a practical example, e.g. a specific goal to improve the serve technique in tennis.

- **S** Specific: if goals are clear and unambiguous they are more likely to be attained.
- **M** Measurable: this is important for monitoring and makes you accountable.
- **A** Achievable: motivation will improve if goals can actually be reached and are within your capabilities.
- **R** Recorded: crucial for monitoring and once achieved can be deleted or checked off, thus improving motivation.
- **T** Timed: the splitting up into short-term goals that are planned and progressive is effective.

▲ Figure 4.2.2 Goal setting is a useful strategy to control anxiety and one that is widely used in sport for training and to improve performance

Section 4 Sports Psychology

Activity

1. Read the 'In the news' feature about exercising during the pandemic. Summarise this article, stating why it is important to exercise and the possible dangers of over exercising/training.

2. Construct a six-week exercise programme for a teenager that could be performed during a pandemic 'lockdown'. Take into account the SMART principle when constructing your programme.

IN THE NEWS

Setting exercise goals during the COVID-19 pandemic

The COVID-19 pandemic had an enormous impact on sports and exercise in 2020. The need to restrict the spread of the virus led to restrictions on people's lives, a reduction of physical exercise and an increase in sedentary behaviour. All forms of organised sport were either cancelled or postponed early on in the pandemic, including events such as marathon races and football matches, e.g. the UEFA European Championship, and even the Summer Olympic Games.

Personal hygiene, social distancing and a healthy lifestyle were all crucially important to reduce the risk of COVID-19 infection. The physical and mental benefits of physical activity were highlighted (within the pandemic restrictions) and exercise was encouraged. However, anyone planning a prolonged endurance activity (for example, long-distance running) was advised to be cautious and to avoid the risks of overtraining. Untrained individuals taking part in high-intensity training can risk a decrease in their own immunity and an increase in their likelihood of contracting COVID-19.

For athletes with positive tests, the advice was to stop exercising for at least seven days. Once any symptoms had cleared up, they were then advised to make a progressive return to training over an additional seven days.

If people exercise simply to lose weight, not because they enjoy it, they will either give up before they achieve their goal or will think 'job done' when it is finally reached, then revert to their old habits of inactivity.

Many surveys have indicated that six months after joining, the dropout rate among new gym members is about 60 per cent. One report suggested that 20 per cent of health club members work out there no more than once a month.

❓ Extend your knowledge

Performance and outcome goals

There are two types of goal that can be recognised and set in sport: performance and outcome goals.

Performance goals

These are directly related to the performance or technique of the activity. For example, performance goals in netball or football might be to improve passing or shooting techniques. Performance goals by their nature tend to be more short term than long term.

Examples of performance goals:

- To improve technique of a front somersault in trampolining.
- To try to stop using a poor golf swing when driving from the tee.
- To improve running technique in sprinting.

- To shorten the back swing in a tennis serve in order to be more accurate.
- To not let lifting technique go wrong when training with heavier weights.

Outcome goals

These are concerned with the end result, whether you win or lose for instance. Outcome goals in netball or football might be to win an individual game or a tournament. A tennis player who is trying to win the grand slam by winning each open tournament is setting another outcome goal. Outcome goals tend to be medium to long term rather than short term. Examples of outcome goals include to:

- win the 100-metre race in an athletics competition
- finish the exercise class without stopping
- try to top the leader board in a cycling race
- win the football league
- get through to the finals of the golf competition.

▲ Figure 4.2.3 A performance goal in netball might be to improve passing technique

Practice questions

1. Describe the SMART principle of goal setting in sport. **(5 marks)**
2. *Using practical examples from your assessed activities, explain how you would use the SMART principle of goal setting to improve performance. **(5 marks)**
3. How might a coach of a sport use goal setting to ensure training adherence? **(3 marks)**
4. Identify why goal setting is important for a sports performer. **(3 marks)**
5. A badminton player wants to improve their serve. As their coach, how would you use the 'timed' aspect of the SMART principle to help to improve their serve? **(3 marks)**

*This question includes an assessment of the quality of your written communication.

SUMMARY
- For goals to result in exercise adherence, motivated performers and improved performance, they need to be appropriate to the performer's needs.
- Goal setting is a very powerful process that can lead to rewards, personal satisfaction and increased motivation levels. By knowing what you want to achieve, you then know what you need to concentrate on and improve, and what distractions to ignore.
- SMART stands for: Specific, Measurable, Achievable, Recorded, Timed.

Chapter 4.3
Mental preparation

Understanding the Specification

You should understand mental preparation techniques and be able to apply practical examples when using these techniques. The mental preparation techniques to be covered, along with practical examples, are:

- imagery
- mental rehearsal
- selective attention
- positive thinking.

Key terms

Anxiety The feeling of fear that we experience that something might go wrong either in the present or in the future.

Cognitive anxiety management techniques Those ways of coping that affect the mind and therefore can control anxiety.

Somatic anxiety management techniques Those ways of coping that affect the body directly such as relaxation. Cognitive can affect somatic and vice versa.

> **STUDY HINT**
> You may be asked to explain how mental preparation can lead to a more successful performance in physical activities and sport.

Mental preparation techniques

Mental preparation techniques are widely used by those who participate in physical activities as well as sportspeople to cope with high levels of cognitive and somatic **anxiety (cognitive and somatic anxiety management techniques)**.

- **Practical example**: controlling the heart rate by relaxation methods before a hockey match can make the player feel more positive about performing (somatic). Positive thinking can, in turn, control our heart rate (cognitive).

The following stress management techniques can be used as coping strategies.

IN THE NEWS

Imagery

Many sportspeople, ranging from grassroots up to elite level, use imagery to enhance their performance. Ronaldinho, the Brazilian football player, likes to use imagery to help him prepare and improve his game and strategy:

'When I train, one of the things I concentrate on is creating a mental picture of how best to deliver the ball to a teammate, preferably leaving him alone in front of the rival goalkeeper. So what I do, always before a game, always, every night and every day, is try and think up things, imagine plays, which no one else will have thought of, and to do so always bearing in mind the particular strength of each teammate to whom I am passing the ball. When I construct those plays in my mind I take into account whether one teammate likes to receive the ball at his feet, or ahead of him; if he is good with his head, and how he prefers to head the ball; if he is stronger on his right or his left foot. That is my job. That is what I do. I imagine the game.'

Imagery

Imagery can improve concentration. The creation of pictures in our minds is imagery. Many people try to get the feeling of movement or capture an emotional feeling, for example, of pleasure or happiness.

Imagery can also help with relaxation. A participant in a physical activity or a performer in sport who feels anxious could go to 'another place' in their minds to try to calm down. Many participants report that they use these techniques to cope with stress and anxiety.

Mental rehearsal

Imagery as a tool for relaxation is a form of mental rehearsal. Mental rehearsal can involve both internal and external imagery:

- External imagery is when you can picture yourself from outside your body, like watching yourself on film. For example, a gymnast may go through all their moves in the floor routine.
- Internal imagery is when you imagine yourself doing the activity and can simulate the feelings of the activity, such as a high-jump athlete visualising the whole activity of run-up, jump and landing.

Mental rehearsal and imagery can result in the following benefits:

- Speeds up your reactions to different situations.
- Enables you to concentrate and focus.
- Keeps you calm and helps to control your levels of arousal.
- Can prepare you to react in different ways depending on the opponent or changing circumstances.
- Encourages you to be motivated and positive in your outlook.

To be effective in using selective attention and imagery, the following points should be taken into consideration:

- Relax in a comfortable, warm setting before you attempt to practise mental rehearsal or imagery.
- If you want to improve skill by using mental rehearsal or imagery, then practise in a real-life situation.
- Mental rehearsal and imagery exercises should be short but frequent.

IN THE NEWS

Penalty misses in highly stressful situations

The England football team in the Women's World Cup 2019 semi-finals were beaten by the USA after their captain Stephanie Houghton's weak penalty was saved by Alyssa Naeher. The penalty had given Houghton the chance to equalise in the last 10 minutes of the game, and to keep hopes of the World Cup alive, but it was not to be.

- Set goals for each session, e.g. concentrate on imagining the feel of a tennis serve in one short session.
- Construct a programme for your training in mental rehearsal or imagery.
- Evaluate your programme at regular intervals.
- **Practical example:** A golfer visualises or uses imagery to picture the course, with all its holes, fairways, rough and other hazards. He goes through the movements he has to perform when he pictures each aspect of the game in his mind. This is an example of mental rehearsal.

▲ Figure 4.3.1 Mental rehearsal and imagery can help in reacting quickly to different situations

Selective attention

When learning skills or performing skills in sport, it is often difficult for the learner or performer to discriminate between information that is relevant and information that is unimportant in the execution of the skill. A beginner basketball player may pay too much attention to the ball and not watch the movement of the opponent he is supposed to be marking. A badminton player may be paying too much attention to the movement of opponents rather than the flight of the shuttle. It is therefore important that when learning or performing a skill that needs more concentration, the performer concentrates on what is relevant and ignores irrelevant distractions. This process is called selective attention.

A goalkeeper in football may receive information that is not required to save the shot. There may be crowd noise and movement; movement of other players and the shouting of opponents to try to distract. The more experienced the goalkeeper, the more likely it is that they will be able to select out and filter this information.

The more tired the player, the less likely they are to selectively attend to or to concentrate on important pieces of information.

Factors that affect selective attention include:

- relevance – the goalkeeper may judge that the striker's foot is more relevant than the waving of the crowd
- expectation – the goalkeeper expects there to be a shot because of the striker's body position
- vividness – a fellow player's loud shout is more likely to be attended to than a passing comment from another.

Positive thinking

This technique, sometimes called 'self-talk' involves the participant in a physical activity or the sports performer being positive about past experiences and performances and future efforts by talking to themselves or thinking through how successful they might be. This technique has been shown to help with self-confidence and to raise levels of aspiration. Unfortunately, for many would-be participants in physical activities and performers in sport, thinking can be far from positive and often can be negative. It is very common for sports performers to 'talk themselves out of winning', for instance a penalty taker saying to themselves, 'I will probably miss this'. It is also common for young people to say that they do not want to exercise because they feel they might look foolish or will be embarrassed in front of others. This is known as negative self-talk or negative thinking and should be minimised if people are to participate in physical activities or for sports performance to be good.

High-level performers cannot afford to be negative and they must develop strategies to change these negative thoughts into positive ones (e.g. by not concentrating on what would happen if they lose, rather what will happen when they win).

There are five categories of negative thoughts:

1. Worry about performance, e.g. 'I think they are better than me.'
2. Inability to make decisions, e.g. 'Shall I pass, shall I hold, shall I shoot?'
3. Preoccupation with physical feelings, e.g. 'I feel too tired, I'm going to give up and rest.'
4. Thinking about what will happen if they lose, e.g. 'What will my coach say when I lose this point?'
5. Thoughts of not having the ability to do well, e.g. 'I am not good enough.'

Activity

Read the five categories of negative thoughts again. Now change each statement into a positive one, e.g. 'I can be just as good as they are.'

❓ Extend your knowledge

The following are examples of activities that help athletes to mentally prepare.

Relaxation

Somatic anxiety can lead to cognitive anxiety, so the more physically relaxed you can get, the more mentally relaxed you can get. There is of course a happy medium in physical activities – you do not want to be too laid back because you often need to react quickly and dynamically.

Section 4 Sports Psychology

> **Activity**
>
> Using progressive relaxation training:
> 1. Sit on the floor with your legs out straight in front of you.
> 2. Now, with your right leg, tense the muscles by pulling your toes up towards your knee using your leg and foot muscles.
> 3. Develop as much tension as possible and hold for about 5 seconds. Concentrate on what it feels like.
> 4. Now completely relax your leg muscles and let your foot go floppy. Concentrate on what the relaxed muscles feel like.
> 5. Now try to relax your muscles even more.
>
> Your leg should feel far more relaxed.

> **Activity**
>
> Construct a psychological skills training programme over six weeks to enhance sports performance for a selected sports performer in one of your assessed activities.

Relaxation exercises before you attempt to train yourself in mental exercises such as imagery can be very useful. It helps the sports person to be calmer and steadier before performance. Relaxation skills are like any other type of skill: you need to practise hard to achieve them.

Self-directed relaxation

Like other techniques, this needs practice to be effective. Each muscle group is relaxed one at a time and the coach can help. The athlete then practises without direct help. Eventually it will take only a very short time for full relaxation. This time factor is crucial if the athlete is to be able to use the strategy just before or during competition.

Progressive relaxation training (PRT)

This is sometimes referred to as the Jacobsen technique, named after its pioneer. The athlete learns to be aware of the tension in the muscles and then releases all that tension. Because the athlete is so aware of the tension in the first place, they have a more effective sense of losing it when it goes.

IN THE NEWS

Positive thinking for the successful England Netball team

In 2018, the England Netball team (The Roses) won gold at the Commonwealth Games for the first time ever, with a 52–51 win against Australia. Helen Housby, who plays goal shooter and goal attack, scored in the final second to secure the win.

Housby stressed that the team did not want that win to be a 'one off', saying that they hoped to inspire young people to take up the sport and ensure that England remain at the top of the world of netball. Housby attributes much of the team's success to 'high energy and positive vibes'.

▲ Figure 4.3.2 Positive thinking can help in team performance

SUMMARY

- Mental preparation techniques can help performers in sport in many different ways.
- Each technique can help them to focus, control their anxiety and motivate them to do well. Imagery can help in controlling your levels of anxiety before and during performance.
- Mental rehearsal and selective attention help with focus and concentration and also help the performer to block out irrelevant stimuli and to attend to relevant stimuli or information.
- As a result, reaction time can be shortened and performance improves.
- Positive thinking helps particularly with motivation and confidence. It helps the performer to stick to the task and to try to do their very best.

Practice questions

1. Explain how imagery can help with mental preparation in sport. **(3 marks)**
2. How can mental rehearsal be beneficial as a mental preparation technique in sports performance? **(2 marks)**
3. Using a practical example from sport, describe the use of selective attention in sport. **(3 marks)**
4. i. Explain 'positive thinking' when preparing for a sports competition.
   ii. Using practical examples, explain the effects of positive thinking in sport. **(6 marks)**
5. *Using practical examples for each, describe mental preparation techniques for sports performance and explain how they might help to optimise sports performance. **(6 marks)**

*This question includes an assessment of the quality of your written communication.

Chapter 4.4
Types of guidance and feedback

Understanding the Specification

You should be able to understand different types of guidance, their advantages and disadvantages, and be able to apply practical examples to their use. The types of guidance that can be examined are:

- visual
- verbal
- manual
- mechanical.

You should also be able to understand different types of feedback and apply practical examples. The types of feedback that can be examined are:

- intrinsic
- extrinsic
- knowledge of performance
- knowledge of results
- positive
- negative.

Effective guidance and feedback will help the learning of sports skills. Guidance is often given before the activity, whereas feedback is given during or after.

Guidance

When a teacher or coach teaches a new skill to a student or seeks to develop the skills of an experienced performer, they need to decide the best way to transmit the knowledge necessary for effective performance. There are four main types of guidance:

- visual, e.g. a coach demonstrating a set shot in basketball
- verbal, e.g. a teacher telling a pupil to watch the ball when receiving a pass in rugby
- manual, e.g. a coach supporting a gymnast in a vault
- mechanical, e.g. a learner swimmer using armbands/a trampolinist using a harness.

▲ Figure 4.4.1 A harness in trampolining is an example of mechanical guidance

The type or combination of types chosen depends on the personality, motivation and ability of the performer, the situation in which learning or development of skills is taking place and the type of skill being taught or developed.

Visual guidance

Visual guidance is widely used when teaching motor or movement skills. During the early phase of skill learning, visual guidance (often a demonstration by the instructor or another competent performer) helps the learner develop a mental image of what needs to be done.

Some instructors use videos, charts or other visual aids to build up the 'ideal' picture of what is required to successfully perform a new skill. The demonstration must be accurate so that there is no possibility of the learner building up an incorrect picture. To avoid confusing the learner and overloading them with information in the early stages of learning, it is important to concentrate on only a few aspects of the skill. The coach may therefore 'cue' the performer on only one or two aspects of the whole movement.

The following points should be considered before using visual guidance:

- Demonstrations must be accurate and should hold the performer's attention.
- Demonstrations must be repeated but should not be too time consuming.
- Videos can be useful, especially if they have a slow-motion facility, but the student must be able to copy the model presented.
- For a learner to gain maximum benefit, their position during training should be considered. For example, the demonstration of a swimming stroke is best viewed from above on the poolside.
- During the early phase of skill learning, visual guidance is important for the learner to develop a mental image of what needs to be done.

Advantages:

- Good for beginners because they can easily visualise the correct movement skill.
- Easier to remember and to form a technical model to copy.
- Quick and effective.

Disadvantages:

- If demonstrations are incorrect then the wrong movement patterns are learned.
- Difficult to get the feel or kinaesthetic sense of the skill.
- May be too complicated for effective understanding.

▲ Figure 4.4.2 A volleyball coach demonstrating skills is an example of visual guidance

Activity

Choose a skill from one of your assessed activities. Describe how you would teach this skill using visual guidance only (with no verbal instructions).

Verbal guidance

This is often associated with visual guidance, being used to describe the action and explain how to perform the activity. Verbal guidance has limitations if used on its own – motor skills are difficult to describe without a demonstration of some kind. Remember that the instructor is trying to create an image in the learner's mind of what needs to be done. Verbal guidance of the more advanced performer is effective when more information, such as tactics or positional play, needs to be given.

Section 4 Sports Psychology

▲ Figure 4.4.3 Verbal guidance can be effective in giving information about positional play

When using verbal guidance the teacher/coach needs to be aware of the following points:
- Do not speak for too long – sports performers are usually action-driven and appreciate brief, clear guidance.
- Some movements simply cannot be explained – stick to visual guidance in these cases.
- Direct verbal guidance is better in the early stages to ensure that the learner has a clear idea of what needs to be done.
- Questioning techniques can encourage personal development and develop confidence if handled in the right way, especially for the more advanced performers.

Feedback from the performers will also test understanding.

Advantages:
- Can be given immediately and quickly.
- Good for fine tuning a skill or developing skilled movements.
- Can be motivating and can, along with a visual, develop a better understanding of the skill.

Disadvantages:
- Might be the wrong information given.
- Can lead to misunderstanding/confusion.
- Cannot easily create a mental picture of movement requirements.

Manual and mechanical guidance

Manual guidance is giving physical support, often by the coach, whereas mechanical guidance involves using equipment to support and guide the performer. This involves two factors:

1. **Physical support for the performer by another person or a mechanical device**. This is commonly known as 'physical restriction'. An example of this is supporting a gymnast over a vault or the use of a twisting belt in trampolining.

2. **The response of the performer being directed physically by another person**. This is commonly known as 'forced response'. Holding the arms of a golfer and forcing their arms through the movement of a drive is an example of forced response.

Advantages:

- Manual/mechanical guidance can reduce fear in dangerous situations. For instance, wearing armbands will help in learning how to swim.
- Can be much safer for the performer and therefore raise confidence.
- This method of guidance can give some idea of the feeling (kinaesthesis) of the movement.

Disadvantages:

- It could give unrealistic 'feeling' of the motion. For example, it is advisable to remove the armbands as soon as possible to be able to teach stroke technique in swimming.
- Performer becomes over-reliant on support and therefore does not learn to perform themselves.
- Can be dangerous if the mechanical guidance malfunctions or the physical guidance is weak or inappropriate.
- The **kinaesthetic sense** of cycling with stabilisers will be different to the feelings that you get from muscles when you are cycling without mechanical help. The same when you are learning to swim with armbands. Therefore, it is important to get the 'true' sense of the skill as quickly as you can in skill learning.

> **STUDY HINT**
> Learn a range of advantages and disadvantages for the different types of guidance and be able to give practical examples to support your statements.

Key term

Kinaesthetic sense This is the feeling or sense that we get through movement. Nerve receptors, called proprioceptors, found in muscles, ligaments and joints, pick up signals that feed back to the brain to tell us where we are and what we are doing.

Feedback

Feedback can be given during the performance of a motor skill or after its completion or even during it. Feedback is most effective if it is given close to the performance so the performance is fresh in the participant's mind. Feedback motivates, changes performance or actually reinforces learning. The more precise the feedback, the more beneficial it is.

There are several forms of feedback:

- **Intrinsic/internal feedback**: this is a type of continuous feedback that comes from within the performer, for example the 'feel' of the skill.
- **Extrinsic/external/augmented feedback**: feedback that comes from external sources, for example from sound or vision.
- **Knowledge of performance**: this is information about how well the movement is being executed, rather than the end result.
- **Knowledge of results**: this is a type of terminal feedback that gives the performer information about the end result of the response.
- **Positive feedback**: reinforces skill learning and gives information about a successful outcome.
- **Negative feedback**: information about an unsuccessful outcome, which can be used to build strategies that are more successful.

Application using practical examples:

- Intrinsic feedback, e.g. a swimmer diving off the blocks feels that their legs are straight.
- Extrinsic feedback, e.g. a hockey player sees the ball go into the net.

> **? Extend your knowledge**
>
> Other types of feedback include:
> - **continuous feedback:** feedback during the performance, either from the coach, instructor or teacher or from the continuous feel of the skill
> - **terminal feedback:** feedback after the response has been completed.

> **STUDY HINT**
>
> It is important to be able to make the links between feedback and performance in sport. Make sure you're able to give relevant practical examples linking different types of feedback to improving performance in physical activities and sport.

- Knowledge of performance – feedback about the quality of the performance, e.g. a coach informs a sprinter that their arms are in the correct position at 90 degrees.
- Knowledge of results – information relating to the end result, e.g. the goal keeper in football saves the penalty.
- Positive feedback, e.g. a teacher saying well done when a pass in netball is performed correctly/an ace is served in tennis.
- Negative feedback, e.g. a coach telling a badminton player that their grip is incorrect/doing a false start in swimming.

Two of these types of feedback are important for learning skills and sports performance:
- knowledge of results
- knowledge of performance.

Knowledge of results

This feedback is external and can come from the performer seeing the result of their response or from another person, usually a coach or teacher. It is extremely important for the performer to know what the result of their action has been. There can be very little learning without this type of feedback, especially in the early stages of skill acquisition.

Knowledge of performance

This is feedback about the pattern of movement that has taken, or is taking place. It is normally associated with external feedback but can be gained through kinaesthetic awareness, especially if the performer is highly skilled and knows what a good performance feels like.

Both knowledge of results and knowledge of performance can help with a performer's motivation and therefore help to improve performance, but if used incorrectly they can also demotivate. If the movement and/or the result is good then the performer will feel satisfaction. Knowing that the movement and results are good will help the performer form a picture of what is correct and associate future successful performance with that picture, image or model.

External feedback should be used with care because the performer may come to depend too heavily upon it and will not develop internal feedback. The type of feedback that should be given depends on the ability of the performer, the type of activity being undertaken and the personality of the performer – different performers respond differently to different types of feedback. For any sort of feedback to be effective, it needs to be accurate, understandable and given in a timely manner.

When performance is measured and this is given to performers as feedback, their motivation can be enhanced and their performance improved. Negative feedback can be used effectively at times as a motivational tool and to encourage self-reflection. Sports performers often set themselves targets from their previous performances, but teachers and coaches can help by constructing performance/goal charts that the performer updates as necessary. These charts serve as feedback on current performance and set clear and progressive targets (see goal setting in Chapter 4.2).

Chapter 4.4 Types of guidance and feedback

> **SUMMARY**
> - There are four main types of guidance and six main types of feedback in the OCR GCSE PE Specification.
> - Visual guidance is used in particular in the early stages of teaching a skill. Demonstrations are the most common form.
> - Verbal guidance is not terribly effective if used on its own, except with very able performers.
> - Manual and mechanical guidance are particularly important in the early stages of learning. They can help a performer cope with fear and can help with safety.
> - Feedback motivates, changes performance and actually reinforces learning.
> - Both knowledge of results and knowledge of performance can help with a performer's motivation and therefore help to improve performance.
> - For feedback to be effective, it needs to be accurate, understandable and given in a timely manner.

Practice questions

1. Using practical examples for each, describe the four types of guidance when coaching sport skills. **(4 marks)**
2. Explain one advantage and one disadvantage of using mechanical guidance when developing a motor skill in sport. **(2 marks)**
3. Give two examples of different types of verbal guidance when coaching skills in sport. **(2 marks)**
4. A coach gives a badminton player verbal feedback about errors in their forehand technique at the end of a training session. Other than being extrinsic, what type of feedback is this? **(1 mark)**
5. *With practical examples from different types of feedback, outline the importance of effective feedback in the learning and development of sports skills. **(6 marks)**

*This question includes an assessment of the quality of your written communication.

Section 5
Health, Fitness and Well-being

5.1 Health, fitness and well-being
5.2 Diet and nutrition

Chapter 5.1
Health, fitness and well-being

Understanding the Specification

You should know what is meant by health, fitness and well-being and understand the different health benefits of physical activity (including physical, emotional and social aspects) and consequences of a sedentary lifestyle.

You should be able to apply physical, emotional and social aspects to different age groups and be able to understand and explain the importance of data about health, fitness and well-being.

Key term

Healthy lifestyle The World Health Organization (WHO) defines health as 'a state of complete physical, mental, and social well-being and not merely the absence of disease or infirmity'.

Healthy lifestyle

Many studies have revealed that a balanced, **healthy lifestyle** will help you to feel better and live longer. Taking exercise, not drinking too much alcohol, eating enough fruit and vegetables and not smoking can add up to 14 years to your life.

? Extend your knowledge

Exercises reduce your risk of major illnesses, such as heart diseases and cancers, by up to 50 per cent and lowers your risk of early death by up to 30 per cent. It can also boost self-esteem, mood, sleep quality and energy, as well as reducing your risk of stress, depression and dementia. It is medically proven that people who do regular physical activity have:

- up to 35 per cent lower risk of coronary heart disease and stroke
- up to 50 per cent lower risk of type 2 diabetes
- around 30 per cent lower risk of early death
- up to 83 per cent lower risk of osteoarthritis
- up to 30 per cent lower risk of depression.

IN THE NEWS

Effect of the pandemic on health, fitness and well-being

The COVID-19 pandemic reinforced the importance of health, fitness and well-being.

Research showed that adults experienced high anxiety levels in the week immediately preceding lockdown and the two weeks which followed. This was around double the average for 2019. It declined through 2020 but was still above 2019 levels.

In April and May 2020, about a third of adults reported doing at least 30 minutes of physical activity on five or more days in the previous week. Later that year, there was a decrease to slightly over a quarter reporting this level of physical activity. Just under a third of parents reported that their children were doing more physical activity compared with before lockdown, although just over a third said they were doing less.

A healthy, balanced lifestyle means different things to different people and different cultures. In the UK, there is general agreement that the following contribute to a healthy, balanced lifestyle:

- eating a healthy and balanced diet
- regular exercise – the current government recommendation is that adults should carry out a minimum of 30 minutes' moderate physical activity on five or more days a week, while children and young people aged 5–18 should participate in physical activity of moderate intensity for 1 hour a day

Chapter 5.1 Health, fitness and well-being

- maintaining a healthy body weight
- not smoking
- sensible alcohol consumption
- minimising stress.

An unhealthy lifestyle often includes the following:

- poor diet, e.g. excess fat, salt, sugar, protein and insufficient complex carbohydrate, vitamin/mineral and fluid intake
- inactivity and lack of exercise
- being overweight, which increases risk of certain types of cancers, high blood pressure, heart disease and diabetes
- smoking, which causes lung cancer, heart disease, chronic bronchitis, emphysema and is a risk factor for many cancers
- excess alcohol consumption, which increases risk of liver disease and mouth, throat and oesophageal (food pipe) cancer and can contribute to obesity
- high stress levels, whether associated with work, ineffective time management, or general lifestyle habits.

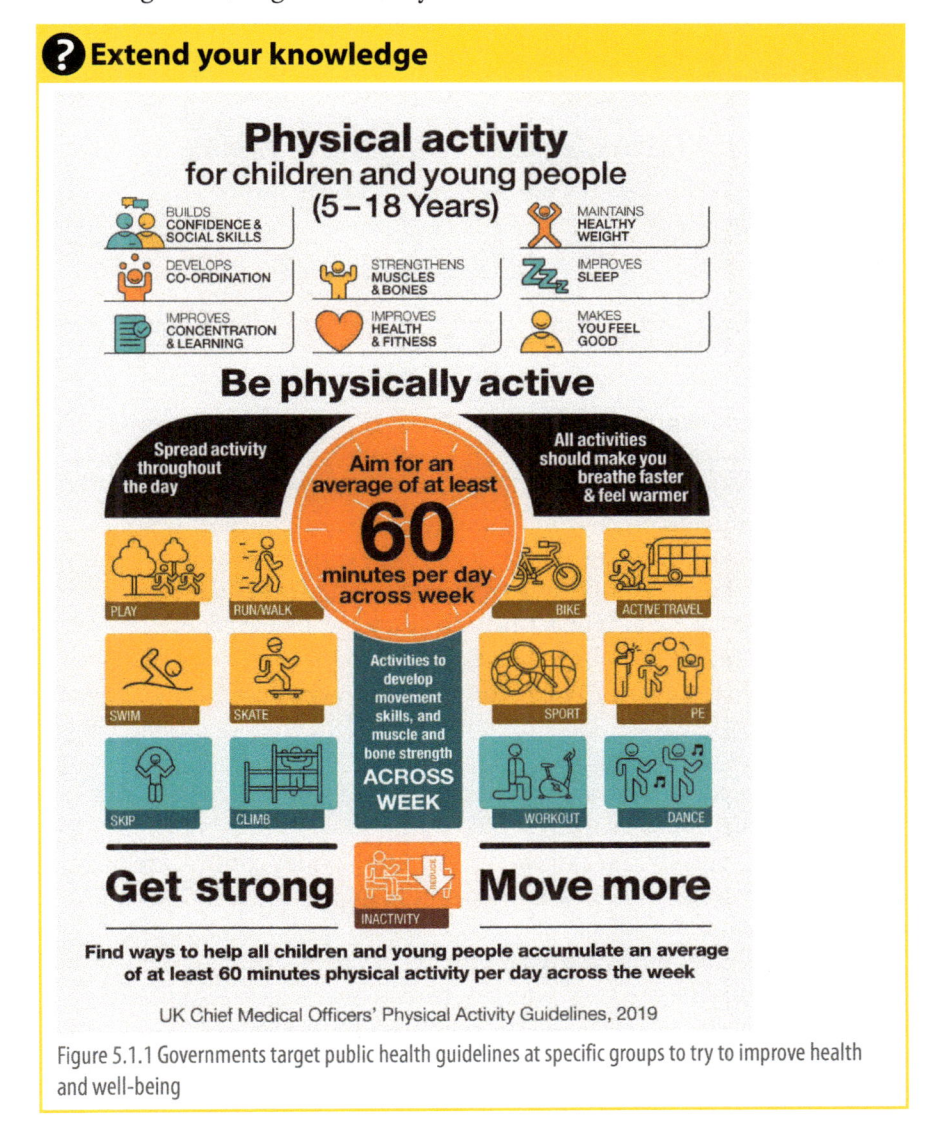

> **? Extend your knowledge**

Figure 5.1.1 Governments target public health guidelines at specific groups to try to improve health and well-being

> **Activity**
>
> 1. Read through the information shown in Figure 5.1.1 about the benefits of exercise on health for young people.
> 2. Identify the main physical, emotional and social benefits of exercise for young people.
> 3. Try to draw your own infographic to show the consequences of following a sedentary lifestyle. Refer to tables 5.1.1, 5.1.2 and 5.1.3 to help you.

Section 5 Health, Fitness and Well-being

Key term

Fitness Usually related to physical fitness, this is a person's capacity to carry out life's activities without getting too tired. It is often used as a measure of the body's ability to function efficiently and effectively.

Fitness

The term **fitness** is often used loosely, and frequently refers to aerobic endurance or how far you can run without getting too much out of breath. Fitness is more complex than that. It involves many different components or parts. Depending on the type of sport you are involved with you may be very fit in one component but not in another. For example, strength and power are very important to the discus thrower in athletics but less important in cross country. All sports activities, however, require a good general level of fitness for all components. For some team games, all components of fitness are equally important, although this may vary depending on what position you play. The following are recognised as the main components of physical fitness (more detail in Chapter 2.1):

- **Strength**: the ability of a muscle to exert force for a short period of time.

▲ Figure 5.1.2 Strength is the ability of a muscle to exert force for a short period of time

- **Muscular endurance**: the ability of the muscle or group of muscles to repeatedly contract or keep going without rest, e.g. being able to keep playing table tennis shots.
- **Aerobic endurance**: the ability to continuously exercise without getting tired, e.g. playing a full game of rugby without resting.
- **Flexibility**: the amount or range of movement that you can have around a joint, e.g. being able to stretch for a low ball in tennis.
- **Power**: a combination of strength and speed, often referred to as fast strength, e.g. being able to throw a javelin with strength and speed.
- **Speed**: the ability of the body to move quickly, e.g. in netball, being able to intercept the ball quickly.
- **Body composition**: the way in which your body is made up, e.g. the physical structure of a rugby prop forward.
- **Agility**: how quickly you can change direction under control, e.g. being able to move your wheelchair into position in wheelchair basketball.
- **Co-ordination**: the ability to perform tasks in sport, for example, running and then passing a ball in rugby.
- **Balance**: the ability to keep your body mass over a base of support, e.g. a gymnast performing a handstand on a balance beam.
- **Reaction time**: the time it takes someone to make a decision to move, e.g. how quickly a sprinter reacts to the gun and decides to drive off the blocks.

Chapter 5.1 Health, fitness and well-being

▲ Figure 5.1.3 Speed is the ability of the body to move quickly

STUDY HINT
Be prepared to comment on and analyse data related to health, fitness and well-being.
For example:
Look at the data referred to in this chapter and draw a graph to show how the risks of major illnesses can be lessened when we undertake regular exercise.

Well-being

Many people report that they feel better after participating in sport. It is accepted that certain hormones are released during exercise and that these can help us to feel more optimistic about life and better about ourselves.

There is of course the additional benefit of meeting and participating with other people. New friends can be made through sport, which is an important factor in our sense of **well-being**.

An active lifestyle often includes the following benefits:

- Keeps the heart muscles in shape and makes the heart a more efficient pump.
- Increases blood flow and contributes to a reduction in risk factors for coronary heart disease.
- Reduces blood pressure, which is good because there is more stress on the arterial walls and this could cause a stroke or kidney failure.
- Reduces stress, which makes us feel better.
- Reduces diabetes risk, because an increase in body fat is often linked with type 2 diabetes.
- Increases 'good' cholesterol, which in this case is beneficial because 'good' cholesterol helps transport 'bad' cholesterol away and reduces the risk of heart disease.
- Promotes a feeling of well-being.
- Promotes a better social life/making friends.

Physical activity and sport can really help people to remain healthy and combat disease. A **sedentary** lifestyle (lack of physical activity) has many disadvantages and can cause mental and physical illness.

Key terms

Well-being This refers to a feeling or mental state of being contented, happy, prosperous and healthy.

Sedentary This describes a lifestyle that is inactive and involves much sitting down. For example, if you worked on a computer all day in an office and then went home to sit and watch TV, your lifestyle could be described as sedentary.

161

Section 5 Health, Fitness and Well-being

▼ Table 5.1.1 A summary of the physical benefits from exercise and the consequences of a sedentary lifestyle

Factor (physical)	Benefit from exercise	Consequence of inactivity
Injury	Exercise will help injuries to heal and enable the body to retain its fitness levels – exercise could also cause injuries (see Chapter 2.3)	More likely to suffer stresses and strains through ordinary life activities because of the lack of physical fitness
Coronary heart disease (CHD)	Less likely to suffer from CHD. Exercise will help to keep the heart and blood supply healthy	Lack of exercise may cause CHD with poor blood and oxygen circulation and build-up of fat in the arteries
Blood pressure	More likely to be the normal levels for a healthy person	More likely to be raised, with health consequences (such as hypertension)
Bone density	More likely for bones to have normal bone density and less likely to be damaged during everyday activities. During sport type exercise, there is less risk of healthy bones being broken	Bone density not as healthy as an active individual with bones more likely to be weaker and more liable to damage
Obesity	Less likely for someone to be obese if regular exercise is a feature of their lifestyle. Exercise will ensure that energy taken in by the body is used well and less likely for fat deposits to be created around the body and its organs	More likely for the body's BMI to show too much body fat and therefore causing diseases such as CHD
Type 2 diabetes	This is less likely for those who exercise regularly with people having lower body fat and more normal blood sugar levels	This is more likely for those who are inactive. The body does not produce enough insulin and too much glucose remains in the blood. It is more associated with obesity and older people
Posture	Posture is more likely to be normal, with fewer problems with the muscles of the back. Activity can of course affect posture through injury	Poor posture can lead to muscle and skeletal damage and this is more associated with those who are inactive
Fitness	The more active you are, the much more likely you are to be fit and therefore have more energy for everyday life	If you are inactive, you are more likely to be unfit and therefore will tire easily and be more likely to suffer from muscle damage

Emotional health benefits of physical activity and consequences of a sedentary lifestyle

▼ Table 5.1.2 The emotional health benefits of physical activity and the consequences of a sedentary lifestyle

Factor (emotional)	Benefit from exercise	Consequence of inactivity
Self-esteem/confidence	Exercise can help you feel better about yourself and feel confident in the way you look and that you can achieve fitness goals. Activity can help to release hormones that make you feel better and happier	Inactive people may well have low self-esteem because they lack energy but also because they are more likely to be obese, which can also be a contributory factor for low self-esteem
Stress management	An active person often feels that the stresses of everyday life can be forgotten or released through exercise and so they manage stress more effectively	When inactive, a person may dwell on life's difficulties and may not have enough outlets to get rid of stress and anxiety
Image	An active person is more likely to have a good level of self-image. In other words, they feel that they look good to themselves and to others	Inactive people can have a poor self-image. This feeling of inadequacy can arise from poor body image, which can, in some cases, be related to obesity or sometimes those who are extremely underweight

Social health benefits of physical activity and consequences of a sedentary lifestyle

▼ Table 5.1.3 The social health benefits of physical activity and consequences of a sedentary lifestyle

Factor (social)	Benefit from exercise	Consequence of inactivity
Friendship	Exercise can help people make friends with others who are involved in physical activities. The improved levels of self-esteem may also help people to make friends with others	A sedentary lifestyle can result in a person not going out very much and not meeting people. Inactive people may also have lower levels of confidence
Belonging to a group	Exercise enables people to belong to a team or an exercise class or a jogging club, for example. There are many opportunities for the more active to join groups and gain a sense of belonging	Inactivity can result in isolation for an individual and therefore that person may not feel they are part of a community and they could become dispirited
Loneliness	Exercise gives many opportunities to meet and be with other participants. Sports teams often have friendship groups within them, but also a collective identity. Those in a team can feel that they belong and therefore are less likely to be isolated	Inactivity can result in a lack of people to talk to and this social isolation can lead to loneliness

Section 5 Health, Fitness and Well-being

? Extend your knowledge

Sedentary lifestyles

The Department of Health has called inactivity the 'silent killer'. Evidence suggests it is bad for your health if you spend long periods sitting or lying down. Another name for this is 'sedentary behaviour' and it can include sitting down for long periods to chat, read, listen to music, watch TV or use a computer. Using your car rather than walking a short distance would also be described as sedentary behaviour.

It is believed that if you spend too much time being immobile, you increase your risk of gaining weight/becoming obese and developing several chronic conditions including type 2 diabetes, stroke and heart disease.

STUDY HINT

When preparing for the examination in this topic area, divide up physical, emotional and social aspects of health and show how health, fitness and well-being can affect each aspect.

Physical	Emotional	Social
Injury Coronary heart disease (CHD) Blood pressure Bone density Obesity Type 2 diabetes Posture Fitness	Self-esteem/confidence Stress management Image	Friendship Belonging to a group Loneliness

? Extend your knowledge

Indicators of health and well-being

- **Satisfaction with aspects of life.** How satisfied do we feel about our lives overall? This does not mean that you will feel deliriously happy about everything, but overall to be a healthy and balanced individual, you need to be pretty satisfied with the way things are generally going.

- **Frequency of positive and negative feelings.** How often do you feel very positive about life around you and how often do you have negative thoughts? The more positive thoughts you have, the more healthy and balanced you are likely to be, both mentally and physically.

- **Frequency of feelings or activities that may have a positive or negative impact on well-being.** Some of the feelings that you have or activities that you are involved in may have a real impact on how you feel; others often do not. For example, if you regularly play sport, you may feel excited and enjoy being with others; this has a positive impact on the way you feel. If you are taking illegal drugs or are consuming too much alcohol, this may also make you feel good in the short term but may have a lasting negative impact on your health and well-being.

- **Access to green space.** Do you have places around you that give you a sense of space? Those who live in overcrowded conditions and do not have anywhere around them that is spacious and has vegetation may well feel less good about their lives, which may have a negative impact on their health and well-being.

- **Level of participation in other activities.** Those who are active in many different ways are often the happiest. This is not always the case, but usually if you have a variety of interests, you have a better view of yourself and others.

- **Positive mental health.** If you feel happy, optimistic about the future and feel proactive, then you are more likely to have positive mental health. Those who are more relaxed, feel interested in other people and deal with problems well are also said to have positive mental health.

> **Activity**
>
> **Well-being: how do you feel?**
>
> Below are some statements about feelings and thoughts. Tick the statements that best describe your experience over the last two weeks.
>
> - I've been feeling optimistic about the future.
> - I've been feeling proactive.
> - I've been feeling relaxed.
> - I've been feeling interested in other people.
> - I've had energy to spare.
> - I've been dealing with problems well.
> - I've been thinking clearly.
> - I've been feeling good about myself.
> - I've been feeling close to other people.
> - I've been feeling confident.
> - I've been able to make up my own mind about things.
> - I've been feeling loved.
> - I've been interested in new things.
> - I've been feeling cheerful.
>
> Once you have thought about your responses, rate yourself out of 10 for how good you feel. Are there any areas listed that you have little control over, and if so, what can you do?

SUMMARY

- Health is a state of complete physical, mental and social well-being and not merely the absence of disease or infirmity.
- Sedentary is a word to describe a lifestyle that is inactive and involves much sitting down.
- Well-being refers to a feeling or mental state of being contented, happy, prosperous and healthy.
- Fitness – usually related to physical fitness – is a person's capacity to carry out life's activities without getting too tired.
- The main consequences of a sedentary lifestyle are injury, CHD, high blood pressure, low bone density, obesity, type 2 diabetes, poor posture and low fitness levels.
- The main emotional consequences include low self-esteem, poor stress management and poor self-image.
- The main social consequences of a sedentary lifestyle include few friends, a lack of a sense of belonging to a group and loneliness.
- Different age groups are affected in different ways.

Section 5 Health, Fitness and Well-being

Practice questions

1. Describe what is meant by health, fitness and well-being. **(3 marks)**
2. Which one of the following is a physical health benefit of participation in physical activity? **(1 mark)**
   a. Having a good sense of well-being.
   b. Bone density is decreased as a result of physical activities.
   c. You are less likely to suffer from type 2 diabetes.
   d. You gain much more confidence.
3. Give two practical examples of how exercise can improve health. **(2 marks)**
4. What is meant by a sedentary lifestyle? **(1 mark)**
5. Describe how posture can be improved through regular exercise. **(2 marks)**
6. *Explain three social benefits of regularly playing a team sport. Analyse how team sports can benefit emotional health. **(6 marks)**
7. It is medically proven that people who do regular physical activity have:
   - up to 35 per cent lower risk of coronary heart disease and stroke
   - up to 50 per cent lower risk of type 2 diabetes
   - around 30 per cent lower risk of early death
   - up to 83 per cent lower risk of osteoarthritis
   - up to 30 per cent lower risk of depression.

   Draw a graph to show the different effects of regular exercise on health.

   Choose two benefits and explain why exercise can lead to a lower risk of major illnesses. **(7 marks)**

*This question includes assessment of the quality of your written communication.

Chapter 5.2
Diet and nutrition

Understanding the Specification

You should know the definition and components of a balanced diet, as well as understand the effect of diet and hydration on energy use in physical activity.

You should be able to apply practical examples from physical activity and sport to diet and nutrition.

Diet and nutrition

The healthy diet

A **balanced diet** is a diet based on:

- starchy foods such as potatoes, bread, rice and pasta
- plenty of fruit and vegetables
- some protein-rich foods such as meat, fish and lentils
- some milk and dairy foods
- not too much fat, salt or sugar.

A balanced diet means eating a wide variety of foods in the right proportions and consuming the right amount of food and drink to achieve and maintain a healthy body weight.

The following are the main nutrients or essential components the body requires to follow an active, healthy lifestyle.

Carbohydrates

These are made up of the chemical elements of carbon, hydrogen and oxygen. Carbohydrates are primarily involved in energy production. There are two forms of carbohydrate:

- simple sugars – these provide a quick energy source and include glucose and fructose
- complex starches – these have many sugar units and are much slower in releasing energy.

Carbohydrates are very important to the athlete, especially in exercise that is highly intense. They are also essential to the nervous system and determine fat metabolism.

Key term

Balanced diet This involves taking the right amount or level of energy and nutrients that the body needs in its expenditure of energy. In other words, you need to have the energy output balancing with energy input. A balanced diet for humans is one that contains the correct proportions of carbohydrates, fats, proteins, vitamins, minerals, and water necessary to maintain good health.

Figure 5.2.1 Carbohydrates are very important to the athlete, especially in exercise that is highly intense

Section 5 Health, Fitness and Well-being

> **? Extend your knowledge**
>
> When exercise takes place, glycogen is broken down to glucose, which supplies muscles with energy. When glycogen stores are depleted, there is less energy available and the participant in exercise will become fatigued. If you are eating about 2 500 calories a day, the recommended daily intake of carbohydrate is at least 313 grams. For 2 000 calories, it is at least 250 g, and for 1 500 calories it is 188 g.

Carbohydrates are stored in the muscles and the liver as glycogen but in limited amounts that need to be replenished. Sources of carbohydrates include:

- complex – cereal, pasta, potatoes, bread, fruit
- simple – sugar, jam, confectionery, fruit juices.

It is recommended that about 60 per cent of an athlete's diet should consist of carbohydrates.

IN THE NEWS

The diet of a legendary gold medallist sprinter – the importance of protein

In the Rio Olympics in 2016, Usain Bolt became the first athlete to win gold in the 100-metre and 200-metre sprints at three consecutive games.

During the run up to the Olympics, Bolt would need more energy than during the actual Olympic Games. Like all sprinters, he would need to maintain a healthy, balanced diet while he was training but, unlike endurance athletes, he would not need to load up with carbohydrates (such as potatoes, pasta, rice, cereals and bread). Rather, he would need to eat plenty of protein which can be found in meat, fish, eggs and dairy, nuts and beans. This is because protein helps damaged muscle fibres to repair, recover and grow after training.

Like all elite sprinters, as the Olympic Games got closer, and having done most of his essential training, Bolt's energy requirements would actually be reduced and he would be in the business of maintaining his weight. He would also have the luxury of being able to eat pretty much what he wanted the night before a medal race. However, apart from sticking to a balanced diet, he would be advised to limit his fibre intake and avoid too much fat (which can sit heavily in the stomach). He would also be wise to only eat food he is familiar with; the night before a big race is not a good time to experiment with new dishes!

Although it is recommended that sprinters eat more protein (to ensure repair and growth), Bolt's recommended diet will be very similar to that of the average person. Most of us need to eat a well-balanced mix of carbohydrates, plus plenty of fruit and vegetables to ensure we get all the vitamins we need.

Figure 5.2.2 Usain Bolt at Rio in 2016 after winning gold in the 100-m and 200-m sprints at three consecutive Olympic Games

Fats

These are a major source of energy for athletes performing low-intensity endurance exercise. They play an important role in insulating the body. Fats or lipids are made up of carbon, hydrogen and oxygen but in different proportions to carbohydrates. There are two types:

- triglycerides, which are stored in the form of body fat
- fatty acids, which are used mainly as fuel for energy production; these are either **saturated fats** or **unsaturated fats**.

When muscles' cells are readily supplied with oxygen, fat is the usual fuel for energy production. This is because the body is trying to save the limited stores of glycogen for high-intensity exercise and therefore delays the onset of fatigue. The body cannot solely use fat for energy and so the muscle is fuelled by a combination of fat and glycogen.

Fat consumption should be carefully monitored and can cause obesity. Fat is very important to protect vital organs and is crucial for cell production and the control of heat loss. It is generally accepted that a maximum of 3 per cent of total calories consumed should be from fatty foods. Examples of sources of fats:

- saturated fats – meat products, dairy products, cakes, confectionery
- unsaturated fats – oily fish, nuts, margarine, olive oil.

Key terms

Saturated fats A saturated fat is in the form of a solid, e.g. lard, and is primarily from animal sources.

Unsaturated fats An unsaturated fat is in the form of liquid, e.g. vegetable oil, and comes from plant sources.

Obesity

The main measurement of obesity is the body mass index (BMI). This is your weight in kilograms divided by your height in metres squared.

$$BMI = \frac{Weight\ (kg)}{Height\ (m^2)}$$

For example, someone who weighs 100 kilograms and is 1.8 metres tall has a BMI of 30.86 (100 divided by 3.25 [1.8 squared]). Individuals are defined as being overweight if their BMI is 25–29.9 and obese if their BMI is 30 or over.

Obesity contributes to a range of problems, including heart disease, type 2 diabetes, osteoarthritis and some cancers. Experts say that obesity is as serious a health problem as smoking or excessive alcohol consumption.

Protein

Proteins are composed of carbon, hydrogen, oxygen and nitrogen and some contain minerals such as zinc. Proteins are known as the building blocks for body tissue and are essential for repair. They are also necessary for the production of haemoglobin, enzymes and hormones. Proteins are also potential sources of energy but are not used if fats and carbohydrates are in plentiful supply.

Protein should account for approximately 15 per cent of total calorie intake. If protein is taken excessively, then there are some health risks, for example kidney damage due to excreting so many unused amino acids. Examples of sources of protein:

- Meat, fish and poultry are the three primary complete proteins.

Vegetables and grains are called incomplete proteins because they do not supply all the essential amino acids.

Protein breaks down more readily during and immediately after exercise. The amount of protein broken down depends upon how long and how hard you exercise. Increased protein intake may be important during the early stages of training to support increases in muscle mass and myoglobin. The following nutrients are essential but needed in small quantities only and are often referred to as micronutrients.

IN THE NEWS

Dangers of being obese during a pandemic

US researchers claim that, if you are obese, you are more likely to develop diseases such as diabetes and high blood pressure. As well as a weakened immune system, this can make you more likely to suffer with severe COVID-19.

The US team's global research considered the data of almost 400 000 patients. Evidence showed that:

- obese people suffering with COVID-19 were twice as likely to need hospital treatment
- 74 per cent of these people were more likely to be admitted to intensive care units
- their risk of dying from COVID-19 was increased by almost 50 per cent.

This is accompanied by a warning that any vaccine against coronavirus would not work as well for obese people (based on the knowledge that flu vaccines are not as effective for people who have a BMI (body mass index) over 30).

Obesity rates are rising globally and 20 per cent of people in all countries are overweight or obese. In the UK and US, this figure is closer to 66 per cent. Therefore, the research concludes, it is critical that we gain an understanding of how treatments and vaccines work in this group.

Vitamins

Vitamins are non-caloric chemical compounds that are needed by the body in small quantities. They are an essential component of our diet because they are vital in the production of energy, the functioning of our metabolism and the prevention of disease. With the exception of vitamin D, the body cannot produce vitamins. Vitamins A, D, E and K are fat-soluble. Vitamins B and C are water-soluble.

A well-balanced diet will ensure sufficient vitamin intake. Vitamins can be found in fresh fruit and vegetables.

Extremely large doses of vitamins can be dangerous. An overdose of vitamin A can cause hair loss and enlargement of the liver. There is little evidence to suggest that supplementary vitamin pills can enhance performance and most excess vitamins are simply excreted via urine.

Minerals

These are also non-caloric and are inorganic elements essential for our health and for chemical reactions in our body. There are two types:

- macro-minerals – needed in large amounts, e.g. calcium, potassium and sodium
- trace elements – needed in very small amounts, e.g. iron, zinc and manganese.

Minerals can be lost through sweating and so there are implications for those who exercise. Minerals should be replaced quickly to ensure good health. Some important minerals are listed below.

Iron

This is an essential component of haemoglobin, which carries oxygen in the blood. Iron-deficiency anaemia can impair performance in endurance events.

> **? Extend your knowledge**
>
> To make sure you get enough vitamins from your food:
>
> - buy good-quality fresh fruit and vegetables
> - wash/scrub food rather than peeling it because vitamins are often found just below the skin
> - prepare just before cooking and boil for a short time and in as little water as possible; steaming or microwave cooking is even better
> - eat soon after cooking.

IN THE NEWS

Research has shown that 36–82 per cent of female runners are anaemic and therefore should seek iron-rich foods in their diets. Only a qualified medical doctor should prescribe iron supplements because too much iron can be dangerous. Iron can be found in meat, fish, dairy produce and vegetables. Main sources are red meat and offal.

Calcium

This mineral is essential for healthy bones and teeth. If there is deficiency in calcium, then there is an increased likelihood of osteoporosis and bone fractures. For calcium to be absorbed, there needs to be sufficient vitamin D, which is found in sunlight.

Calcium is found in milk and dairy products, green vegetables and nuts.

> **? Extend your knowledge**
>
> **Calcium deficiency**
>
> Calcium deficiency can be found in females who are underweight, smokers, alcoholics, vegans and those who overdo training and exercise.

Fibre

Fibre is essential to ensure a healthy, balanced diet. Fibre in foods is known as dietary fibre and is found in foods such as fruit and vegetables as well as cereals, beans, lentils and wholemeal bread.

For the digestive system to work effectively, it is important to consume dietary fibre. For the large intestine to work properly and waste to be excreted effectively by the body, dietary fibre should be part of your everyday diet. A high-fibre diet has also been shown to reduce cholesterol and to limit the risk of diabetes and obesity. The NHS advises that we consume about 18 grams of fibre per day. However, most do not reach this level.

Water and hydration

This is also a nutrient and is crucial for good health, particularly for those who participate in sport. It carries nutrients in the body and helps with the removal of waste products. It is also very important in the regulation of body temperature. The body loses water through urine and sweat. This

Section 5 Health, Fitness and Well-being

> **? Extend your knowledge**
>
> **Heat exhaustion**
>
> Heat exhaustion is a result of the body overheating, with heavy sweating and a rapid pulse. Without treatment, it can lead to heatstroke which can be very dangerous. The signs of heat exhaustion (NHS 2021) include:
>
> - a headache
> - dizziness and confusion
> - loss of appetite and feeling sick
> - excessive sweating and pale
> - clammy skin
> - cramps in the arms, legs and stomach
> - fast breathing or pulse
> - a high temperature
> - being very thirsty.
>
> If someone is showing signs of heat exhaustion, they need to be cooled down to avoid heatstroke. Contact a doctor if the symptoms worsen or if they do not improve within one hour. If you are with someone showing signs of heat exhaustion, seek immediate medical attention if he or she becomes confused or agitated, loses consciousness, or is unable to drink. They will need immediate cooling and urgent medical attention if their core body temperature reaches 40 °C or higher.

water loss accelerates depending on the environment and the duration and intensity of any exercise.

On average, individual daily consumption of water should be about 2 litres. Those involved in exercise should take more to ensure a good state of hydration. Studies show that individuals who are dehydrated become intolerant to exercise and heat stress. The cardiovascular system becomes inefficient if there is dehydration and there is an inability to provide adequate blood flow to the skin, which may lead to heat exhaustion. Fluids must be taken in during prolonged exercise. This will minimise dehydration and slow the rise in body temperature.

There are a number of commercially available sports drinks containing electrolytes and carbohydrates. Some of the claims that are made about these drinks have been misinterpreted. A single meal, for instance, can replace the minerals lost during exercise. Water is the primary need in any drink taken before, during and after exercise because it empties from the stomach extremely quickly and reduces dehydration associated with sweating. Thirst is not a reliable indicator for fluid intake; therefore it is best to drink small amounts regularly even if you are not thirsty. Under cooler conditions, a carbohydrate drink may give the extra energy needed in events or periods of exercise lasting over an hour.

Composition of a healthy diet

Healthy eating involves a daily calorie intake in approximately the following proportions:

- 50 per cent carbohydrate
- 30–35 per cent fat
- 15–20 per cent protein.

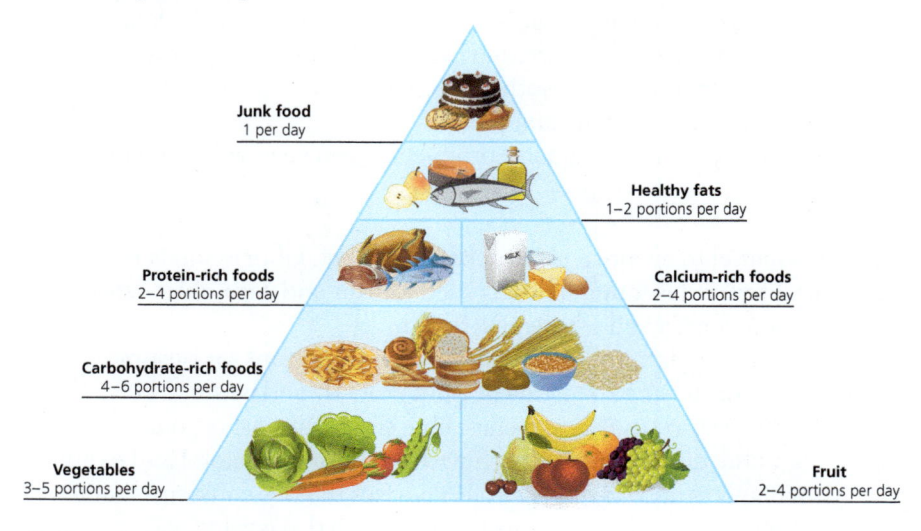

▲ Figure 5.2.3 The nutrition pyramid

When planning your diet, you should also take the following into consideration:

- Food is meant to be enjoyed.
- Avoid too much fat.
- Avoid too many sugary foods.

- Include vitamins and minerals.
- Eat plenty of fibre.
- Keep alcohol within prescribed limits (for those over 18).
- Maintain balance of intake and output.
- Eat plenty of fruit and vegetables.

The Health Development Agency and the National Institute for Health and Clinical Excellence recommend the following as the maximum intake of alcohol for adults (over 18s):

- males – 3–4 units per day
- females – 2–3 units per day.

Most advisers agree that 'binge drinking', a growing habit among teenagers and young adults, is particularly bad for you. If you are of the legal age to drink, it is better to spread your alcohol consumption across the week and to leave some alcohol-free days.

One unit:

- half pint 'ordinary strength' beer = 3.0–3.5 per cent alcohol = 90 calories
- 1 standard glass of wine = 11 per cent alcohol = 90 calories
- single measure spirits = 38 per cent alcohol = 50 calories.

Extend your knowledge

Alcohol and exercise

Whatever your level of exercise, it is important to understand the two main detrimental effects of alcohol on your sporting performance:

1. Alcohol makes your kidneys produce more urine (it's a diuretic) – so the more alcohol you drink, the more dehydrated you can become. If you exercise soon after drinking, the problem is compounded when your body temperature rises and you lose more fluid through sweat. It is important to stay well hydrated during exercise to maintain your blood flow, ensuring that oxygen is circulated and your muscles receive all the nutrients they need.
2. Alcohol gets in the way of your body making energy. When the body is trying to break down alcohol, the liver is unable to produce as much glucose, and in turn this reduces blood sugar levels. You need high sugar levels when you are exercising to give you energy. Therefore, sporting performance is affected if the liver cannot produce enough glucose, with an accompanying reduction in reaction times, concentration and co-ordination.

Each of these effects happen immediately so you should not exercise or take part in any competitive sport soon after you have drunk alcohol.

There are no healthy or unhealthy foods, there are only bad uses of food. The right balance in a diet is essential for health and fitness. Enjoyment is an important aspect of eating; a healthy diet does not mean that you have to give up all your favourite 'bad' foods – it is the overall balance that counts. Balanced meals contain starchy foods with plenty of vegetables, salad and fruit. Your fat content should be kept to a minimum by using low-fat or lean ingredients.

Section 5 Health, Fitness and Well-being

> **? Extend your knowledge**
>
> What is a portion of fruit or vegetables?
> - 2 tablespoons of vegetables
> - 1 dessert bowlful of salad
> - 1 apple/orange/banana
> - 2 plums
> - 1 cupful of grapes/cherries
> - 2 tablespoons of fresh fruit salad
> - 1 tablespoon dried fruit
> - 1 glass fruit juice

Factors that also affect choice of foods include:
- culture, morals, ethics
- family influences
- peer-group influences
- lifestyle
- finance.

Eating sufficient fruit and vegetables is important for a healthy diet. It helps to reduce the likelihood of coronary heart disease and some cancers. Government guidelines suggest that you should eat at least five portions of fruit and vegetables each day. This is not a scientifically proven formula but it gives us useful guidance about roughly the right levels of intake.

Most healthy eating guidelines warn against eating too much salt. If your diet contains too much salt, this may lead to high blood pressure, which can cause heart and kidney disease.

NICE (National Institute for Health and Care Excellence) recommends eating a healthy diet, which means you and your family should:

- base your meals on starchy foods such as potatoes, bread, rice and pasta, choosing wholegrain where possible
- eat plenty of fibre-rich foods such as oats, beans, peas, lentils, grains, seeds, fruit and vegetables, as well as wholegrain bread, and brown rice and pasta
- eat at least five portions of a variety of fruit and vegetables a day in place of foods higher in fat and calories
- avoid foods containing a lot of fat and sugar, such as fried food, sweetened drinks, sweets and chocolate (some takeaways and 'fast' foods contain a lot of fat and sugar)
- eat breakfast
- watch the portion sizes of meals and snacks, and how often you are eating
- avoid taking in too many calories from alcohol.

Effective nutritional strategies for those who exercise regularly

Glycogen stores

Ensuring that the body has enough glycogen is crucial for optimum energy supply. One method of increasing the glycogen available is through glycogen 'loading', sometimes known as carb-loading. This process involves the sports person depleting their stores of glycogen by cutting down on carbohydrates and keeping to a diet of protein and fat for three days. Light training follows, with a high-carbohydrate diet for three days leading up to the event. This has been shown to significantly increase the stores of glycogen and helps to offset fatigue. When carb-loading, the diet should consist mainly of foods like pasta, bread, rice and fruit. Generally a high-carbohydrate diet will ensure that glycogen will be replenished during exercise.

Other energy-giving strategies:
- Consume carbohydrates 2–4 hours before exercise.
- Consume a small amount of carbohydrates within the first half an hour of exercise to ensure refuelling of glycogen.
- Eat carbohydrates straight after exercise for up to two days to replenish stores.

Fluids

> **? Extend your knowledge**
>
> ### Hydration and exercise
> In order to gain the best sporting performance and recovery, it is vital that you drink enough fluid. When you exercise, your body sweats in a bid to cool itself down, and you lose water and salts. People differ in how much sweat they produce and this depends on:
> - genetics – it is a fact that some people produce more sweat than others
> - clothing – if you are wearing more clothing, you will warm up more quickly and so produce more sweat
> - the amount and intensity of exercise – the longer and harder you exercise, the more you will sweat
> - the ambient temperature – you will produce more sweat if you are exercising in a hot and humid climate.
>
> It is estimated that on average between 0.5 to 2 litres of sweat are produced per hour during exercise. Therefore, the more you sweat, the more you should drink to replace lost fluids.
>
> It is especially important that athletes, and people who are very active, manage their hydration levels carefully, particularly when they are training or competing. It is recommended that they drink before, during and after exercise. In order to rehydrate, they should aim to drink 1.25 to 1.5 litres of water per kilogram of their body weight lost through sweat when exercising. However, some sportspeople take part in exercise which is more intense and lasts longer than one hour (e.g. footballers and long-distance/marathon runners). During this kind of extended exercise, stores of carbohydrates and sodium can be significantly depleted. It may benefit them to consume drinks that include carbohydrates and electrolytes such as sodium.

You may lose up to 1 litre of water per hour during endurance exercise; therefore rehydration is essential, especially if there are also hot environmental conditions. As we have discovered, thirst is not a good indicator of dehydration, therefore the athlete needs to drink plenty during and after exercise even if they don't feel thirsty.
- Take fluids, preferably water, before exercise to ensure full hydration.
- Take fluids continuously during exercise even if not thirsty.
- Small amounts often is best.
- Take fluids straight after exercise before alcohol is consumed.
- Some sports-specific drinks may be useful for high-intensity and long-duration exercise.

Section 5 Health, Fitness and Well-being

▲ Figure 5.2.4 You may lose up to one litre of water per hour during endurance exercise; therefore rehydration is essential

Vitamin and mineral supplements

There is an increase in the body's requirements for vitamins and minerals if regular, intensive exercise takes place. This means that the athlete will eat more food because of the need for more energy. This in itself will mean that the body is receiving more vitamins and minerals. As we have already seen, large quantities of extra vitamins and minerals can damage health. Supplementing the athlete's diet can be beneficial in certain circumstances.

❓ Extend your knowledge

Supplements

(Please note that supplementation is best undertaken with medical supervision.)

- Smokers should consider extra vitamin C.
- If you are planning to become pregnant, it is recommended that you take folic acid.
- If you are on a diet and consuming less than 1 200 calories per day, supplements in low doses have been found to be beneficial.
- If you are vegan or vegetarian and your diet is therefore restricted, multi-vitamins and mineral supplements could be useful.

Factors to consider with sports performers and nutrition

Sports performers, especially at the top level, have certain aspects to their lifestyles that should be considered when planning nutritional intake:

- timing of meals to fit around training and events
- ensuring that there is balance in the diet
- ensuring adequate fluid intake
- ensuring adequate iron intake

- diet should be suitable for very high workload, depending on the activity
- psychological well-being – if an athlete is unhappy with the diet, then even if physiologically beneficial, it could negatively affect performance because of psychological pressure
- there should be a sharing of ideas between coach/dietician and performer to agree the best strategy, depending on an individual's needs and perceptions
- obsession with food is common with high-performance athletes and should be avoided.

IN THE NEWS

Interview with a Paralympian about their diet

Ross Wilson is GB's bronze medal winner for table tennis in the Rio Paralympics. He is the reigning World and Commonwealth Games champion and looking to add Paralympic gold in the Paralympic Games in Tokyo.

Figure 5.2.5 Ross Wilson, Paralympic table tennis player

Typical daily diet when training for a big event?
Breakfast: I have cereal most mornings at about 8 a.m.
Lunch: I tend to eat good carbohydrates for lunch to give me plenty of energy – something like chicken and rice, usually at around 12.30 p.m.
Dinner: I try to eat something healthy like an omelette at around 8 p.m.
How do you keep your diet varied and do you ever get bored with eating for your sport?
I ensure I shake up my menu every two to three days to ensure I don't get bored of the foods I'm eating.

Section 5 Health, Fitness and Well-being

> What super food/juice/meal helps you get out of bed and motivated on those particularly dreary mornings?
> *Just the thought of my regular breakfast helps me get up in the mornings. My usual breakfast would probably include orange juice, an apple and some cereal.*
> What's your trusted snack for an energy boost?
> *I make sure I have a cereal bar on hand as the simple carbohydrates release energy quickly into the body and give me the boost I need.*
> How do you stay hydrated when training?
> *I drink a lot of water to ensure I stay hydrated but sometimes have an energy drink as well.*
> When competition season is over what are your favourite food indulgences?
> *I love takeaways, so will usually treat myself to one or two when not getting ready for a competition.*
> What would be your top diet and exercise tip for the amateur athlete?
> *Eating a balanced diet full of foods that you love would be my tip – it's the only way I can stick to a healthy eating plan.*
>
> Source: bbcgoodfood.com

STUDY HINT
Know the components of a balanced diet and be able to give examples for each:
- ✔ carbohydrates
- ✔ proteins
- ✔ fats
- ✔ minerals
- ✔ vitamins
- ✔ fibre
- ✔ water and hydration.

SUMMARY
- A balanced diet involves matching the energy being expended with that being consumed.
- The main measurement of obesity is the body mass index (BMI).
- Water carries nutrients in the body and helps with the removal of waste products. It is also very important in the regulation of body temperature.
- Carbohydrates are primarily involved in energy production, fats are a major source of energy and insulating the body, proteins help to build body tissue and are essential for repair.
- Vitamins are an essential component of our diet because they are vital in the production of energy and the prevention of disease.
- Minerals are essential for our health and for chemical reactions in our body.
- One method of increasing the glycogen available is through glycogen 'loading', sometimes known as carb-loading.

✔ Check your understanding

1. What is the definition of a balanced diet?
2. What are the components of a balanced diet?
3. What is the function of each component and why is each so important for an athlete?
4. What is the effect of hydration on energy use in physical activity?

Practice questions

1. Is this statement true or false? **(1 mark)**

   A balanced diet is the amount of energy expended matching the amount of energy taken in through food.

2. Vitamins make up one component of a balanced diet.

   Give three other components of a balanced diet and give a food example for each. **(3 marks)**

3. Which one of the following is the main function of proteins? **(1 mark)**
   a. To deliver oxygen to muscles
   b. To fight disease
   c. To enable bones to repair
   d. To provide fibre for the digestive system.

4. What might happen if a sports performer lacks hydration during competition? **(1 mark)**

5. Other than water, which other component of a healthy diet is important for a marathon runner and why? **(3 marks)**

6. *You are a coach to a long-distance swimmer.

   Using your knowledge of diet and nutrition, explain the advice about daily nutrition that you would give to a long-distance swimmer the week before a major competition. **(6 marks)**

*This question includes an assessment of the quality of your written communication.

Glossary

Adrenaline – This is a hormone released from the adrenal glands and its major action is to prepare the body for 'fight or flight'.

Agonist – This is the muscle that initiates a movement. It is also called the prime mover.

Anaerobic – This is when the body is working without the presence of oxygen, for example, lifting something quickly off the floor or doing an activity such as sprinting for a ball. This type of activity can be carried out only for a short amount of time because of the lack of oxygen and the build-up of lactic acid.

Anticipatory rise – This is the raising of the heart rate before exercise begins. It is caused through the release of adrenaline, which is a hormone.

Antagonistic pair – This is a pair of muscles that work together: as one muscle contracts, the other muscle relaxes.

Anxiety – The feeling of fear that we experience that something might go wrong either in the present or in the future.

Articulating bones – These are the bones that move within a joint.

Axes of rotation – The centre around which something rotates.

Balanced diet – This involves taking the right amount or level of energy and nutrients that the body needs in its expenditure of energy. In other words, you need to have the energy output balancing with energy input. A balanced diet for humans is one that contains the correct proportions of carbohydrates, fats, proteins, vitamins, minerals and water necessary to maintain good health.

Ballistic stretching – This uses the momentum (a tendency for the body to keep moving) of a moving body or a limb in an attempt to force it beyond its normal range of motion. This is different from dynamic stretching, which involves controlled gradual stretching up to but not beyond the normal range of movement.

Blood viscosity – This refers to the thickness of the blood and how resistant the blood is to flow freely. The more viscous the blood, the more it resists free flow. The amount of plasma or water content of the blood affects the viscosity. Therefore to ensure fast blood flow, the plasma level needs also to be high.

Body dysmorphia – An obsessive mental health disorder where someone cannot stop thinking about an imagined or slight flaw, or flaws, in their physical appearance. (Muscle dysmorphia is when someone perceives themselves to be thin, physically weak and small, regardless of their actual physical size, and despite often being large and muscular.)

Breathing rate – Sometimes called the respiratory rate or ventilation rate, it is the frequency of breathing measured in breaths per minute. Normal breathing rate at rest is approximately 12 breaths per minute.

Cardiovascular – Cardio means heart, vascular means circulatory networks of the blood vessels.

Cognitive anxiety management techniques – Those ways of coping that affect the mind and therefore can control anxiety.

Cognitive skills – These are skills that involve the intellectual ability of the performer. These skills affect the perceptual process and help us to make sense of what is required in any given situation. They are essential if the performer is to make correct and effective decisions.

Commercialisation – This refers to the influence of commerce, trade or business on an industry (e.g. sport) to make a profit.

Co-ordination – This is the ability to repeat a pattern or sequence of movements with fluency and accuracy.

Deviance – This involves human behaviour that is against your society's norms and values. Behaviour of this kind is often against the law.

Epiglottis – The main function of this flap of tissue is to close over the windpipe (trachea) while you are eating, to prevent food entering your airways.

Etiquette – This is about the customs we observe surrounding the rules and regulations of the physical activity and also about what is socially acceptable in a particular culture. It involves a convention or an accepted way of behaving in a particular situation.

Fast twitch muscle fibres – Sometimes called type 2 fibres. They are used to generate short bursts of speed or strength but these fibres fatigue very quickly.

Fitness – Usually related to physical fitness, this is a person's capacity to carry out life's activities without getting too tired. It is often used as a measure of the body's ability to function efficiently and effectively.

Gamesmanship – The use of unethical, although often not illegal, methods to win or gain a serious advantage in a game or sport.

Haemoglobin – This is iron-rich protein and transports oxygen in the blood. The more concentrated the haemoglobin, the more oxygen can be carried. This concentration can be increased through endurance training.

Hazard – Something that has the potential to cause harm.

Healthy lifestyle – The World Health Organization (WHO) defines health as 'a state of complete physical, mental, and social well-being and not merely the absence of disease or infirmity'.

Heart rate (HR) – This refers to the speed at which the heart beats (contractions of the ventricles) and is measured by beats per minute (bpm).

Hypertrophy – This term means that there is an increase in the size or the mass of an organ in the body or a muscle. Hypertrophy often occurs as a result of regular training or exercise and can lead to an increase in muscular strength and power.

Insertion – This is the end of the muscle attached to the bone that actively moves, e.g. the biceps insertion is on the radius.

Kinaesthetic sense – This is the feeling or sense that we get through movement. Nerve receptors, called proprioceptors, found in muscles, ligaments and joints, pick up signals that feed back to the brain to tell us where we are and what we are doing.

Lactic acid – With the absence of oxygen, lactic acid is formed in the working muscles. Lactic acid causes muscle pain and often this leads us to stop or reduce the activity we are doing.

Limiting disability and long-term health conditions – Defined as an individual reporting they have a physical or mental health condition or illness that has lasted or is expected to last 12 months or more, and that this has a substantial effect on their ability to do normal daily activities. (Sport England 2020).

Mechanical advantage – Some levers (first class and second class) provide mechanical advantage. This means that they allow you to move a large output load with a smaller effort. Load and effort are forces and are measured in Newtons (N).

Mechanical advantage is calculated as follows:

Mechanical advantage = Load ÷ Effort

For example, where the load = 500 N and the effort = 100 N, the mechanical advantage would be:

500 N ÷ 100 N = 5

Meniscus cartilage – In the knee, these are areas of cartilage tissue that act like shock absorbers in the joint.

Metabolism – This involves the many continuous chemical processes inside the body that are essential for living, moving and growing. The number of kilojoules the body burns is regulated by the rate of metabolism.

Mitochondria – These are parts of each muscle cell and places where energy is produced – sometimes referred to as 'powerhouses' of muscle cells. Those who exercise regularly and participate in endurance activities such as long-distance cycling often have more mitochondria.

Moderate activity – In September 2019, the Chief Medical Officer updated the guidelines on physical activity. Instead of the measure of children and young people doing 60 + minutes of moderate activity every day, this has now changed to 60 + minutes a day across the week. This effectively means they need to do 420 moderate minutes or more a week to meet the guidelines.

Motor skill – An action or task that has a target or goal and that requires voluntary body and/or limb movement to achieve this goal. There are two main ways of using the word 'skill':

a. To see skill as a specific task to be performed.
b. To view skill as describing the quality of a particular action, which might include how consistent the performance is and how prepared the performer is to carry out the task.

Muscular endurance – This is the ability of the muscle or group of muscles to repeatedly contract or keep going without rest.

Myoglobin – This is related to haemoglobin and is found in muscle cells that transport oxygen to the mitochondria to provide energy. Those who are more active – especially those who exercise regularly for endurance events such as marathon running – have higher levels of myoglobin.

Origin – This is the end of the muscle attached to a bone that is stable, e.g. the scapula. The point of origin remains still when contraction occurs.

Glossary

Osteoporosis – This is a disease in which bones become fragile and more likely to break. If not prevented or if left untreated, osteoporosis can progress painlessly until a bone breaks. These broken bones, also known as fractures, occur typically in the hip, spine and wrist.

Oxyhaemoglobin – Haemoglobin combines with oxygen in the lungs to form a bright red chemical called oxyhaemoglobin. When the blood gets to places where oxygen is being used up, oxyhaemoglobin releases the oxygen and turns back into haemoglobin.

Participation rates – This refers to the number of people within a group who are involved in sport compared with those who are not. For example, in a school the participation rates of girls in extra-curricular sport could be 30 per cent. In other words, three out of every ten girls in the school are regular members of a sports team or club.

Perception – A complex concept that involves interpretation of stimuli. Not all stimuli are perceived and what is perceived depends on experience and attention ability.

Personal protective equipment – PPE (including correct clothing and footwear) is defined by the government's Health and Safety Executive as 'all equipment (including clothing affording protection against the weather) which is intended to be worn or held by a person at work and which protects him (or her) against one or more risks to his health or safety'.

Power – This is a combination of strength and speed.

Prehabilitation – This term is not explicit in the OCR GCSE PE Specification but nevertheless is often used in the context of physical preparation in sport.

It is a term used to describe exercises before medical surgery but has been adopted by sports trainers to describe strength and conditioning exercises for specific muscles that help to reduce injury risks, before an injury occurs.

Prime mover – This is the muscle that initiates the movement and is also often called the agonist. A prime mover does not act alone – it acts simultaneously with other muscles to perform a specific movement.

Reaction time – This is the time it takes for you to initiate an action or movement, or the time it takes someone to make a decision to move, for example, how quickly a sprinter reacts to the gun and decides to drive off the blocks.

Recreation – Activities that you enjoy that are not work-related.

Redistribution of blood – This is also known as the vascular shunt mechanism, and involves two processes:

- The arterioles (smaller arteries) experience vasodilation (diameter increases) and this increases the blood flow. Vasoconstriction (diameter decreases) of the arterioles that supply other organs such as the liver means that blood flow is lessened to these organs that do not require as much blood supply.

- In the capillaries that supply the skeletal muscles the precapillary sphincters (valves) open up and blood flow is again increased. In the capillaries that supply other organs, the precapillary sphincters close, thus decreasing the blood flow.

Risk – The chance that someone will be harmed by the hazard.

Risk assessment – This is the technique by which you measure the chances of an accident happening, anticipate what the consequences would be and plan actions to prevent it.

Rooney Rule – This dictates that sporting authorities must interview a Black, Asian and Minority Ethnic (BAME) applicant when recruiting for senior coaching positions. There is no quota or preference given to minorities in the hiring of candidates. The rule is not restricted to sport and has been adopted across a number of other industries. The rule is named after Dan Rooney, former owner of the Pittsburgh Steelers in the USA and former chairman of the NFL's diversity committee.

Saturated fat A saturated fat is in the form of a solid, e.g. lard, and is primarily from animal sources.

Sedentary – This describes a lifestyle that is inactive and involves much sitting down. For example, if you worked on a computer all day in an office and then went home to sit and watch TV, your lifestyle could be described as sedentary.

Slow twitch fibres (sometimes called type 1 muscle fibres) –These are muscle fibres that can produce energy over a long period of time. They have high levels of myoglobin and mitochondria and are used for mainly aerobic activities.

Somatic anxiety management techniques – Those ways of coping that affect the body directly such as relaxation. Cognitive can affect somatic and vice versa.

Glossary

Sport – This involves organised competition between individuals or teams that includes physical activity.

Sport England – Previously known as the English Sports Council, this organisation tries to help communities develop sporting habits for life. It funds other organisations and projects to get people more involved in sport and to help those who wish to pursue sport to the highest level.

Sportsmanship – This involves behaviour that shows fair play, respect for opponents and gracious behaviour, whether winning or losing.

Synovial joint – This is a freely movable joint in which the bones' surfaces are covered by cartilage, called articular cartilage, and connected by a fibrous connective tissue capsule (joint capsule) lined with synovial fluid.

Tendons – Muscles are attached to bones by tendons. These tendons help to 'pull' the muscle to the bone and help with the power of muscle contractions. Tendons are attached to the periosteum (a membrane that covers the outer surface of bones) of the bone through tough tissue called Sharpey's fibres.

Trachea – This is sometimes called the windpipe. It has 18 rings of cartilage, which are lined with a mucous membrane and ciliated cells, which trap dust. The trachea goes from the larynx to the primary bronchi.

Unsaturated fats An unsaturated fat is in the form of liquid, e.g. vegetable oil, and comes from plant sources.

Vascular shunt – This is the redistribution of blood (see definition).

The result of these processes is to significantly increase the supply of oxygen to the working muscles during exercise.

Vasoconstriction – This occurs when the artery walls decrease their diameter.

Vasodilation – This occurs when the artery walls increase their diameter.

VO_2 max – The maximum amount of oxygen an individual can take in and use in 1 minute.

Well-being – This refers to a feeling or mental state of being contented, happy, prosperous and healthy.

Index

1RM (one repetition maximum test) 55–6
5 A Day 113
30-metre sprint test 52–3
abdominal muscles 11, 12
abduction 6
Active Communities 112–13
addiction 126
adduction 6
adrenaline 34
aerobic endurance 160
aerobic exercise 29
age, and participation in sport 98
agility 61–2, 160
agonists 13
alcohol consumption 114, 173
alveoli 27
anabolic steroids 127, 130
anaerobic exercise 30, 53
antagonistic pairs 13
antagonists 14
anti-doping regulations 127
anxiety management 144–5
arteries 21–2
axes of rotation 18–19
balance 62–3, 160
balanced diet 167, 172–4
ball and socket joints 4–5
    types of movement 5, 6
benefits of exercise 105
    emotional 163
    physical 161–2
    social health 163
    see also effects of exercise on the body
beta blockers 127
biceps 11, 12
blisters 86
blood 21
blood cell production 3
blood pressure (BP) 26, 38, 162
blood vessels 21–2, 23
BMI (body mass index) 169

body dysmorphia 127
bones
    effects of exercise 40, 162
    fractures 85–6
    location of 2–3
breathing 28–9
bronchi and bronchioles 27
calcium 171
capillaries 22
carbohydrates 167–8
    glycogen loading 174–5
cardiac output (CO) 25
cardiovascular endurance (stamina) 44–5
    tests for 45–8
cardiovascular system
    blood and blood vessels 21–2
    double circulatory system 20–1
    effects of exercise 34, 37–8
    heart 22–5
cartilage 8–9
    effects of exercise 40
Change4Life 113–14
circuit training 72
circumduction 7
closed skills 137
clothing 82
cognitive skills 136
commercialisation 117
    media influence 117–18
    sponsorship 118–20
complex skills 137
concussion 84–5
continuous training 69–70
cool-down 78, 83
Cooper 12-minute run/walk test 45–7
co-ordination 63, 160
culture, and participation in sport 102–3
deltoid muscle 11, 12
Department for Culture, Media & Sport (DCMS) 110
deviance 125–6
    drugs in sport 126–8
    violence 129–30

diabetes 161, 162
diet 114, 167–72
    healthy 172–4
    nutritional strategies 174
    and sports performers 176–8
disability, participation in sport 93, 95, 104–5
    encouragement of 111
dislocations 86
double circulatory system 20–1
drugs in sport 126–7
    prohibited substances 127–8, 130
effects of exercise on the body 161
    long-term 36–40
    short-term 33–5
elbow joint 4, 5, 6
emotional health 163
endurance training 36
epiglottis 27
equipment, safety issues 82–3
ethics 123
    deviance 125–30
    gamesmanship 124–5
    sportsmanship 123–4
ethnicity, and participation in sport 93, 95, 102–3
etiquette 123
expiration (breathing out) 28
extension 6
family influences 103
fartlek (speed play) 70–1
fast twitch muscle fibres 36, 49, 52
fats 169
feedback 153–4
    knowledge of performance 154
    knowledge of results 154
fibre, dietary 171
fitness 44, 160, 162
    agility 61–2
    balance 62–3
    cardiovascular endurance (stamina) 44–8
    co-ordination 63
    flexibility 58–60
    muscular endurance 49–51

Index

power 57–8
reaction time 64
speed 52–3
strength 53–6
FITT principle 68–9
fixators 14
flexibility 58–9, 160
test for 59–60
flexion 5, 6
fluid intake 171–2, 175–6
footwear 82
forced response 153
fractures 85–6
friendship 163
frontal axis 18
frontal plane 17
funding, sources of 121
sponsorship 118–20
gamesmanship 124–5
gaseous exchange 27–8, 38
gastrocnemius muscle 11, 13
gender, and participation in sport 93, 94, 99–101, 112
gender equity (equality) 112
gluteal muscles 11, 13
glycogen 168
glycogen loading 174–5
goal setting 139–40
effective strategies 141–3
goals, achievement of 140–1
'golden triangle' 117–18
governing bodies 111
government healthy living initiative 113
grip strength dynamometer test 54–5
guidance 150–1
manual and mechanical 152–3
verbal 151–2
visual 151
haemoglobin 21
hamstrings 11, 12
hazards 87–8
head injuries 84–5
health promotion initiatives 113–14
healthy diet 167, 172–4
healthy lifestyle 158–9

heart 22–5, 162
heart rate (HR) 24–5
anticipatory rise 34
heart valves 24
heat exhaustion 172
high-intensity interval training (HIIT) 74–5
hinge joints 4
types of movement 5
hip joint 4, 5, 6, 7
hydration 171–2, 175–6
hypertrophy 36, 53
Illinois agility test 61–2
imagery 145–6
injury prevention
clothing and footwear 82
level of competition 82
lifting and carrying 82
personal protective equipment (PPE) 81
warm-up and cool-down 83
injury types 84–6
inspiration (breathing in) 28
interval training 71–2
high-intensity (HIIT) 74–5
iron 171
joints 3
components of 7–9
dislocations 86
synovial 3–5
types of movement 5–7
kinaesthetic sense 153
knee joint 4, 5, 6, 8
lactic acid 29, 33
latissimus dorsi muscle 11, 12
level of competition 82
levers 15–16
lifting and carrying 82
ligaments 7
loneliness 163
longitudinal axis 18
lungs 27
manual guidance 152–3
mechanical advantage 15
mechanical guidance 152–3

media coverage 106–7
media influence 117–18
meniscus cartilage 8
mental preparation techniques 144
imagery 145
mental rehearsal 145–6
positive thinking 147
relaxation techniques 147–8
selective attention 146–7
metabolism 33
minerals 171
supplements 176
minute ventilation 29
mitochondria 49
motivation 139–40
motor skill 134
movement analysis
axes of rotation 18–19
planes of movement 16–17
multi-stage fitness test ('bleep'/'beep' test) 47–8
muscular endurance 49, 160
tests for 49–51
muscular system
effects of exercise 33, 36
location of main muscle groups 11–13
roles in movement 13–14
myoglobin 49
nutrition 167–72
healthy diet 172–4
and sports performers 176–8
nutrition pyramid 172
nutritional strategies
fluids 175–6
glycogen loading 174–5
vitamin and mineral supplements 176
obesity 99, 162, 169
one repetition maximum test (1RM) 55–6
open skills 137
osteoporosis 40
outcome goals 143
overload 67

Index

participation
    and age 98
    barriers to 108
    benefits of 105
    current trends 92–7
    and disability 104–5
    and ethnicity, religion and culture 102–3
    family influences 103
    and gender 99–101
    improvement strategies 109–13
    influencing factors 97–108
    media coverage, effect of 106–7
pectorals 11, 12
perception 136
personal protective equipment (PPE) 81
physical restriction 152
planes of movement 16–17
plyometrics 73
positive thinking ('self-talk') 147
posture 162
power 57, 160
    tests for 57–8
prehabilitation (prehab) 69
press-up test 50–1
prime movers 13
private sector facilities 109–10
prohibited substances 127–8, 130
promotion of sport 109–13
protein 169–70
public sector facilities 109–10
pulmonary circulation 20
quadriceps 11, 12
reaction time 64, 160
    test for 65
red blood cells 21, 38
relaxation techniques 144, 145, 147–8
religion, and participation in sport 102–3
respiratory muscles 28
respiratory system
    breathing 28–9
    effects of exercise 34–5, 38
    pathway of air 27–8

risk assessment 86–8
Rooney Rule 102
rotation 6
    axes of 18–19
ruler drop test 65
safety
    injury prevention 81–3
    risk assessment 86–8
sagittal plane 17
saturated and unsaturated fats 169
sedentary lifestyle 161
    consequences of 162–4
selective attention 146–7
self-esteem 163
shoulder joint 5, 6, 7, 8
simple skills 137
sit and reach test 59–60
sit-up test 51
skeletal system
    functions 3
    joints 3–9
    location of major bones 2–3
skilful movement 134–5
skilled performers, characteristics of 134–6
skills, classification of 137
slow twitch muscle fibres 36, 53
SMART principle 139, 141
smoking 113
social health 163
social media 117
socio-economic status 93, 94–5
speed 52, 160
    test for 52–3
spinal injury 85
sponsorship 118–19
    advantages and disadvantages 120
sportsmanship 123–4
sprains 86
standing jump test 58
stimulants 127
stork stand test 62–3
strains 86

strength 53–4, 160
    tests for 54–6
stress management 144–5, 163
stroke volume (SR) 25
synovial joints 3–5
systemic circulation 20–1
television coverage 117–18
tendons 9
tidal volume 28
Top Tips for Mums 113
trachea 27
training
    goal setting 139
    optimising 68–9
    principles 67–8
    types of 69–78
transverse axis 18
transverse plane 17
trapezius muscle 11, 12
triceps 11, 12
UK Sport 110
UK Sports Institute (UKSI) 110
vasoconstriction 22
vasodilation 22
veins 22
verbal guidance 151–2
vertical jump test 57–8
violence in sport 129–30
visual guidance 151
vitamins 170
    supplements 176
VO_2 max 44
voluntary sector facilities 109–10
wall throw test 63
warm-up 76–7, 83
water consumption 171–2, 175–6
weight 99, 114
weight training 73
well-being 161, 164
Women in Sport 112
Youth Sports Trust (YST) 110–11